STUDIES IN CULTURE AND COMMUNICATION

General Editor: John Fiske

AN INTRODUCTION TO
LANGUAGE AND SOCIETY

IN THE SAME SERIES

AN INTRODUCTION TO LANGUAGE AND SOCIETY

Second Edition

Martin Montgomery

London and New York

First published 1986
by Methuen & Co. Ltd

Second edition published 1995
by Routledge
11 New Fetter Lane, London EC4P 4EE

Simultaneously published in the USA and Canada
by Routledge
29 West 35th Street, New York, NY 10001

© 1986, 1995 Martin Montgomery

Typeset in Garamond by
Florencetype Ltd, Stoodleigh, Tiverton, Devon
Printed and bound in Great Britain by
Clays Ltd, St Ives plc

British Library Cataloguing in Publication Data
A catalogue record for this book is available from the British Library

Library of Congress Cataloguing in Publication Data
Montgomery, Martin.
     An introduction to language and society/ Martin Montgomery, –
[2nd rev. edn]
     p. cm. – (Studies in culture and communication)
Includes bibliographical references (p.) and index.
1. Sociolinguistics. 2. Language acquisition. I. Title.
II. Series.
P40.M66 1995
306.4'4–dc20 95–7513

ISBN 0–415–07238–7

To Magda

CONTENTS

GENERAL EDITOR'S PREFACE

This series of books on different aspects of communication is designed to meet the needs of the growing number of students coming to study this subject for the first time. The authors are experienced teachers or lecturers who are committed to bridging the gap between the huge body of research available to more advanced students, and what new students actually need to get them started on their studies.

Probably the most characteristic feature of communication is its diversity: it ranges from the mass media and popular culture, through language to individual and social behaviour. But it identifies links and a coherence within this diversity. The series will reflect the structure of its subject. Some books will be general, basic works that seek to establish theories and methods of study applicable to a wide range of material; others will apply these theories and methods to the study of one particular topic. But even these topic-centred books will relate to each other, as well as to the more general ones. One particular topic, such as advertising or news or language, can only be understood as an example of communication when it is related to, and differentiated from, all the other topics that go to make up this diverse subject.

The series, then, has two main aims, both closely connected. The first is to introduce readers to the most important results of contemporary research into communication together with the theories that seek to explain it. The second is to equip them with appropriate methods of study and investigation which they will be able to apply directly to their everyday experience of communication.

If readers can write better essays, produce better projects and pass more exams as a result of reading these books I shall be very satisfied; but if they gain a new insight into how communication shapes and informs our social life, how it articulates and creates our experience of industrial society, then I shall be delighted. Communication is too often taken for granted when it should be taken to pieces.

John Fiske

PREFACE TO THE
SECOND EDITION

Profound changes have taken place in technologies of communication since this book was first written. Satellite television is now well established, cable is assuming an ever-increasing role, many new applications are being developed for techniques of 'virtual reality', and the data or information superhighway is imminent. None the less, even though many new techniques have become available for communicating in a mediated way, communication itself remains rooted in and dependent on our everyday ability to interact through language.

For this reason, it is important to keep sight of these everyday bases of interaction and communication even while the technologies of communication are changing apace. This book, then, focuses on language in everyday social life, beginning with the process of acquisition, then exploring social differences in language use, its role in social interaction, and finally the part it plays in representing or constructing social reality.

This broad field of inquiry has changed a great deal since the first edition of this book. In preparing this second edition I have tried to fill some of the gaps that have emerged in its treatment of the field. The most notable gap relates to issues of language and gender. In the last ten years there has been a burgeoning of work on sex differentiation in language use: it is now probably the liveliest area of research within sociolinguistics. As such, it clearly needed a chapter devoted to it.

In addition to a new chapter on gender and language, further material has been added to the chapters on register, the speech community, language and subcultures, and language and representation.

I would like to record my debt to colleagues and students at the University of Strathclyde, and to Michael and Anna: if this second edition is an improvement on the first, much credit must go to them.

Arran 1994

ACKNOWLEDGEMENTS

Thank you to the following who read and commented on portions of the book in typescript: David Bevan, John Beynon, Tracy Byrne, Deborah Cameron, Malcolm Coulthard, Brian Doyle, Robin Fawcett, John Fiske, John Hartley, Magda Montgomery, Helen Reid-Thomas, Tim O'Sullivan, Andrew Tolson, Gordon Wells, and Peter Wilson. I received much useful advice which I didn't always follow (my favourite piece of marginalia was 'EEK!'), so the book's faults remain obstinately my own.

Especial thanks are due to John Fiske, who got me started on the book in the first place; and to John Hartley (first reader of the complete manuscript and perpetrator of 'EEK!') for being such an intellectually challenging colleague while the book was being written.

I would also like to thank the parents and the children, recordings of whose speech furnished many of the examples in part one; and John Sinclair and Malcolm Coulthard, who made the recordings – and much else – possible. John Beynon, Andrew Tolson, Phil Yates, Judith Wrench, Sue Franklin and Chiu Ying Wong generously supplied examples from their own data or experience. Thank you to them, and to all those lecture and seminar groups who listened to me, questioned me, argued and discussed as the book took shape. I would be well pleased if it adequately reflects the quality of their interest and insights.

Grateful thanks are also due to the following for permission to reproduce copyright material in this book: J. M. Atkinson and

P. Drew, *Order in Court*, Macmillan (1979), p. 137; K. Basso, 'To give up on words: silence in Western Apache culture', in P. P. Giglioli (ed.), *Language and Social Context*, Penguin (1972), p. 74; L. Bloom, *One Word at a Time*, Mouton (1973), pp. 253–4; E. V. Clark, 'What's in a word? On the child's acquisition of semantics in his first language', in T. E. Moore (ed.), *Cognitive Development and the Acquisition of Language*, Academic Press (1973), p. 85; *Company* for the four advertisements; T. Demisse and M. L. Bender, 'An argot of Addis Ababa unattached girls', *Language and Society*, 12 (1983), pp. 343–4; S. Ervin-Tripp, 'Sociolinguistic rules of address', in J. B. Pride and J. Holmes (eds), *Sociolinguistics*, Penguin (1972), p. 225; R. Fowler, *Language and Control*, Routledge & Kegan Paul (1979), p. 65; M. Gregory and S. Carroll, *Language and Situation*, Routledge & Kegan Paul (1978), p. 47; M. A. K. Halliday, *Learning how to Mean*, Edward Arnold (1974), p. 158; M. A. K. Halliday, *Language as Social Semiotic: the Social Interpretation of Language and Meaning*, Edward Arnold (1978), p. 174; Joseph Heller, *Catch 22*, Corgi (1964), p. 87; Jennifer Johnson, 'Ballad for You', in D. Sutcliffe, *British Black English*, Basil Blackwell (1982), pp. 24–7; T. Kochman, ' "Rapping" in the black ghetto', *Trans-Action*, February 1969, p. 27; W. Labov, *Language in the Inner City: Studies in the Black English Vernacular*, University of Pennsylvania Press (1972), pp. 309–11 and 316; P. Menyuk, *The Acquisition and Development of Language*, Prentice-Hall (1971), p. 106; Sis Zuleika Moore, letter in *Voice of Rasta*, 18, in D. Sutcliffe, *British Black English*, Basil Blackwell (1982), p. 32; *New Larousse Encyclopedia of Mythology*, Hamlyn (1969), pp. 92, 133, and 205; Julie Roberts, extract in D. Sutcliffe, *British Black English*, Basil Blackwell (1982), p. 81; J. McH. Sinclair and R. M. Coulthard, *Towards an Analysis of Discourse: the English used by Teachers and Pupils*, Oxford University Press (1975); B. L. Whorf, *Language, Thought and Reality*, MIT Press (1956), pp. 214 and 221. Where it has not been possible to contact copyright holders, we apologize to those concerned.

TRANSCRIPTION CONVENTIONS

The examples drawn upon throughout the book come from a range of different sources, so it has not been possible to operate with a completely standard set of conventions. However, the most common ones are listed below. For fuller detail on transcript procedures and notation see Schenkein (1978).

Pauses

Length of pause is inserted within parentheses to the nearest half second:

    your erm (1.0) breathing thing was (4.0) a year ago

Pauses of less than half a second are indicated by a dash or a dot:

    so (.) take your coat off

Unintelligible speech

Where an interpretation is in doubt it is enclosed within single parentheses:

    and erm (.) see you (make an appointment)

Where no interpretation is possible the parentheses are left empty:

    and erm (.) see you (   )

Overlapping speech

The point at which overlap begins is marked by a vertical bar dropped down from one line to another:

    P: yes same to you
    D: └and erm (.) see you make an appointment

Contextual information

This is enclosed within double parentheses:

    D: anyway (.) there y'are (.) ((Hands patient prescription))

Points of interest

These are indicated by an arrow to the left of the line at issue:

    M: what's broken down? (.)
         um?
    C: a van
    →   a blue van

Sustained syllables

These are indicated by double colons after the vowel in question:

    C: icecre::m today

Emphasis

Particularly strong emphasis may be indicated by capitals:

    M: you DIDn't

INTRODUCTION

The electronic media – in particular such innovations as cable and satellite television or the word processor – are often said to be rapidly transforming the world in which we live; and, partly because they are so conspicuous, they come to occupy a privileged position in shaping our understanding of communication. In the present climate of continuous technical innovation in the electronic media, our oldest technology of communication – the power of speech – goes almost unnoticed. The attention that it does receive is often restricted to the rehearsal of local prejudices about what counts as 'good' or 'bad' or 'correct' speech.

For the most part we can take speech for granted, because its most basic use in everyday conversation seems ephemeral and transitory. And yet it is absolutely central to the social process. As human beings in society we talk our way through our lives – from home to school, from school to work; from childhood to maturity; through friendships, jobs and marriage. Even in a 'post-industrial', 'information-oriented' society such as our own, most people spend much more time in face-to-face conversation than in any other form of communication .

The electronic media themselves can be understood as merely technological extensions of pre-existing forms of communication. There would, in fact, be little point in developing them at all, were we not people who had in the course of some long evolutionary development come to have things to say to each other.

In an important sense, then, speech (or any related form of linguistic expression) constitutes the prototypical medium of communication: it is the one implicated in all the others.

Each new medium of course is more than simply parasitic upon the old. It is important to recognize that each new medium transforms the nature of, and the relationships between, the older media. It is noticeable, however, that they often refer back to and re-emphasize older forms. This may be illustrated by reference to the field of broadcast television, for instance, which is becoming progressively more reliant upon the public performance of conversation, ranging from the dramatized conversations of soap opera, through 'phone-ins' and chat-shows, to discussion of current affairs; or by reference to the field of computing, where strenuous attempts are currently in progress to make both computer programs and the machines themselves more interactive and 'user friendly'. In the long term this will entail adapting them to accept and simulate spoken communication.

Speech, therefore, is at the heart of communication, even in the area of the new technologies. As conversation it is never far from the centre of the social process – shaping relationships, confirming our common-sense realities, ratifying or shifting the boundaries of the world we take for granted. There is behind speech, however, another presence – language. Speech is merely its manifestation (and not the only manifestation that human language can adopt: it can equally well be expressed in the marks of writing or in the gestures of deaf-and dumb sign language).

Language is the more generalized capacity on which speech depends. The relationship of one to the other may be partially understood by reference to various analogies – none of them perfect. Language stands to speech like a pattern in relation to the garments that can be produced from it, like a musical score in relation to the actual performances of the work, like the rules of chess in relation to the playing of specific chess games. All these analogies emphasize the abstract characteristics of language. But the chess analogy probably best illuminates its rule-governed character. Just as playing chess depends upon participants sharing the same basic set of rules for the manipulation of its pieces, so language is constituted as a meaningful human activity only by virtue of shared conventions for the manipulation of its symbols. We make sense to each other when we speak, only in so far as we share the same abstract set of underlying conventions.

These abstract patterns or conventions or rules that constitute a language operate on various levels. The sounds of any given language are organized into patterns and each language tends to work with its own particular configuration. Cantonese Chinese, for instance, makes do perfectly well without the sound in English that occurs at the beginning of such words as 'red', 'rain', etc. Although the human vocal tract is capable of forming a very wide range of sounds, each language tends to adopt only a limited set from the total possibilities; and each language tends to have its own particular restrictions on the way such sounds can be combined. Consonants such as /m/, /v/ and /b/ may all be found in English, as – for example – the initial sounds of the words 'man', 'van' and 'ban'. But a consonant cluster such as /mvb/ cannot be found in Standard English, although there is no reason in principle why such a sequence should not occur – and indeed it may do so in some other language.

Similar constraints operate at other levels of linguistic organization. Words combine into sentences according to basic patterns or rules, referred to as the syntax of a language. Some orderings of items into sentences are permissible within a language; others are not. A sequence such as

o'clock is news nine the here

does not count as a sentence within English, whereas the following is a perfectly well-formed sequence:

here is the nine o'clock news.

Some sequences, therefore, are excluded as not conforming to the basic patterns. This makes the rule system, the syntax, sound somewhat restrictive. What the syntax does, however, is to specify a set of possibilities for sentence construction, the adherence to which ensures some degree of mutual interpretability. Indeed, from the basic core patterns of the syntax an indefinite variety of sentences can be composed. And as long as they conform to the patterns, the sentences will be interpretable even though they stand as 'one-off' creations – unique events. For example, readers of this book will have little difficulty interpreting a sentence such as 'The chocolate mouse opened his eyes, yawned, and went back to sleep' even if this is the first occasion – as is most likely – on which they have encountered it. Many of the sentences that we put together and understand are similarly novel and unique. It is the underlying rule system that enables us to produce this novelty and handle this uniqueness. Language in this respect again conforms to the analogy with chess. Every time a game is played it may turn out to be unique, even though the rules followed in each case are identical.

The major difference between language and chess, of course, is that chess does not really refer to anything outside itself. It is difficult to point to anything other than chess that is involved in the playing of it: perhaps it has a connection with personal or national prestige; or it may be seen as the solution of semi-mathematical problems. Unlike language, however, we do not use chess to flirt, or insult, or argue, or compliment, or describe what happened on the way to work. Although language may be more self-referential than we sometimes suppose, it is also typically embedded in, and sometimes constitutive of, other activities.

The capacity of language to refer to things outside itself is an important one, not least because whatever is referred to may be absent. It may be displaced in time or space. Language may be used to refer to events of the previous year or of the previous millenium; or to things happening on the other side of the planet. It may even be used to refer to events that have never happened at all, and are never likely to happen except in a fiction – like the yawning chocolate mouse of our example above. It thus has the capacity to transcend its immediate situation of use. In this sense language is more than a purely gestural, reflex signalling system.

Although language may stand for things outside itself, it does so in a somewhat oblique fashion. Smoke may be taken as an indication of fire; and a square emblem containing pictures of tongues of flame when attached to a liquid container may be taken as indicating that its contents are inflammable. In both these cases there is some clear connection between that which does the indicating and that which is indicated. Language, however, as a means of signification produces meaning in more arbitrary ways. In language there is no necessary connection between a linguistic form and that which is signified by it. There is no particular reason, other than convention, why the combination of sounds 'snake' should stand for a notion of 'limbless reptile'. The notion itself does not determine the sounds we use to signify it. If this were the case, all languages would settle on the same sound cluster to signify equivalent notions, which they clearly do not: 'snake' in German, for example, is 'Schlange', and in Polish 'waz' – both of which are quite remote in pronunciation from each other and from the English word. Thus, even though a word may sound particularly appropriate to us, it is none the less only by convention that it carries its particular meaning. The link between its sound and its meaning is for the most part quite arbitrary.

However, the way in which language stands for something outside itself – the way it signifies – is not just an issue of arbitrary connections between a sound image and a concept, between a linguistic form and a meaning. It is also a question of inter-relationships between one linguistic form and another. Language, indeed, is best understood as a set of interlocking relationships in which a linguistic form takes on the meaning it does by virtue of its place within the total system of forms. Consider, for example, the hypothetical case of a small child developing expressions for animals. The first expression the child develops may be 'bow-wow' for 'dog(s)'. But finding a need to talk about other animals such as 'cows', 'horses', 'sheep', 'cats', the child first overextends the use of 'bow-wow' to these other animals. Then gradually s/he adds further expressions to cover this domain – expressions such as 'moo', 'horsie', 'kitty'. Studies of the way in which several individual children developed expressions in this particular domain led to the following composite picture being proposed:

	Expression		*Domain of application*
stage I	bow-wow	=	dog(s)
stage II	bow-wow	=	dogs, cows, horses, sheep, cats
stage III	(a) bow-wow	=	dogs, cats, horses, sheep
	(b) moo	=	cows
stage IV	(a) bow-wow	=	dogs, cats, sheep

	(b) moo	=	cows
	(c) gee-gee	=	horses
stage V	(a) bow-wow/doggie	=	dogs, cats
	(b) moo	=	cows
	(c) gee-gee/horsie	=	horses
	(d) baa lamb	=	sheep
stage VI	(a) doggie	=	dogs
	(b) moo	=	cows
	(c) gee-gee/horsie	=	horses
	(d) baa lamb	=	sheep
	(e) kitty	=	cats

Source: based on Clark (1973).

It is particularly striking that, as each new expression is added from stage III onwards, the significance of the other expressions – their range of meaning – is subtly altered. The range of 'bow-wow', for instance, is progressively narrowed down as each new expression is added. Although we are dealing here with very simple expressions drawn from accounts of young children's speech, we have every reason to believe that the significance of linguistic forms within the adult system alters in similar ways. The introduction of 'Ms', for example, has probably altered the sense in which the terms 'Mrs' and 'Miss' are now understood. Once a new form enters the system the significance of the related forms will shift accordingly. Thus, the meaning of a linguistic form is partially a product of its place in the total system of forms.

For in the last analysis, of course, language is a system in flux. On the one hand – as an abstract system of signs, rules and relationships – it underpins our capacity to speak and guarantees our mutual interpretability. On the other hand, those very acts of speaking, continuous and pervasive as they are, always bring pressure to bear on the shape of the abstract system, to mould and change it.

This book explores some of the ways in which the life of language intermingles with the life of society. Each, of course, is an integral part of the other; so much so that learning one's first language is intimately bound up with becoming a social being. Each of us becomes a full member of society only by learning its language.

It is for this reason that part one deals directly with the topic of early language development. The way in which children take on language from those around them is examined, in particular as an interactive process – one which involves both the child and others with whom s/he can engage communicatively.

This whole process lays down for the child the outlines of the abstract linguistic system which thereby in turn radically extends his or her capacity to communicate with members of the society at large. In developing a linguistic system, children are developing a resource for making sense of the world of people and things which they inhabit: and they are also developing a resource for interacting in more complex ways with those who people that world.

The wider society into which the child is beginning to move does not, however, typically possess one single, uniform language. Even a small but densely populated country such as the United Kingdom possesses a striking degree of diversity in languages and in linguistic expression. Part two examines some aspects of this diversity – ways, for instance, in which social factors help to produce and reproduce it; and how it can become charged with social significance. In this respect even quite trivial features of pronunciation can become the focus for a sense of solidarity or of social distance.

However, language is more than a marker of group membership: it enters crucially into the conduct of our everyday encounters. Part three examines some aspects of the way in which language opens, closes and regulates encounters. More generally it considers how utterances may be seen as accomplishing actions such as challenging, warning, questioning, requesting, accusing, complaining, and so on. In this respect language is more than the ground on which encounters are worked through and negotiated. It lies at the heart of making and shaping social relations themselves.

At the same time as language provides the principal means of realizing our social relations and organizing our encounters, it also provides us with our most fundamental framework for making sense of our everyday world. Part four explores some of the ways in which the categories, systems and patterns of our language help to shape our habitual ways of seeing, feeling and thinking about the persons and the things with which we engage.

This brings us, however, face to face with a most fundamental paradox. In our everyday transactions we seem able to manipulate language for our personal and individual purposes – fluently, and apparently without pause for conscious reflection. It seems to provide each of us as individuals with a personally distinctive means of expression. And yet none of us really creates it anew – at least, not in its entirety. It comes to us already shaped by the society of which we are a part and with the impress on it of the previous generations who formed its history. In this respect the language shapes us, as much as we shape the language: we operate within constraints – linguistic ones – which are not of our own individual making. This book is about some of the ways in which society shapes us through its language, in the belief that by knowing something about the constraints exerted on us by language we can avoid becoming its prisoners.

Background sources and further reading

Major sources for further discussion of basic characteristics of language would be:

Aitchison, J. (1987) *Linguistics,* Teach Yourself Books, Sevenoaks: Hodder & Stoughton.

Hockett, C.F. (1958) *A Course in Modern Linguistics,* New York: Macmillan.

Hudson, R.A. (1984) *Invitation to Linguistics*, Oxford: Basil Blackwell.

Saussure, F. de (1974) *Course in General Linguistics,* London: Fontana.

All of these are classic texts on what language is, and how it should be studied. Saussure's *Course* was first published in 1916. An excellent explication and commentary on it may be found in:

Culler, J. (1976) *Saussure,* London: Fontana.

Perhaps more accessible as an account of basic aspects of language would be:

Bolinger, D. and Sears, D.A. (1981) *Aspects of Language,* New York: Harcourt Brace Jovanovich.

A difficult but searching account of the relationship between social change and developments in technologies of communication may be found in:

Williams, R. (1974) *Television: Technology and Cultural Form,* London: Fontana.

PART ONE
THE DEVELOPMENT
OF LANGUAGE

In the beginning was the word.

(John 1:1)

In the beginning was the deed. The word followed as its phonetic shadow.

(Leon Trotsky*)

*Trotsky, L. (1925) *Literature and Revolution*

1 THE BEGINNINGS OF LANGUAGE DEVELOPMENT

Learning language: the first words

It first becomes obvious that children are actually learning to talk some time between twelve and eighteen months of age when they begin to use single-word utterances of the following type:

juice	dada	biscuit
there	no	that
byebye	big	wassat
hi	shoe	allgone
car	look	dirty
hot	up	ball

Such simple single-word utterances may look like a very primitive and rudimentary communication system. The vocabulary in the early stages is limited in range and its application is restricted to the immediate here and now. Consequently, it is hardly possible for the child to express or give shape to complex relationships, such as:

the conditional ('if . . ., then . . .');
the temporal ('before', and 'after');
notions of probability ('might', 'may', 'could', etc.)

But the first one-word utterances are not as simple as they look. For one thing, children use them in a variety of ways. Thus, whilst

3

the list above includes expressions for salient objects in their immediate environment (items such as 'shoe', 'car', 'juice', 'biscuit', etc.), it also includes items for opening and closing encounters ('byebye', 'hi'), items for attracting someone's attention ('dada') and focusing it in a particular direction ('look'), items for refusing or resisting a particular course of action ('no!') and for commenting on a particular state of affairs ('dirty', 'allgone'). Furthermore it is not uncommon for the child to have at least one question form (e.g. 'wassat?') and to be able to use some of the items to request actions of others (e.g. 'up' as meaning 'lift me up'). And, while some of the items seem only ever to be used for one purpose (e.g. 'hi' as a greeting), others can serve a variety of purposes: for example, 'dada' can be used as a call, a greeting or a comment (as meaning 'there's a man in the photograph'); 'biscuit' can be used as a request (I want a biscuit now'), or as a comment ('that's a biscuit on the table'), or even as a kind of acknowledgement, as in the following interchange:

ADULT: here's your biscuit
CHILD: biscuit   ((takes biscuit))

There is, then, more to the child's first words than might at first appear. They are from the beginning much more than merely names for objects, ways of referring to things around them. Indeed, even such a restricted range of items provides a highly subtle means of engaging with and responding to others. They enable the child to establish and maintain contact with others and they allow for the expression of diverse dispositions such as hunger, interest, curiosity, pleasure, warmth and anger. So, although the range of items that initially comprise the child's vocabulary may be small, the purposes that such items can be made to serve in use are highly varied.

Studies of child language development usually refer to these oneword utterances as 'holophrases', implying thereby that these single items carry a broader and more diffuse range of meaning than do their equivalents in the language of adults: basically, children at this stage make single words do the work of the fully constructed sentences they will probably be producing a year or so later.

Some precursors of language development

Language development, however, does not begin suddenly out of the blue with the 'holophrastic stage'. Children can, for instance, understand and respond in appropriate non-verbal ways to the utterances of others long before they begin to produce holophrases. This is partly because in the everyday routines of feeding, washing, dressing and play the infant will be exposed to myriad repetitions of identical linguistic forms in recognizably similar contexts; and so, by the time the child begins to speak, s/he has already begun to grasp the basic outlines of the language system of his/her culture.

The infant cry

The first year of life sees the gradual emergence of very generalized capacities to interact – capacities that precede and provide a basis for the specifically linguistic developments later on. From the moment of birth, for example, infants can impinge dramatically on those around them: they can cry. Indeed, from the first weeks of life they have a repertoire of at least three distinguishable types of cry – the hunger cry, the pain cry, and a cry associated with fatigue, boredom or discomfort – each sounding subtly different from the other. The hunger cry, or 'basic cry' as it is sometimes known, is a moderately pitched loud cry that builds into a rhythmic cycle made up of the cry itself followed by a short silence, then an intake of breath followed by another short silence before the next cry resumes the cycle. Repetition of the series through successive cycles gives the cry its rhythmic quality. The discomfort cry or 'grumble' is lower in pitch, more variable in volume, though generally quieter than the basic cry. Its rhythm is slower and may be interspersed with grunts and sucking noises. The pain cry is markedly different again, taking the form of an inward gasp followed by a high-pitched, long-drawn-out rising shriek.

These cries are, of course, most important for survival in the first weeks of life. They provide a key resource, perhaps the only resource, open to the infant for signalling crucial physiological states such as hunger or pain; and as such they seem pitched at a level likely to evoke most disturbance in another human. Initially they may well be purely reflex responses to physiological states; but, if matters are ever that simple, they do not remain so for long. For one thing the different forms of cry often shade into one another. A child may begin with a grumble that gradually shifts into a hunger cry, or begin with a pain cry that gradually subsides into the basic cry rhythm. An adult accustomed to looking after a particular child or children may know instantly what a specific cry indicates, but just as often there is some indeterminacy and it requires the exercise of several kinds of awareness simultaneously to interpret what a particular instance of crying is all about. Thus, any one cry has to be gauged against the others that may have preceded it. It has also to be interpreted in the context of the recurring cycle of child care (Is it long since the last feed? How long since the last nappy change? etc.). And finally any particular cry is interpreted in the light of any known special circumstances affecting the child; for instance, a tendency to get fretful after a wakeful period late in the day. Basically, those involved in the care of the child find themselves discriminating between the different noises that the child makes, and arriving at different interpretations of them.

The noises themselves, of course, do not as yet amount to fully fledged acts of communication. They seem to be reflex responses to physiological states, rather than acts performed with the deliberate intention of conveying a specific meaning to a recipient. Even so, there is some evidence to suggest that infants are highly responsive to the human voice, and that a 'grumbling' infant, for example, will often break off from crying if spoken to by an adult. Indeed, it is not long before those who look after the child detect what seems best described as a 'fake' cry – one that is related to no clear physiological need but is apparently designed to provoke attention from the adult. This marks the crucial beginnings of a growing displacement of the child's vocalizations: they are no longer so firmly entrenched in bodily needs but become available for use as a social and interactive resource.

Further developments in vocalization

The child, of course, has still many steps to take before developing the fully articulated powers of speech. There will be a phase of 'cooing' around three months and this gives way in turn to a period of 'babbling' from around six months onwards. Vocalization now

6

begins to take on features of the speech of the surrounding community, especially in terms of the tone of voice and intonation with its attendant stress and rhythm patterns. The babbling can sound at times almost conversational but it is hard to detect anything meaningful in its performance. Indeed, both cooing and babbling are indulged in by at least some children irrespective of whether or not there is someone around prepared to respond to it: it is not necessarily addressed to anyone in particular. On the contrary, it sounds and looks at times as if the child is actively manipulating these vocalizations for her/his own practice and pleasure, irrespective of communicative intent, almost as if s/he were doodling with her/his voice like a writer with a pen.

From vocalization to communicative expressions

At around nine months, however, some particular expressions begin to emerge out of all this foundation work and begin to assume consistent and recognizable meanings for those who are daily involved with the child. Initially, these expressions may bear little resemblance to the words of the adult language – and even when they do sound similar, they are not necessarily used in conventional ways. The child, in fact, seems to select fairly arbitrarily some (any) particular configuration of sounds from the large repertoire with which s/he has been experimenting and settles on it to do some particular, necessary kind of work. This work will not be so much a matter of 'telling' people things; while this might be the most obvious and recognizable use of language from an adult viewpoint, it is by no means the first use of language that children settle upon. Rather, they develop particular sounds for getting particular things done. One child (reported in Halliday, 1975) fastened on the sound 'nanana(na)' and used it to mean 'give me that toy/biscuit/toothbrush', etc.: and for the more particular demand 'give me my toy bird', he used a sound something like 'buh'. While the latter sound may be indirectly related to the adult word for the object, the other expression ('nanana') has no obvious antecedent in the language (English) that this child was taking over.

The communicative functions of the early expressions

The kind of work being performed by these two examples is

primarily *instrumental*: they fulfil an 'I want' function for the child, serving to satisfy material needs and to gain the goods and services that are required from an immediate situation. Other functions that emerge around this time are the *regulatory*, the *interactional* and the *personal*. The child who developed the examples given above also developed expressions explicitly oriented towards influencing the actions of a particular addressee (e.g. 'uh', for 'do that again'), where the emphasis is more on regulating another's behaviour, than on obtaining goods and services. This function, in fact, is a kind of turning back by the child on to the adult of a dominant way in which the language is used on him, as in 'Leave the cat's dinner alone'; or in 'Put your coat on, we're going to the shop'; or in 'Don't touch that, it's hot.' *Interactional* resources are developed with expressions for opening and sustaining encounters with others. The same child again, for example, employed a sound something like 'dor' to mean 'good to see you', and other typical expressions realizing this function are forms for 'hello' and 'goodbye', responses to calls, and so on. Finally, expressions that serve a more purely *personal* function, that register feelings of pleasure (e.g. 'ah', for 'that's nice') and of interest, annoyance, anger and so forth, also emerge around this time.

The early communicative expressions as a *protolanguage*

We can, in fact, see a qualitative change taking place during the last half of the child's first year. Around about six months children seem to be preoccupied with developing a broad repertoire of sound and intonation, and generally with exercising a growing control over the capacity to vocalize almost as an end in itself. Then, from around nine months onwards they seem to narrow down and refine these resources, by fastening on a few particular expressions from the stream of sound they are capable of producing, and deploying them consistently for specific purposes in the ways outlined above.

With some children babbling and 'vocal doodling' fade out completely with the advent of these functionally oriented expressions or 'protoforms'. With others, babbling continues side by side with the protoforms on into the development of speech. In either case, however, there are still clear differences in kind between the vocalization of babbling and the sounds of the protoforms. For instance, when children are babbling they are typically capable of producing a wide variety of sounds and intonations, and as far as the latter is concerned the pitch of the voice will display combinations of rising, falling and level contours characteristic of the conversations of the local speech community. The intonation of the initial protoforms, however, tends to be predominantly falling in the direction of pitch movement and it will be some time yet before the child begins to use even the simple opposition between rising and falling on the protoforms. So, it is as if, when the protoforms emerge, the child's rich potential for vocalization is initially pressed into very narrow moulds.

The forms adopted by the child may not as yet correspond to those used by the adult in similar circumstances: for the most part they amount to rather idiosyncratic innovations. How can we be so sure, then, that the child means anything by them at all? Clearly, the innovatory and idiosyncratic nature of the protoforms requires from those engaged with the child a fair degree of sympathetic interpretive work, involving attention to – amongst other things – the immediate situation of the utterance and the non-verbal behaviour of the child. So even though we cannot ask the child what he means by 'nanana', if he is using it in the presence of what is for him a favoured object – such as a chocolate button or a cuddly toy – while reaching for it with outstretched hand, then it is a reasonable supposition that he means 'I want that'. If he cannot obtain it by his own devices and the object is still not provided and he repeats 'nanana' more insistently, while still reaching out for it and looking at the adult, then the supposition grows yet stronger. If, over the course of a few days, the child uses 'nanana' on different occasions but always in the context of gaining a desired object and for that purpose only, then we seem to have very strong grounds for claiming that the child has systematically coupled the sound with the meaning. Indeed, it is precisely this consistent and systematic application by the child on several occasions of particular sounds (sometimes also a particular posture or gesture independently of a vocal expression) for particular meanings that constitutes a watershed in the child's growing capacity to communicate – that constitutes, indeed, the emergence of a *protolanguage*.

Conditions that aid the emergence of a protolanguage

There are, it should be noted, special circumstances associated with child–parent interaction that help this primitive communication system to establish itself fully. For one thing, the child is typically interacting predominantly with a small circle of 'significant others', and the world of persons and objects with whom and about which the child communicates is usually relatively constant and familiar. Furthermore, the activities that the child is engaged in with others over the course of a day are often repetitive and even ritualized. Finally, the communication itself is always embedded in the immediate here and now, rather than concerning itself with absent objects or past and future events, sometimes forming little more than a sympathetic accompaniment to known and familiar actions.

Thus, it need not even require – especially for those who comprise the child's special circle of intimates – much conscious intellectual effort to tune in on the child's emerging protoforms. What seems to occur, in fact, is a mutual accommodation between the child and his/her closest associates: they learn to interpret his/her protolanguage, while s/he is learning their language.

Expanding the protolanguage

Given these special circumstances, the child is able to accumulate expressions, thereby refining the distinctions in meaning that s/he can make in each of the four functional areas. For example, the child who produced 'nanana' at around nine months (see Halliday, 1975) continued over a six-and-a-half-month period to accumulate roughly ten protoforms for expressing *instrumental* purposes, adding expressions for meanings such as

'I want the clock'
'I want a rusk'
'I want some toast'
'I want some powder'

to the basic two expressions that he began with in this area. At the same time, he was extending his repertoire in the other functional areas, by developing further expressions for regulating others' behaviour, for opening and sustaining interaction with them, and for expressing personal points of view: so that by sixteen months he had at his command in his *protolanguage* something over forty expressions.

During this time, he also expanded the range of functions that the protoforms could be used to realize, since he was beginning to create them for the enactment of two new kinds of purpose. First, he was developing protoforms as an accompaniment to, and initiator of, play: for example, he used a sound 'eee' for 'peepo' and another sound for 'let's pretend to go to sleep'. He was thus beginning to use language as a way of entering an imagined world, a function that will eventually turn into one of make-believe and story. Second, he was also beginning to extend his communicative system in the direction of exploring his environment, initially by the use of the form 'a::da' (more common with other children might be the form 'wassat?') meaning 'what's that [called]?' This is the first sign of the *heuristic* function, that will later develop into a variety of question forms. The child will use these to find out about the social and physical world and the way it operates – a function most noticeable with questions beginning 'why . . .?' For the moment, significantly, the first step in this direction is by means of an expression that demands the *names* of objects, and is thus not so much to do with the world in itself, but rather with how the vocabulary of the adult language system maps on to the familiar objects of his everyday experience. With this expression the child is able to elicit focused and situationally relevant linguistic labels, tailored directly to his needs and interests. This kind of process can be seen at work in a more developed way in the following extract from a transcript of a slightly older child (about twenty-three months):

DATA EXTRACT 1.1

CHILD:	wassat? (.) wassat? (.) wassat? (.)	1
PARENT:	what's that? that's the other tape (.)	2
CHILD:	wassat?	3
PARENT:	that's what we call (..) those are called spools	4
CHILD:	wassat? wassat? (..) wassat?	5
PARENT:	that's a spool darling (..)	6
CHILD:	'sat? 'sat? 'sat? 'sat? (.) 'sat mummy?	7
PARENT:	what love?	8

	show me	9
CHILD:	'sat mummy?	10
PARENT:	what are you pointing to?	11
CHILD:	look	12
PARENT:	oh	13
	that's a switch	14
CHILD:	sitch	15
	'sat?	16
PARENT:	and that's another one isn't it?	17
CHILD:	'sat? 'sat? 'sat?	18
PARENT:	and that's a little button that you press	19
	a little red button isn't it?	20
CHILD:	((whispers))	21
PARENT:	no	22
	don't you press it now	23
	because it'll (.) it won't work if you do	24

This kind of activity can, in fact, occur much earlier than the twenty-three months of this example and partially as a result of it we see a very rapid growth in the range of expressions open to the child in each functional area. Moreover, the expressions themselves now approximate more and more closely to the adult forms. The child is now on the verge of leaving behind his own protolanguage and gradually replacing it with the more economical possibilities of the adult system – and with the first steps into this system come the holophrases of the type we examined at the beginning of the chapter.

From *protolanguage* to *holophrases*

Initially the holophrases operate in similar ways to the protoforms that comprise the protolanguage, tending to slot into, and be an enactment of, one or other of the already established repertoire of functions, be it the *instrumental, regulatory, personal, heuristic, interactional* or *imaginative* function. Initially, then, the holophrases fit into place alongside the protoforms of the existing protolanguage. They do, however, constitute a new departure for the child, who now begins to assimilate expressions ready-made from the speech of those around him/her, instead of making up protoforms afresh as s/he goes along.

The protolanguage, with its gradually developing functional potential, has provided an important platform for the subsequent projection into the adult system. But as long as those around the child can make sense of what s/he is saying, why should it be necessary for him/her to make the transition into the adult system at all? After all, there are well-documented cases of private languages such as those adopted by some identical twins, where young children can seem actually resistant to taking over the conventional and publicly accepted forms of the adult system.

In the case of the transition from the protolanguage to the adult system the shift seems to be motivated in part by the communication situation itself – by the fact that the child's interlocutors don't actually speak his/her language, even though they may understand it. Just as important, however, is the basic nature of the proto-linguistic system itself. While the child remains within it – with its basic principle of one sound, one meaning – s/he is committed to coining a new expression for every new meaning s/he wants to convey. Because of the inherent unwieldiness of this process, it is as if a law of diminishing returns sets in and it thereby becomes more economical to take over adult forms, rather than to go on creating them uniquely for him/herself. For what the adult system ultimately provides is a basic and relatively fixed set of patterns, which can be mobilized for the production of an unlimited range of utterances, each with a possibly unique meaning. Instead of uniquely creating a system as s/he goes along, s/he can take over a system that has creativity built in to it as an inherent and fundamental property. Meanwhile, however, the holophrases themselves enhance the communicative potential of the child: for, as was seen earlier (pp. 3–4), while some of them are relatively fixed in function (e.g. 'hi' as a greeting), others can serve a variety of purposes (e.g. 'dada' as call, greeting, or comment).

Two-word utterances as the beginnings of *syntax*

The child is now faced with the task of finding ways of organizing these single words of the holophrastic stage into the sentences of the adult language. The holophrastic phase has enabled the child to lay down a set of possibilities for doing things with language – a functional basis, in effect, for later developments. Now s/he must find ways for realizing these functions not just in words but in the word sequences that are such a crucial component of the adult language system. In essence the child has to develop a *syntax:* a way of combining single words into sentences. For it is the syntactic element that has been lacking so far in the child's attempts at communication. Until s/he develops such a syntactic component, the child has only partial access to the creativity and flexibility of language in its fullest sense. So s/he has to move from a simple two-level model of language, where meanings are realized directly in sound, to a more complex three-level model, where meanings are realized in sentences, and sentences are realized in sound.

The emerging control of syntactic structure proceeds fairly rapidly: estimates vary but it seems likely that the majority of children develop the basic core structures of the language they are learning by about three and a half years. This is a mere two years from the onset of recognizably adult single-word utterances. But the child does not accomplish this in a single step: s/he moves through intermediate and overlapping stages on the way, each stage being characterized by a different kind of syntactic model, as the child searches out and builds up the regular patterning of the adult system.

The movement from holophrases to two-word utterances is begun with little more than a loose association of two holophrases of the type

ride	horse
doll	there
climb	up
mommy	help
down	there

where each half of the utterance takes a discrete, though similar, intonational configuration characteristic of the individual holophrases. The relations between the individual parts, and whatever unity the utterances have, is given more by the situation than by anything else: and it is just as likely for the ordering of the discrete parts to be reversed as in

| mommy | help | *versus* | help | mommy |
| down |there | *versus* | there | down |

and still convey quite comparable meanings. As yet these apparent two-word utterances are merely two separate holophrases in loose tandem. However, they soon develop into two-word utterances with a unified intonational contour and it is these which constitute the child's first real step into syntax – into the complex activity of combining words in consistent ways into interpretable utterances.

The two-word utterance in situation

Typical instances of two-word utterances with their unified contour – such as '| ride horse |', '| see shoe |', or '| build tower |' – remain on the page inherently ambiguous: '| build tower |', for example, might mean:

(1) 'I'm building a tower'
(2) 'Build a tower for me'
(3) 'Are you building a tower?'

As actual situated utterances, however, the range of ambiguity is considerably reduced. Here is 'build tower' in context:

DATA EXTRACT 1.2

	((The child shakes a cup; then turns it over))
MOTHER:	what are you doing?
	((The child continues to shake cup))
MOTHER:	what are you doing?
	oh careful
	be careful
	((The child puts cup on juice can))
CHILD:	build tower!
MOTHER:	build tower!
	((The child takes cup off can; puts cup back on can))
MOTHER:	you gonna build a tower?
	oh that's a nice tower

```
            is that a big tower?
            ((The child hits at cup))
    CHILD:      tumble
```
Source: after Bloom (1973).

The interplay between the child's actions, the child's utterances and the mother's utterances, especially the latter's question ('what are you doing?') and her subsequent expansion ('you gonna build a tower?'), provide strong grounds for supposing that what the child meant was '[I am] build[ing] [a] tower'.

It is important to note, however, that the utterance itself only provides minimal indications to confirm this interpretation, basically because its syntax is extremely rudimentary. The child lacks as yet some of the syntactic elements necessary to make this meaning explicit and to mark it off from the other possibilities.

Developments after the two-word phase

An indication of the kinds of syntactic structures the child will have to develop can be gained by considering for the moment just one aspect of the adult linguistic system. The adult system makes a distinction between:

declaratives (used normally for stating or asserting);
interrogatives (used normally for questions); and
imperatives (used normally for commands).

The distinctions are carried by aspects of word order and by the presence or absence of certain syntactic markers, as can be seen in the following examples: here the basic content has been held constant, but each utterance does something different depending on how the items are arranged and what formal elements have been introduced or deleted:

declarative: She's opening the box.
interrogative: Is she opening the box?
imperative: Open the box.

And these, of course, can be negated in a variety of ways:

She's not opening the box.
She isn't opening the box.

16

Isn't she opening the box?
Don't open the box.

In the case of the child these distinctions are not clearly signalled during the two-word phase and s/he must build them up progressively in something like the following manner:

Table 1

	A: Early 20–24 mths	B: Intermediate	C: Late 3½–4 yrs
declarative	that box big boat	that's box that big boat	that's a box that's a big boat
interrogative	see shoe? truck here?	mommy see shoe? truck's here? *or* where's truck?	do you see the shoe? is the truck here? where's the truck?
imperative	want baby		I want the baby give me the baby
negative	no play	I no play	I won't play

Source: Menyuk (1971).

Basic meaning relations during the two-word phase

In the meantime, despite the limitations in syntax during the two-word phase, the child's utterances in situation clearly become capable of rendering more complex meanings than were possible with the holophrase. The situation of utterance remains, of course, most important. Indeed, an identical two-word utterance may occur in quite different situations to mean quite different things. The utterance

17

| mommy sock |

for example, occurred in the speech of one child on one occasion when the child was picking up her mother's sock; and on another occasion when the mother was putting the child's sock on for her (see Bloom, 1970). The most precise way of specifying the difference between these two occasions is in the following terms: on the first occasion the relationship expressed is one of *possessor* + *possessed entity* ('that's mommy's sock'); on the second occasion the relationship is *agent* + *object* ('mommy's putting my sock on').

These two kinds of meaning relation are only two out of a range of recurring and prominent patterns of meaning that emerge in the child's speech during this period. Perhaps most common early in the two-word phase are various expressions for location either of entities or of actions – expressions such as:

| down dere |
| doll dere |

Also common are simple expressions of quantity, such as:

| more glasses |
| another switch |

Then there are utterances that express action relationships of various kinds, such as:

| cut it |
| push it |
| ride horse |

and so on. During this phase the child also develops ways of attaching qualities or attributes to entities, as for example in:

| naughty boy |
| nice drink |

We can summarize the major meanings of this phase as follows (with examples from data):

Table 2

A *Various action relations; e.g.*	
1 *ACTION + OBJECT*	ride horse
	push it
	cut it
	hear bells
	make bridge
	find bear
2 *AGENT + ACTION*	mommy help
	mommy sleep
	Michael crying
3 *AGENT + OBJECT*	mommy sock
B *Various possession relations; e.g.*	
POSSESSOR + POSSESSED ENTITY	mommy sock
	my milk
	Michael hanky
C *Various locational relations; e.g.*	up dere
	over dere
	down dere
	on dere
	doll dere
	Michael dere
	climb up
	went away
D *Quantity relations;*	
QUANTIFIER + ENTITY	more melon
	more glasses
	more switch
	another switch
	two switch
E *Quality relations;*	
QUALITY/ATTRIBUTE + ENTITY	pretty boat
	naughty boy
	sore botty
	nice drink
	big bridge

Also common during this period are utterances concerned with disappearance ('juice allgone', 'allgone now'), with refusal ('no play' meaning 'I don't want to play'; 'no dinner' meaning 'I don't want any dinner'), and with securing attention preparatory to talk or action ('watch me', 'look mummy'). Thus, we can see that, even though children during the two-word phase have at their disposal only the most rudimentary syntactic structure, they are none the less capable of expressing a wide and complex range of meanings.

A problem of method

There is a wide measure of agreement among researchers that relationships such as these are commonly expressed in the child's speech during the two-word phase. An interesting problem arises, however, in specifying the precise character of such relationships. In the first place the whole approach depends upon going beyond the strict limits of what the child has actually said, and 'reading them in' to the child's utterance. Given the relevant information about the situation, this is not difficult to do, as the extract on p. 15 illustrates. And anyway, it is precisely by making such interpretations that adults in close contact with children manage to communicate reasonably fluently with them at all. Indeed, they often overtly indicate the interpretive work they are doing by reformulating what they think the child meant, as for example:

    1 CHILD: build tower!
       MOTHER: build tower!
                 you gonna build a tower?
    2 CHILD: Michael hanky
       MOTHER: that's right
                 those are Michael's aren't they
                 that one

Or the adult may display the sense in which the child's utterance is taken quite clearly, though by implication rather than directly, as in:

    3 CHILD: book mummy
       MOTHER: all right
                 I'll go and get you one

None the less, a further problem remains. The categories employed to specify relationships such as those involving *possession* or *attribution* are drawn from descriptions of the adult system. It is therefore quite possible that although the broad claims of such an approach are indisputably worthwhile, adult meanings are nevertheless being imposed on the child's production. It consequently runs the risk of overlooking distinctively childlike properties in the meaning systems that are taking shape. This is one of the most intractable problems in formulating a satisfactory account of child language development: whether or not, at what stage, and in what respects, we should assume that children's language resembles that of adults. If we assume very little, especially in interpretive terms, then we tend to produce rather impoverished accounts. If we take our chances and assume a lot, then we tend to do so in terms of the linguistic practices with which we are most familiar – those of the adult system – and thereby face the possibility of seriously distorting what the child is doing. It is not so much the case that the child's meanings are necessarily simpler or less sophisticated than those of adults. They may well be subtly complex but developed in order to express different concerns and organized on rather different terms to those of adults.

Consider the kind of meaning system we have attributed to the child during the two-word phase. It contains categories and distinctions such as *possession, attribution, action* and so on – common enough in descriptions of the adult system – and examples are listed to illustrate the distinctions, which seem to fit the presumed categories quite neatly. It is quite possible, however, to recast some of these distinctions in slightly different terms. For example, there is a category *quantity* for handling relations of the type 'more glasses', 'another switch', etc. And a category *non-existence/disappearance* was posed for handling utterances such as 'knife gone', 'peas gone', 'juice allgone', 'allgone now' which are quite common with many children for a time during the two-word phase. However, posing the distinction between the two types in this way may actually disguise a fundamental similarity. For the child, it may be that these two types are merely reverse sides of the same coin, amounting to something like the arithmetical relations of plus and minus, or addition and subtraction, so that fundamentally *disappearance* is a kind of *zero* or *minus quantity*.

21

Similarly, a category *possession* was posed for handling utterances such as 'mommy sock', 'Michael hanky', 'my milk', etc. The actual label, however, may disguise a fundamental difference in the way in which children construct this kind of relationship. An utterance such as 'Michael hanky', for example, may be not so much a combination of *possessor* + *possessed entity* – the object plus its owner – but rather consist of the object coupled with its habitual user. Thus, 'Michael hanky' may be the child's way of saying not so much 'That handkerchief belongs to Michael' but rather 'Michael uses that handkerchief'. If this is so, then the relationship involved might be better seen as a subvariant of *agent* (customary) + *object* rather than *possessor* + *possessed entity*. Alternatively, it might be argued that the child sees 'possession' as a kind of *quality* to be associated with *entities* in a way which helps to discriminate one superficially similar entity from another, in which case the utterance 'my milk' has much in common with an utterance such as 'nice drink' *(quality + entity)*.

In one way the situation gets more complicated as the two-element stage proceeds and the range of meanings being signified becomes more extensive and interwoven one with another. Is 'two there' a *quantity* relation or a *locational* one? Clearly it is both. But surely it must also involve a presumed *entity* that can be both 'counted' and 'positioned', so that a satisfactory account of it will involve three categories, two explicit and one latent (enclosed within brackets):

quantifier (+ entity) + location

This seems most likely, especially since by this time the child will already be producing some three-word utterances of the type 'mummy do it', 'Michael rolled it', or even a four-word string such as 'me a wet boy'. A quite credible hypothesis would be that the meaning base expands slightly in advance of the child's capacity to give shape to it in actual utterances, and so for a while s/he goes on squeezing it into the two-word phrase, consolidating as s/he goes along.

In another way, from the point of view of the ambiguities posed above, the situation gets easier, because the child begins to develop formal markers of some of the relations, as grammatical inflections (such as -ing, -ed, -'s, -s) begin to emerge and 'word order' contrast (e.g. agent before *action* in English) becomes more stable and predictable. Hence

'Martin cover'	becomes	'Martin's cover'
'Wendy daddy'	becomes	'Wendy's daddy'
'big bidge'	becomes	'a big bridge'
'two egg'	becomes	'two eggs'
'me swim'	becomes	'I'm swimming'

and so on. In the last analysis, whatever the difficulties associated with procedures involving the rich interpretation of children's speech and the subsequent assignment to it of semantically loaded categories, the approach has undeniable merits, not least because it seeks to take account of what adults ordinarily assume anyway when interacting with a child during this stage of development.

Background sources and further reading

Pre-speech

Bullowa, M. (ed.) (1979) *Before Speech,* Cambridge: Cambridge University Press.

Lock, A. (ed.) (1978) *Action, Gesture and Symbol: the Emergence of Language*, London: Academic Press.

Both these collections include a wide range of material on prelinguistic developments in communication. For developments around the infant cry see:

Wolff, P.H. (1969) 'The natural history of crying and other vocalizations in early infancy', in Foss, B.M. (ed.) (1969) *Determinants of Infant Behaviour*, IV, London: Methuen.

The early communicative expressions as protolanguage

The term *protolanguage* and the description of it in terms of use or function are drawn from:

Halliday, M.A.K. (1975) *Learning How to Mean,* London: Edward Arnold.

This interesting and highly influential account of early language development shows the foundation of the child's linguistic system being established before the child can actually communicate in words.

Early developments in syntax

Key sources for the discussion of syntactic development during the two-word phase are:

Bloom, L. (1975) *One Word at a Time,* The Hague: Mouton.
Brown, R. (1976) *A First Language: the Early Stages*, Harmondsworth: Penguin.

Basic introductions to child language

Cruttenden, A. (1979) *Language in Infancy and Childhood,* Manchester: Manchester University Press.
Crystal, D. (1976) *Child Language, Learning and Linguistics,* London: Edward Arnold.
Dale, P.S. (1976) *Language Development: Structure and Function*, New York: Holt, Rinehart & Winston.
Foster, S. (1990) *The Communicative Competence of Young Children*, London: Longman.
Harris, J. (1990) *Early Language Development*, London: Routledge.
Macaulay, R. (1981) *Generally Speaking: How Children Learn Language*, Rowley: Newbury House.
Painter, C. (1984) *Into the Mother Tongue: a Case Study in Early Language Development*, London: Frances Pinter.
Painter, C. (1985) *Learning the Mother Tongue*, Victoria: Deakin University Press.
Villiers, P.A. de and Villiers, J.G. de (1979) *Early Language*, London: Fontana.

Examples of child speech quoted in the chapter are either drawn from Halliday, Brown or Bloom (see above), or from my own data – some twenty hours of audio recordings of five children aged from eighteen months to forty months. Most of the examples from p. 11 to the end of the chapter are drawn from here. All the examples of child speech in this (and the next chapter) are thus attested in data.

Fieldwork projects

The best way of exploring early language development, if you happen to know a helpful parent, is by actually recording children talking and then transcribing the speech. Restrict yourself initially to situations involving only one child – more than one can make transcription difficult, unless you know the children well. If you are not familiar with the child, and are not used to conversing with small children, then record the parent with the child. But try not to put the parent under pressure to get the child talking. If possible use video, because in this way some at least of the features of the situation that are so important for understanding children's speech get recorded too. If video is not available, then quite interesting material can be recorded on even the most simple audio equipment. And though you may lose something in detail, you can gain here in terms of informality. All recording distorts the situation so try to do it as unobtrusively as possible – but always ask permission. Sometimes parents will let you switch on recording equipment and leave it with them, which is slightly less intrusive than having you there as well. In any case play back and transcribe soon afterwards and, if possible, consult the parents over incomprehensible passages.

(1) The following two-word utterances are drawn from nearly an hour's recording of a child aged twenty-three months. (The child also produced several one-word and some three-word utterances.) For each example, attempt to specify the meaning relation being expressed (see Table 2, p. 19). If there are ambiguities, what sorts of information would help to resolve them? What are the most frequent kinds of meaning relation being expressed? What factors might influence the apparent preference for certain kinds of meaning relation?

cover off (×2)	pulling David
Martin('s) cover	two man
two there (×2)	on dere
one there (×2)	big bridge
over there (×2)	naughty boy
in there (×2)	hear bells
out there (×2)	blue van

daddy home	petrol gone
it('s) Wendy	made bridge
in dere	make glasses
under dere (×3)	Michael('s) hankies
Wendy doing	milky there
nice drink	fall down

Useful comparisons can be made with material you collect yourself.

(2) In the following transcript we have the same child in conversation with his mother. They are in the living-room near the tape recorder and also near a window from which they can see people passing along the road. What kinds of function(s) are the child's utterances performing? Comment on the role of the mother's utterances and generally upon the distinctive features of language between adult and young child.

JAMES: TWENTY-THREE MONTHS [M = Mother; C = Child]

M now (.) there's mister Box gone by in his car (6) Wendy's daddy – um

C Wendy's daddy (5) (   ) (2) (   )

C (working) 'sat 'sat 'sat

M   └that's a tape recorder darling

C   'sat mummy

C   └'sat

M that's a switch – now love (.) come on – are you going to come and play with your cars now

C no::

   (1)

M aren' t you

C (what are dose)

M   um

C   (maybe dose) (babydose)

M   there's no more boys and girls – they've all gone now (.) haven't they (2) they've all come home from school

C Wendy

M and Wendy (.) yes (.) Wendy came home too

```
        (3)
M   what
C     └(      )
        (5)
M   who's this – who's that going up there (5) can you see –
    going up through there (2) gone now I think (3) who is
    it (3) heh (4)
C   Wendy
M   it's not (2) it's not Wendy (3) look – who is it – eh
C   Brenda
M   that's right
        (7) ((chuckles))
C   (Chr)issy
M   and Chrissy – yes (.) and Chrissy
        (½)
C   um – darden – a darden (1) a darden
M   um (.) they've gone into the garden (.) haven't they
C   wassat (1) wassat – mummy
M   that's a *switch* (.) darling (.) that you push down
        (½)
C   a bayem pint
M   a what
C   (      )
        ((mother lifts child up away from tape recorder))
C   NO::
M   now – come on (.) are you going to come over here and
    play with your cars
C   NO:: (do it)
M   wouldn't you like to build a garage
C   NOO::
M   I beg your pardon
C   no no
M   um (1) wouldn't you like to build a garage
C   no (1½) wassat – wassat
M   that's a *tape* recorder my darling
C                                           └wassat
M   and those are all the switches on it
C   (      ) – wassat
```

(1)

C   os – oh – boys – boys – boysde dolls

M   boys and girls (.) yes (.) all coming back still some more to come – those are the bigger ones (.) aren't they – um (3) ((noise of aeroplane))

C   an aeroplane

M   yes (.) can you see it anywhere James

C   dere (.) dere (.) dere

M   └where (.) show me where

C   └dere dere

M   ooo yes – it's not an aeroplane is it – you look – what is it

(2)

M   it's a helicopter (1) can you see

C   └yes

M   └it's a bit difficult

C   dissy (1) dissy

M   no (.) I don't think that's Chrissy

(1)

C   no

C   wassat – switches – wassat – wassat

M   what did mummy say they were – what are they

C   switches

M   switches – that's right

C   wassat – wassat mummy (1) wassat – wassat

M   oh that's a little dial

C   wassat

M   what did mummy say that was

C   dale

M   no (.) not that one (2) that's a little knob – that you press (2) DON'T you press it now darling

C   no

M   you just look – just look at it

2 DIALOGUE AND LANGUAGE DEVELOPMENT

Further developments in meaning

During the two-word phase, therefore, children become capable of expressing a relatively wide range of different meaning relations. They have begun the crucial enterprise of making sense in words of their everyday world in communication with others. The kinds of meaning relation entailed in these developments are sometimes referred to as *ideational* (see Halliday, 1975, 1978) – a term used usually more particularly to describe that aspect of the adult language system concerned with expressing and giving shape to events and the external world and of the internal world of consciousness. In taking over the representational properties of speech, by using it to enact notions of *action, agency, quantity, possession* and so forth, the child is thus moving into the *ideational* sphere of the adult system, and is thereby significantly transcending the limitations of the earlier protolanguage.

It is not the case, however, that the earlier modes of meaning are totally supplanted. Indeed, the development of this *ideational* component probably has its roots in, and grows out of, the conflation of the *heuristic* and *personal* functions of the protolinguistic phase. Nor do the other functions of the earlier phase atrophy and disappear, for simultaneously with developments in the *ideational* potential of language the child is also increasing and extending his capacity for engaging linguistically with others, for opening and sustaining dialogue with them. This parallel development amounts to a growing facility in the *interpersonal* dimension of language use. In other words the child is gaining greater access to those aspects of the adult system concerned with ways in which utterances contribute to speech events – informing, directing, querying; and also to ways in which utterances adopt specific roles with respect to the contributions of others – replying, commenting, acknowledging and so forth.

If developments in the *ideational* sphere can be seen as having their roots in the *heuristic* and *personal* systems of the protolinguistic phase, then developments along the *interpersonal* dimension can also be seen as growing out of this earlier phase – in this case as a drawing together of the *instrumental,* the *regulatory* and the *interactional* functions. We can summarize these developments very crudely and schematically as follows:

Table 3

FUNCTIONS IN THE PROTOLANGUAGE		FUNCTIONS IN THE ADULT SYSTEM
Instrumental ('I want')	→	
Regulatory ('Do as I say')	→ →	*Interpersonal*
Interactional ('You and me')	→	
Heuristic ('Tell me why')	→	
Personal ('Here I come')	→ →	*Ideational*

Source: based on Halliday (1975).

On the face of it this can seem like a rationalization plan on the part of the child, a kind of scaling down of what s/he could do before. It has the effect, however, of considerably enhancing his/her communicative potential. The earlier range of functions was discrete and each utterance by the child performed only one function. The evolving system, however, both assimilates the old range into two new functions, and allows these to be simultaneously enacted in a single utterance. Many of the child's utterances now are not just *ideational* but at one and the same time *interpersonal* as well. Within the same utterance the child can now express meaning relations, such as *agent + object,* while at the same time enacting some interpersonal purpose, such as 'demand', as a contribution to a dialogic process.

Ideational *and* interpersonal *meanings in extracts of dialogue*

We can illustrate the way in which the *ideational* and *interpersonal* components operate together by considering some actual examples of dialogue between child and adult. In the first example that follows the child is playing with modelling clay or plasticine, out of which he's shaping the figure of a man. Then he decides to decapitate the figure – an action that he gives linguistic shape to in the utterance 'cut it', perhaps in order to release some clay for the completion of another figure. In *ideational* terms 'cut it' is *agent + object*. But the utterance also works *interpersonally;* in the first instance (ll. 3 and 4) it works partially as a response to the mother's expression of interest and in the second case (ll. 22 and 24) it works as a way of engaging her attention:

DATA EXTRACT 2.1

MOTHER:	that's very clever (.)	1
	isn't it?	2
→ CHILD:	cut it (.)	3
	cut it	4
→ MOTHER:	what are you going to cut it for? (.)	5
	um?	6
CHILD:	man (.) man (10)	7
	another man (.) another man	8
MOTHER:	is that his head? (.)	9

	is that his body?	10
CHILD:	(yes) (1)	11
MOTHER:	stick it on his body then (2)	12
CHILD:	yeh	13
MOTHER:	yes	14
CHILD:	no	15
MOTHER:	yes (.)	16
	I think we'll put it that way up	17
	shall we?	18
CHILD:	no (1)	19
	I do it	20
MOTHER:	oh all right love	21
→ CHILD:	cut it (.) cut it (1)	22
	oh mum (.) mum (.)	23
→	cut it (.)	24
	oh mum	25
MOTHER:	what d'you want? (4)	26
→ CHILD:	cut it (5)	27
MOTHER:	going to cut his head off are you?	28
CHILD:	yeh!	29
MOTHER:	well that's a funny thing to do isn't it	30
	why are you doing that? (3)	31
	um?	32
CHILD:	((no reply))	33

It can be seen, then, that the child's turns at talk are not just designed from the point of view of representing salient features of his situation; each turn at talk is also designed as a contribution to a dialogue, as one part of an ongoing exchange of utterances between himself and his mother, in which the child is variously initiating the dialogue and responding to it – announcing, agreeing, disagreeing, and so on. The successive repetitions of 'cut it', for example, at ll. 22 and 24, seem clearly oriented to gaining some kind of response, though the precise nature of the response required – whether actions or words – remains unclear. (The child is still at the 'early' stage of Table 1 on p. 17 and consequently lacks some of the formal markers useful for making a clear distinction between 'request action' and 'request acknowledgement'.) Later on the same occasion he uses the same utterance 'cut it', again in a response-demanding way, but this time it seems more clearly to be demanding actions rather than words from the mother:

DATA EXTRACT 2.2

	CHILD:	oh (.)	1
→		cut it mum (.)	2
→		cut it	3
	MOTHER:	cut what love?	4
	CHILD:	that (.) that (.) that (4)	5
		mummy	6
	MOTHER:	um?	7
→	CHILD:	cut it	8
		fatter mum	9
	MOTHER:	what d'you want?	10
		to make it fatter?	11
	CHILD:	um	12
	MOTHER:	well it's not got very much plasticine	13
		here have you?	14

In all of these episodes the child is doing more than describing states of affairs in the world at hand: he is doing more than giving voice to, for example, an *action* ('cut') to be performed on an *object* ('plasticine'). He is also, at one and the same time, assigning and adopting roles in relationship with his conversational partner.

This *interpersonal* dimension to the child's utterances can be emphasized by reference to one further extract. Here the dialogue is built around the coupling of 'nice' with 'drink' *(attribute + entity)* and the child's utterance (1.7) seems to carry little implication for action on the mother's part. Instead, 'nice drink' seems to serve as a kind of free floating comment by the child on his own play (he's pretending that the cup of water for dampening the ironing is in fact a cup of tea). At the onset of the extract, however, the child needs to establish the mother's attention ('look mummy'). Towards the end of it he is faced with a query to which he responds affirmatively ('um': 1.12). Neither of these utterances convey much about ongoing events. But they are, none the less, crucial in opening and sustaining the dialogue between the two participants: as such they are almost exclusively *interpersonal* in orientation:

DATA EXTRACT 2.3

CHILD:	look mummy (.)	1
	nice (.) nice mum	2
MOTHER:	it's nice?	3
	good	4
CHILD:	look mummy (.)	5
	look (1)	6
	nice drink	7
MOTHER:	a nice drink	8
	can mummy put a bit of water on her	9
	blouse?	10
	to wet it?	11
CHILD:	um	12
MOTHER:	ta	13

Thus, towards the end of the two-word stage children have not only taken significant steps into the *ideational* sphere: they have also extensively advanced their linguistic potential in the *interpersonal* dimension. Whereas, previously, interchanges between child and 'other' tended quickly to lose a sense of connectedness (and where there was coherence, it was often supplied by the adult), now the dialogues are far more sustained – with the child quite often making the running. They are like conversations in embryo, even if the talk is still rooted in the immediate present.

The child's strategies for dialogue: establishing shared attention

The 'here and now' nature of the talk is still an important feature, a fact highlighted by the child's use of 'look' in the extracts above. (See, for example, extract 2.3: ll. 1, 5 and 6.) Since the dialogues typically grow out of the immediate context, their successful accomplishment depends crucially on both parties attending to the same features of what is there present for both of them. The device, 'look', is a useful and economical way of attempting to secure this joint attention. The same child had a companion strategy, 'watch me', for use especially when his own actions were to provide the 'field' for the dialogue to work within – as can be seen in the following extract:

DATA EXTRACT 2.4

CHILD:	watch me	1
MOTHER:	watch you?	2
	go on then I'm watching (.)	3
	come on (.)	4
	what've I got to watch? (1)	5
CHILD:	dancing	6
MOTHER:	so you're dancing (.)	7
	let's see you dance then (.)	8
	go on	9
CHILD:	((6 sec. pause, then throws a lego brick))	10

Children, of course, also use 'mum' or 'mummy' (or a similar naming device), often in association with 'look' and 'watch me': there are examples in data extract 1.1: ll. 7 and 10; data extract 2.1: ll. 23 and 25; 2.2: ll. 2 and 9, and 2.3: ll. 1, 2 and 5. At first sight this might seem a rather obvious element in the child's speech. It takes on a special significance here, however, inasmuch as it displays that the child is shaping his utterance with an 'other' in mind. This is not always the case: quite often children's utterances constitute a mono-logic stream with no apparent recipient intended. It is as if the child is talking with himself. Equally, those who surround the child are not always in a clear state of engagement with him: maybe they're painting the ceiling, doing the ironing, or are bored with the effort of conversing with a two-year-old. Given these kinds of possibilities, the child clearly needs a device that marks off certain of his own utterances as an attempt at dialogue by invoking attention, naming who is to be the recipient and thereby positioning that recipient as next speaker when the child has finished his own turn.

Further dialogic strategies: responses

Children, through these and other devices, are making a claim to partnership in the process of talk. By now, late in the two-word stage they can intervene in the talk in a variety of ways. As shown above, they can open the dialogue, engage a recipient, establish a shared field of interest. They can also respond within dialogue. They can respond affirmatively, when a proposition is presented to them for confirmation:

EXAMPLE 2.1

    MOTHER: going to cut his head off are you?
    CHILD: yeh!

EXAMPLE 2.2

    MOTHER: Michael rolled that did he?
    CHILD: yeh!

They can register a disinclination to comply with suggestions or commands:

DATA EXTRACT 2.5

    MOTHER: d'you want to play with the plasticine   1
               um?   2
    CHILD: no   3
    MOTHER: do you?   4
    CHILD: no (2)   5
    MOTHER: shall I bring it in for you? (2)   6
    CHILD: no   7
    MOTHER: no you don't want to play with it?   8

They can now also produce clear and appropriate answers to a variety of questions:

EXAMPLE 2.3

    MOTHER: where are your tights?
    CHILD: there

EXAMPLE 2.4

    MOTHER: what colour are they?
    CHILD: pink

EXAMPLE 2.5

   MOTHER: whose is it?
   CHILD: Ian's

EXAMPLE 2.6

   MOTHER: what d'you think it is?
   CHILD: a bag

EXAMPLE 2.7

   MOTHER: who's a wet boy? (.)
                eh?
   CHILD: me:: (.) a wet boy
   MOTHER: yes
   CHILD: wet boy (.) wet boys
   MOTHER: you're a wet boy aren't you? (2) um?
   CHILD: (laughs)

Questions of the *why*-form, however, still seem to present some problems.

EXAMPLE 2.8

   MOTHER: well that's a funny thing to do isn't it?
                why are you doing that? (3)
                um?
   CHILD: ((no reply))

(Data extract 2.1, ll. 29–32)

These developments constitute important steps into dialogue for the child. Indeed, learning to participate in dialogue is a very crucial aspect of the child's development of language, not least because language itself is as much for talking *with someone* as it is for talking *about something*.

Ideational and *interpersonal* developments are closely interdependent

Even when the orientation of an utterance seems clearly to be more in one dimension than the other, matters may be more complex than they appear to be on first consideration. Take for example the use of 'wassat?', which is an important source of information for the child about the conventionally accepted linguistic labels for objects. Children may use it – or something like it – as early as fourteen months, and still be getting mileage out of it a year later. Certainly they use it to find out about the world and the way in which it is mapped in language: and thus it can be seen as a continuous strand of development running from the *heuristic* function of the protolinguistic phase into the later emergence of the *ideational* function. But what is the twenty-four-month-old child in the following extract doing? (This is the same child as in data extract 1.1, pp. 11–12, but here transcribed from a recording made some four weeks later.)

DATA EXTRACT 2.5

	CHILD:	wassat? (2)	1
→		swi (3) switches (.) switches	2
	MOTHER:	that's right (.) those are switches (.)	3
		yes	4
	CHILD:	oo (.) whatsat? (2)	5
	MOTHER:	what's that? ((sighs)) (2) no don't (.)	6
		don't touch anything darling	7
	CHILD:	wassat?	8
	MOTHER:	that's a switch darling	9
→	CHILD:	wassat? (.) more pish	10
	MOTHER:	another switch	11
	CHILD:	more pitch	12
	MOTHER:	umhum	13
	CHILD:	pish	14
	MOTHER:	umhum	15

They've been through all this before, as we know from the recording made a month earlier (see data extract 1.1, pp. 11–12). Even more significantly, however, the child displays in some of his utterances that he knows the answer to the question he has asked before the mother actually supplies it (see ll. 2 and 10). This suggests that on this particular occasion the *ideational* orientation of 'wassat?' is considerably curtailed and that it is almost exclusively its *interpersonal* possibilities that are being exploited. Basically it is a handy way of keeping the mother engaged, although that sigh at line 6 suggests she might not put up with this particular strategy for much longer.

Dialogue as an arena for language development

Building up utterances in dialogue

So language does not merely shape a material and mental world for the child; it also shapes and explores the possibilities of relationship with others (sometimes to their limit). It can even be argued that the *ideational* shaping of experience is necessarily dependent upon developments in the *interpersonal* sphere, and that it is dialogue that provides the ground in which the development of meaning relations in the two-word stage can take root. For it is not unusual to see two-word utterances being built up on the wing, so to speak, in successive utterances of an unfolding dialogue, as below.

DATA EXTRACT 2.6

MOTHER:	now (.)	1
	that'll just about go in (.) that old car	2
	won't it?	3
→ CHILD:	ode Morris	4
→	that ode Morris	5
MOTHER:	that's an old Morris is it?	6

DATA EXTRACT 2.7

→ CHILD:	a Morris (1)	1
→	new Morris (.)	2
→	new Morris there	3
MOTHER:	um?	4

DATA EXTRACT 2.8

CHILD:	look (.) look (.)	1
	look mum	2
MOTHER:	yes	3
→ CHILD:	broken	4

	broken down	5
→		
MOTHER:	what's broken down? (.)	6
	um?	7
→ CHILD:	a van	8
→	a blue van	9

DATA EXTRACT 2.9

	CHILD:	ice cream	1
	MOTHER:	are you licking it?	2
	CHILD:	yeah	3
	MOTHER:	um?	4
→	CHILD:	ice cream	5
→		(? lick it)	6
→		a dinner	7
→		ice cream a dinner	8
	MOTHER:	ice cream for dinner?	9
		did you have ice cream for dinner today?	10
	CHILD:	yeah	11
	MOTHER:	you didn't!	12
	CHILD:	yeah (.)	13
		ice cream (to)day	14
	MOTHER:	not today	15
		you had it yesterday didn't you?	16
	CHILD:	ice cream a day	17
	MOTHER:	not today	18
		you had rhubarb today	19
	CHILD:	rhubarb	20

In all of these episodes the child puts together quite complex structures not in one attempt, but in successive stages: 'a Morris' becomes 'new Morris' becomes 'new Morris there'. It is as if in the actual ebb and flow of talk the child builds up to utterances such as 'that ode Morris', 'new Morris there', 'ice cream a day' from earlier versions, each of which provides a kind of platform from which to mount each new attempt. In this piecemeal construction work the child's conversational partner gives crucial support by providing a kind of dialogic scaffold. She both prompts his attempts and returns them back to him in expanded form for him either to accept or reject. Occasionally, but very rarely – if indeed at all – she corrects surface features of grammatical accuracy. As long as what the child says can be made to seem meaningful in the context of the world they both inhabit, then it's allowed to pass as an appropriate contribution to the joint construction of the dialogue. If it doesn't seem to match the world of shared events, then there may be grounds for dispute, as in the last extract above concerning 'ice cream' or 'rhubarb'.

The negotiation of meaning within dialogue

An intricate process is at work between child and other, perhaps best described as a 'negotiation of meaning', in which *ideational* and *interpersonal* are closely interwoven. Dialogue provides the arena for this negotiation of meaning, and thereby provides the arena for the various systems of language to develop.

This notion can cast some light on the problem (discussed in chapter 1, pp. 20–3) concerning the precise definition of the meaning relations of the two-word stage. In presenting such meaning relations it is difficult to avoid implying that somehow they are 'fixed quantities' present in the child's speech; that utterances such as 'nice drink' or 'make bridge' – despite their incomplete and almost telegraphic character – are realizations of precise and specific situated meanings, meanings which we can decode and identify and which are reducible to abstract categories such as *attribute + entity* and *action + object*. It is difficult also not to imply that for any particular stage or indeed moment in the child's development there is a limited and stable set of basic meanings manifest in the child's speech, and that we can encompass these meanings in a small number of abstract categories.

This, however, would be to oversimplify what is in effect a more complex process: one in which the meaning of an utterance as spoken by the child is not necessarily closed off in advance, but can be relatively fluid and unstable at the time of speaking. It only becomes fixed or stabilized to any degree by the conversational partner in the continuous negotiation that dialogue provides. Thus, the child in effect is actually discovering what some of his/her utterances can mean in the act of using them. S/he remains for a long time an active innovator and experimenter with language. In this active appropriation of language, however, s/he requires the dialogue provided by a conversational partner in order to be able to assess the felicity or otherwise of the innovations and experiments that s/he is making.

This does not mean that the categories proposed to handle the *ideational* meanings of the two-word stage are redundant or irrelevant. For one thing, not all of what the child does is innovatory or experimental. There are some things s/he will be relatively sure of, and these relative certainties can provide a provisional framework within which to operate less stable meanings. After all, for communication to proceed in even the simplest form, there has to be some mutually adopted and shared set of conventions. None the less, it is perhaps more illuminating to consider the *ideational* meanings at this stage of development as broad guidelines or parameters that the child has available to him/her to experiment within, rather than as absolute and fixed categories, especially if we accept that this skeletal framework is provisional and is subject to revision as the child's active search for the basic regularities of the language system continues.

Mutual accommodation within dialogue: the recycling of patterns from parent to child

In this active search, dialogue not only constitutes an arena for the negotiation of meaning and for experimentation in the possibilities of the system: it also provides the child with a source of fresh insights into how language in both its *ideational* and *interpersonal* aspects can be made to work. Often s/he takes over at one stage of development, patterns that s/he has been the recipient of earlier.

THE EXAMPLE OF 'LOOK'
In extract 2.3, p. 34, for example, we saw a child using the device 'look' as a way of establishing a shared field of attention with his conversational partner. He used this apparently simple though effective discovery several times in a recording made at twenty-three months and again at twenty-four months. However, in an earlier recording of one hour's duration made at twenty-two months there is little sign of it. What we do find is the *parent* using this device and using it with a frequency that exceeds even that of the child a month later.

CHILD:	((pulling cushions off seat))	1
→ MOTHER:	oh look	2
	who's this coming?	3
	who's this coming?	4
→	look now	5
→	look	6
CHILD:	dadda	7

DATA EXTRACT 2.11

CHILD:	((playing with toy bricks))	1
	AAAR! ((followed by screams))	2
→ MOTHER:	darling (.) look (.) listen (.)	3
	it won't stay on top of there	4
→	look let mummy show you	5
	if you put them this way around	6
CHILD:	no	7
MOTHER:	it'll stay on top	8
→	look let mummy show you	9
→	look	10
	like that (.) see?	11

The use of 'look' by the mother is thus very similar to its subsequent adoption by the child, the only difference being that the mother's use is slightly more marked than the child's and seems to constitute a more positive attempt to switch the field of attention: it is used particularly in contexts where the child has run into trouble of some sort or is imminently likely to do so.

There is in fact one instance of 'look' by the child on this recording and it comes as follows:

DATA EXTRACT 2.12

CHILD:	((close to a hot electric iron))	1
MOTHER:	don't touch it darling don't touch it	2
→	come on (.) look (.)	3
	shall we get your construction set out?	4
	um?	5

CHILD:	NO	6
MOTHER:	hum ?	7
CHILD:	no	8
MOTHER:	come on	9
	let's get your construction set out	10
CHILD:	OH!	11
→	LOOK!	12
MOTHER:	what've you put on the floor?	13
CHILD:	milky	14
MOTHER:	mummy get a cloth and wipe it up then	15

This solitary example from the child on this recording does in fact seem closer to his mother's usage than examples from his speech a month later. In general terms, however, we can see how a prominent dialogic strategy evolved by the mother in response to the special requirements of the communicative situation subsequently becomes appropriated and refined by the child.

THE EXAMPLE OF 'WASSAT?'
A similar process seems to underlie the genesis of the child's first question form, 'wassat?', which figured so prominently in extract 1.1, pp. 11–12, and in extract 2.5, p. 36, and which this same child used nearly seventy times in the course of an hour's recording at twenty-three months. Its antecedents may be found early in the holophrastic stage. As the first words begin to emerge, one way for adults to elicit them is simply by asking the child 'what's that?'

There will be many other question forms used as well, of course, depending upon the purpose and circumstances of the communication. There's the kind of minimal question often used by adults, made up by expanding the child's immediately prior utterance and adding a tag at the end: 'gonna build a bridge, are you?' And then there are trouble-oriented questions, such as: 'what's the matter?'; 'what happened?'; 'what are you doing?' Also commonly used by adults to children from early in their development are location or *where*-type questions, such as: 'where's the digger?'; 'where are you going?' It is, however, unusual during the two-word phase to find questions of the *when-, how-* or *why*-type being used with genuine dialogic intent and with any real chance of success. This is primarily

44

because the child has little means at his disposal to provide an answer until later in development. Questions such as these presuppose development of, for example, *temporal* or *causal relations,* which rarely emerge within the limits of two-word utterances.

On the other hand, questions such as 'what's that?' from the adult are particularly effective during this period, especially in focused settings such as looking at a picture book or playing with objects. Suppose a child has a verbal repertoire which includes an expression for 'ball'. An adult who is looking at a book with the child and is familiar with the child's potential, on seeing a picture of a ball is most likely to ask 'what's that?' In some ways, it is a curious strategy, since language is much more than a list of names for objects. Furthermore, the adult has no need to know the name and quite likely reckons that the child knows it anyway. But their mutual knowledge ensures that this particular dialogic opening has some chance of a response, whereas at this stage of development 'why do you want to visit grandma's?' in all likelihood would not. The device can be seen in play in the following edited extract of a parent with a nineteen month-old child who is firmly in the holophrastic stage.

DATA EXTRACT 2.13

	MOTHER:	shall we read a book?	1
	CHILD:	ock	2
	MOTHER:	book	3
		all right	4
	CHILD:	bock ock	5
	MOTHER:	come on then	6
	CHILD:	ock ock	7
		....	
		((they settle on a picture rather than a nursery rhyme book))	
		....	
	MOTHER:	right	8
→		what's that then?	9
→		what is it ?	10
	CHILD:	((no reply))	11
	MOTHER:	it's what?	12

	you tell me what it is (.) go on	13
→	what's that?	14
CHILD:	(?? unintelligible)	15
MOTHER:	that's a vase	16
	....	
→ MOTHER:	and what's that? (2)	17
	you forgotten?	18
CHILD:	tick tock	19
MOTHER:	yes	20
	tick tock tick tock	21
CHILD:	tick tock	22
MOTHER:	it's a clock isn't it? (.)	23
→	er (.) what's that?	24
CHILD:	(?? eggs)	25
MOTHER:	that's not eggs is it?	26
	or are you looking for eggs?	27
	is that what you mean?	28
CHILD:	((no reply))	29
	....	
→ MOTHER	and what's that?	30
CHILD:	ba—oon	31
MOTHER:	yes balloon	32
	and	33
CHILD:	tick tock	34
MOTHER:	yes we've had the clock	35
CHILD:	cwock!	36

It should be clear from this what a fragile enterprise any sustained verbal dialogue between child and other can be in the early stages of development. In this particular episode there seems to be some uncertainty between the two over the precise procedure they are following; whether the child has free choice over elements to which to supply a name, or whether the mother is to elicit them from her. At one point the latter remarks 'you're determined to find your own aren't you – all right well you find them and you tell me what they are.'

But despite the fragility of the exercise, the mother's question 'what's that?' does seem to work in a fair proportion of instances.

Although it has overtones of being an overt teaching strategy on the parent's part, it should be emphasized that in the last analysis it is more than merely rehearsing the names of objects. What is at stake here, and in dialogues such as this, is the selection by the adult of the optimum opening likely to secure a sustained dialogue in the light of the child's present communicative possibilities. In so far as the parent's strategy is both repetitive and effective in this respect, it is hardly surprising that children quickly discover how to do it in return, even to the extent of asking the adult the names of objects which they both already know they know. (See extract 1.1, pp. 11–12, and extract 2.5, p. 36.)

THE EXAMPLE OF 'WHERE'
A similar genesis can be traced for another question form, *where . . .?*, which does not emerge with any degree of consistency in the speech of the child till late in the two-word stage – say, around twenty-six months. In the following examples from a child of twenty-eight months they are well established: she used over twenty in the course of an hour (along with, incidentally, over fifty occurrences of 'wassat?'):

DATA EXTRACT 2.14

→ CHILD:	where's Martin?	1
MOTHER:	he's gone (.) erm (..) back to school	2
CHILD:	oh	3
MOTHER:	do his lessons	4
CHILD:	oh	5
MOTHER:	like Juliette	6
CHILD:	oh (1)	7
→ CHILD:	where's Moire?	8
MOTHER:	she's gone back to school with	9
	Martin as well	10
CHILD:	oh	11

DATA EXTRACT 2.15

→ CHILD:	where's my book?	1
MOTHER:	er (..) here look (.)	2
	on the washing	3

→ CHILD:	where's it?	4
MOTHER:	there (.)	5
	here look (.) Sarah (.) look (.)	6
	here (.) on these clothes (.)	7
	in the corner	8
CHILD:	oh	9

This kind of question that *seeks* locational information may only become firmly established in the child's speech late in the two-word stage. A good deal earlier than this, however, as far back as the holophrastic phase and before, the child has been able to *give* locational information. Indeed, one of the earliest meaning relations to emerge in the two-word phase is represented by locational expressions such as 'up dere', 'on dere' and so on (see pp. 18–19). The availability of these expressions to the child provides the adult conversational partner with another effective way into dialogue from the holophrastic phase onwards. Thus, we find adults opening and sustaining dialogue in the following way:

To child of eighteen months:	'Where's Anna gone?'
To child of nineteen months:	'Where's it gone now?'
	'Where's the dog?'
	'Where's the tree?'
To child of twenty-two months:	'Where you going love?'
	'Where's that milk?'
	'Where's Jamie's?'
	'Where is the digger?'
	'Where is it?'
	'Where are you going with your satchel?'
	'Where are the trousers?'
	'Where's he been?'

The incidence of this type of question gradually increases as the two-word stage proceeds and a subvariant of it is quite likely to appear, in which it is used for checking the field of attention in response to an utterance from the child, as in the following conversation with a child at twenty-three months.

DATA EXTRACT 2.16

CHILD:	(?? an aeroplane)	1
MOTHER:	yes	2
	can you see it anywhere Jamie?	3
CHILD:	dere! (.) dere!	4
→ MOTHER:	where? (.)	5
	show me	6
→	where?	7
CHILD:	dere! (.) dere! dere!	8
MOTHER:	oo yes	9
	it's not an aeroplane is it? (.)	10
	you look	11
	what is it?	12
CHILD:	((no reply))	13
MOTHER:	it's a helicopter	14
CHILD:	oh	15

Once again the effectiveness and consequent prominence of a device in the speech of the adult seems to prepare the ground for its subsequent appropriation by the child. And this appropriation may well include the kind of checking just noted above, as with this child at thirty months:

DATA EXTRACT 2.17

CHILD:	where the top is (.) mum	1
MOTHER:	here it is (.)	2
	on this side	3
→CHILD:	where? (.) where mum?	4
MOTHER:	this side here (2)	5
	on this other side of the box	6
CHILD:	on here?	7
MOTHER:	um	8

The overall evolution of the locational question form ('where . . .?') for the child would seem to be similar to the genesis of 'wassat?' Because from early on in the one-word phase the child has growing control over an expanding range of locational expressions (such as 'down', 'on there', etc.), then a favoured mode of opening dialogue for the adult will be by way of a question directed precisely towards an area such as this in which the child can readily respond.

Adult and child, then, share a mutually determining communicative circuit in which forms pass from one to another in ascending complexity as development proceeds. Certainly, the range of access that the child has at a particular developmental moment to the communicative possibilities of language exerts constraints on what adults can effectively introduce into the talk: they are forced to frame their utterances in the light of their estimate of the child's linguistic potential. Whatever way the adult engages in dialogue with the child, however, provides a resource from which the child can then construct a new set of possibilities to which the adult must in turn again adjust. And in this way adult and child together progressively advance what can be encompassed in their joint universe of discourse.

Theoretical paradigms of language development

The imitation hypothesis

In this account of early stages in the development of language a rudimentary explanation seems to be emerging of how this development takes place. At times, indeed, the foregoing account might almost be taken to imply that children learn language simply by imitating what they hear spoken around them. I would not, in fact, wish to propose or imply such an explanation, associated as it is with certain crucial difficulties which may be summarized briefly as follows.

Problems with the imitation hypothesis

THE STRUCTURAL NATURE OF LANGUAGE
First, there is the peculiar nature of language itself, imbued as it is with certain characteristics that are difficult to reproduce by purely imitative strategies. In particular, language is made up out of, and

constituted in, structures: rules, for example, that govern the combination of words into sentences. Out of the set of rules or structures speakers of a language are able indefinitely to produce new sentences from essentially limited resources. A sentence, for example, such as 'The ant crawled across the table cloth and bumped into a dormant moth many times its own size' is unlikely to have been encountered before by the reader of this book. It is the shared rules and conventions that make possible this creativity in the formation and comprehension of quite unique utterances. In taking over a language, then, the child is not learning by rote whole utterances or even words alone. S/he is discovering the regular principles that underlie the construction and formation of sentences out of words. In this respect, what s/he is after is not merely the bricks and mortar construction elements of a language: s/he requires the blueprints as well. Imitative learning strategies cannot in themselves yield up this creativity to the child.

THE CHILD'S INTELLIGENT MISTAKES

The second consideration is less abstract and philosophical than the first, though closely related to it, and takes account of what children actually do as they learn a language. It is difficult to trace an imitative origin for many of the early utterances produced by children. As they move beyond the two-word stage, for instance, children begin to register distinctions between singular and plural, present and past by the use of inflections such as /-s/, /-d/ and so on. Thus, they are now more likely to say 'more cars' than 'more car', if they wish to indicate the plural; and 'me walked home' rather than 'walk home', if they wish to indicate a past event. But having grasped a generalization such as 'form the plural by adding /-s/ (or a variant such as /-z/ or /-Iz/)', they then proceed to apply it even to irregular cases with results such as 'sheeps', 'foots' and 'mans' (as in 'there's three mans'). Similarly, having grasped a generalization such as 'indicate past event by adding /-d/ (or a variant such as /-t/, etc.)', instances then begin to appear of items such as 'comed', 'goed', and 'maked' (as in 'maked a bridge'). These kinds of intelligent mistakes – from which we may infer that children have detected two broad types of pattern but not yet filtered out those cases to which it does not apply – are very difficult to account for within imitative theories of language development.

A CRITICAL LEARNING PERIOD

The third consideration is of a very different order. There is an accumulating body of evidence that learning a first language can only be accomplished within a critical developmental period. So called 'feral' children, for example, who have managed to survive the first few years of life with little known human contact, have great difficulty advancing beyond the most limited linguistic expressions, even when subjected to explicit language training. Similarly, children who are born profoundly deaf respond less well to speech training than those in whom severe loss of hearing occurs later, especially if this happens after the critical learning period has passed. In the light of factors such as these, there is now a growing consensus that the critical period for beginning the development of a first language comes within the first three years of life. If through some special set of circumstances a child is unable to begin the process by this point in the maturational cycle, then s/he will develop language only slowly and with great difficulty, whatever his/her other abilities.

The notion of a critical learning period is not easily accounted for within the imitation perspective, since the generalized procedures of imitation, memorization and selective reinforcement imply no attendant time limit on when they can be applied.

An alternative position: 'nativism' – an innate capacity for language

These criticisms of the imitation perspective have lent weight to a counter position which argues that humans in general have a special and distinctive language-learning faculty which makes possible the learning process: it equips us with an unconscious awareness of certain basic properties of language itself and it comes into play at a predetermined stage in the maturational cycle. This innate knowledge, it is claimed, is part of every human's genetic inheritance, transmitted at conception, and merely activated at a particular moment in the early years of life by the necessary linguistic environment. All that is required is a context of others speaking a human language for us to begin the task of breaking the language code and implementing it in use. In this sense, discovering the patterns and structures of a language – such as, for example, the markers of plural or of past events – is only possible on the basis of a subtle preparedness. For, in framing and refining such hypotheses, the child is working within a generally inherited, genetically endowed, predisposition to learn language. It is his/her special and distinctive language-learning faculty that dictates what to look for and where to look: by virtue of it s/he already possesses part of the language blueprint.

In further support of this position it is claimed that, as long as there is no gross physiological impairment and as long as the necessary linguistic environment is present to work upon, all children learn language with equal facility despite circumstantial differences in ethnic or social background or in intelligence. And in so far as it is possible to compare progress in different languages, it is further claimed that all children pass through broadly similar stages in their development of language: individual rates of acquisition may differ but the broad steps remain the same for all children.

Problems with nativism

These arguments have generated a great deal of controversy, more recently by the apparent ability of some chimpanzees to develop a linguistic potential when trained to express it in the form of sign language of the type prevalent amongst the profoundly deaf. That such considerations should provoke debate is partly because the issues are complex and because conclusive evidence is still lacking to settle some of the more contentious points. It is also, however, a measure of the significance of the positions adopted: discussion of them inevitably and rightly leads us on into fundamental questions of what is a 'human' being and the role played by language in defining and constituting that 'humanity'.

While the theory of an innate language-learning faculty gained much support as a rival to imitation-based theories, there is still much about language development that it overlooks. It tended to reduce the whole process to an internal psychological one based on pre-existing mental dispositions. Accordingly, it fostered a picture of development that focused almost exclusively on the types of linguistic structure displayed by children in their speech at certain developmental moments. The development of linguistic structure came to be seen as either motivated purely in and for itself or as primarily motivated by maturational tendencies within the child. It thus gave little emphasis to what purposes were being enacted by these linguistic structures, nor why children said what they did, when they did. In this respect it tended to overlook a great deal that was special and noteworthy about the social context of language development: how the child is learning language in the act of communicating with another person, and how this process is an essentially interactive one involving mutual accomplishments and adjustments by both child and other.

Conclusion

The question of innate psychological tendencies has yet to be satisfactorily resolved but meanwhile there has been a burgeoning interest in the communicative context of language development, and it is this that this chapter reflects. What I have tried to emphasize is that children, while developing language, are already heavily involved in dialogue: they learn language in the act of talking with others. Indeed, there is an important sense in which they learn language actually to fulfil the needs and purposes of dialogue. For it is the dialogic situation that exerts a continuous pressure on the child to extend and refine his/her communicative competence.

But dialogue does not merely frame and create communicative needs as an impetus to development. It also provides a rich, but carefully adapted, source of insights for the child into ways of modifying and developing his/her own linguistic potential. For, in the last analysis, the child is learning much more than a sense of how to put words together into sentences: s/he is both learning how to mean; and learning how to accomplish actions with words. In the act of engaging with others in dialogue s/he is learning the prevalent modes of relationship as given in the language of the surrounding society. And at the same time, that society is imparting to him/her in language its own dominant meanings and preferred ways of looking at the world.

Background sources and further reading

The ideational/interpersonal *distinction*

The terms are drawn from the work of the linguist Michael Halliday. See:

Halliday, M.A.K. (1975) *Learning How to Mean,* London: Edward Arnold.
Halliday, M.A.K. (1978) *Language as Social Semiotic: the Social Interpretation of Language and Meaning,* London: Edward Arnold.

Dialogue and language development

The following emphasize the interactional and communicative dimension in first-language learning:

Ervin-Tripp, S. and Mitchell-Kernan, C. (eds) (1977) *Child Discourse,* New York: Academic Press.
French, P. and MacLure, M. (eds) (1981) *Adult–Child Conversation,* London: Croom Helm.
Garvey, C. (1984) *Children's Talk*, London: Fontana.
Wells, G.C. *et al.* (1981) *Learning Through Interaction: the Study of Language Development*, Cambridge: Cambridge University Press.

Nativism versus environmentalism

The classic statement of the nativist position may be found in the linguist Noam Chomsky's review of a book on language by B.F. Skinner, a behaviourist psychologist. See:

Chomsky, N. (1959) 'Review of Skinner's *Verbal Behaviour*', *Language,* 35, 26–58. It is reprinted (along with an extract from Skinner's book) in:

Cecco, J.P. de (ed.) (1961) *The Psychology of Language, Thought, and Instruction,* New York: Holt, Rinehart & Winston.

Two collections of papers on child language development show renewed interest in the nativist position:

Deutsch, W. (ed.) (1981) *The Child's Construction of Language,* New York: Academic Press.

Wanner, E. and Gleitman, L.R. (eds) (1982) *Language Acquisition: the State of the Art,* Cambridge: Cambridge University Press.

Fieldwork projects

(1) The following are extracts from recordings of two separate children (both girls; one aged thirty months and one aged thirty-four months) with their respective mothers. For each extract:
(a) which features of which turns help to sustain the talk;
(b) which participant plays the leading role in sustaining the talk;
(c) which child would you consider to be the elder and why?

Extract A

C   they come home (.) in a minute – when – they go in the car. Sarah – Sarah – (mustn't cross it) when (.) when they come – back home – won't they?

M   L(   ) not
so much traffic when you come back home (.) traffic when you go to school

C   (   )

M   eh?

C   you and I (go in) (traffic) when we go to school won't we?

M   um (.) yeah – not as much as Daddy got

C   no (2) Daddy hasn't got – tra – any traffic has he?

M   no not when he comes home (.) but when he goes to work

C   oh

M   when he comes home everyone else is home
     (5)

M   he went a different way this morning
C   um?
M   I SAID he went a different way
C   oh
M   didn't he?
C   – 'cos- 'cos the (light) was there (.) and (   ) he didn't
     go – a different way (.) did he?
M   he went a different way
C   yes he did go a ( ) 'cos he didn't go the school way didn't
     he – in't he?
M   └he didn't what love?
C   └didn't he (1½) didn't he?
M   └he didn't what?
C   (he-he) didn't
M   (1) yes I think he went (.) yes he did go to school
C   └he didn't
     I did go to school didn't I?
M   you? (.) not today
C   (1) didn't I (1) didn't I (1) didn't I – go to playgroup
     Mummy?
M   yes (.) yesterday
C   (2) didn't I – go – go – I did not go to playgroup with
     Sarah didn't I?
M   oh no (.) not yesterday. Sarah was at school
C   (1) (   )
M   yeah
C   (6) we go:: (.) we go that way – a::nd (.) we not go that
     way are we?
M   yes (.) we can go that way (.) 'cos there's not so much
     traffic now
C   no
M   └it's just when everyone's going to work there's a lot of
     traffic
C   (5) and (   ) we will meet them – won't we?
M   um

Extract B

C   where the top is (.) Mum?

M   here it is (.) on this side?

C   where – where Mum

M   ⌐this side here (2) on this other side of
       the box

C   on here?

M   um

C   oh (   ) Mum (.) I'm making some (.) porridge – for
       you

M   thank you

C   it's cooking now

M   good

C   wheresa spoon? (3) wheresa SPOon?

M   it'll (.) be – in the box somewhere open your eyes and
       look for it (3)

C   (   ) it's not there Mum
       (2)

M   well look in the other box
       (1)

C   in here?

M   um
       (1½)

C   wait a minute (1) I found something (.) here

M   oh yes (1)

C   where that goes?

M   on the kettle

C   where? (   )

M   ⌐(on the) – I don't know where the kettle is –
       but it goes on the kettle
       (1)

C   where's the kettle?

M   I think it must be upstairs somewhere

C   you – you find the kettle

M   when?

C   you FInd the kettle

M   when? (.) now?

C   yes
M   o::h (I'm) not going just for a minute

(2) If possible make your own recording of a younger child with its parent and compare the transcript with the extracts above for differences in the way the dialogue is structured and sustained. (A recording of child peer-group interaction would give another interesting point of comparison.)

PART TWO
LINGUISTIC DIVERSITY
AND THE SPEECH
COMMUNITY

The development of labour necessarily
helped to bring the members of society
closer together by increasing cases of
mutual support and joint activity, and by
making clear the advantage of this joint
activity to each individual. In the short,
humans in the making arrived at the point
where *they had something to say* to each other.
(Frederic Engels*)

Now the whole earth had one language and
few words . . . And the Lord said, 'Behold
they are one people, and they all have one
language; and this . . . [tower reaching to
the heavens] . . . is only the beginning of
what they will do; and nothing that they
propose to do will now be impossible for
them. Come, let us go down, and there
confuse their language, that they may not
understand one another's speech.
(Genesis 11: 1–9)

*Engels, F., 'The part played by labour in the transition from ape to man' in
Marx, K. and Engels, F. (1968) *Selected Works,* London: Lawrence & Wishart.

3 LANGUAGE AND REGIONAL VARIATION: ACCENT AND DIALECT

Regional variation within a speech community

In learning a first language the child assumes active membership of society. Initially, of course, the child enters not society as a whole but a particular localized subgroup. In this respect, access to his/her first language is by way of a highly specific network of speakers who pass on to the child their own version of the language in question. The child, in effect, does not learn 'a language' whole and entire such as Urdu, Swahili, German or English: s/he learns a way of communicating with an immediate social group. For, just as there are extreme and obvious differences between one language and another – between, for example, English, Farsi (Persian), Gujarati, Urdu, Welsh, Serbo-Croat, and German – there are also significant if less obvious differences within languages. Thus there are important distinctions between High and Low German, between Serbian and Croatian, between British and American English. A child growing up somewhere in Britain does not necessarily learn a uniformly standard form of English as a first language. In the first place, it might not be English at all: It might be Welsh or Urdu or Punjabi. And, even if it is 'English', it may well be a very different English if learnt in parts of Liverpool, Glasgow, Oxford, or Belfast.

For one thing it will sound different. To some extent such differences in pronunciation are part of the geographical dispersal of a language – the degree of difference roughly corresponding to the way in which localities are separated from each other. These variations in pronunciation can become powerful indicators of regional identity and affiliation. Indeed, they form part of our everyday commonsense knowledge about language. Most of us can quite accurately tell the difference between a 'Geordie' accent and a 'Scouse', between a West Country accent and a North Country accent. Our ability to make such apparently simple, often unconscious, almost trivial acts of recognition does, however, have important interpersonal consequences.

Regional variation and social structure

Whenever differences are registered between groups of speakers who use ostensibly the 'same language', these differences become a site for the interplay of social judgements as part of the intricate symbiosis between language and society. For just as any one language encompasses a variety of ways of speaking it, so any one society encompasses a variety of ways of living within it – or on its margins. Distinct groups or social formations within the whole may be set off from each other in a variety of ways; by gender, by age, by class, by ethnic identity. And these differences most frequently go hand in hand with differing degrees of access to material resources, to knowledge, to power. If the society is stratified, then as language enters into the life of that society to shape, cement and reproduce it, it too will display stratification. Particular groups will tend to have characteristic ways of using the language – characteristic ways of pronouncing it, for example – and these will help to mark off the boundaries of one group from another.

In the realm of language this stratification can work itself through on a variety of levels. At the level of pronunciation some individual sounds will assume a prestige value as 'correct' or 'pleasant'; others come to be stigmatized as 'incorrect' or 'ugly'. In this way features that appear at the outset to be merely regional characteristics get taken up and woven into the fabric of social life, especially amongst large urban populations.

The social stratification of pronunciation

In New York City, for instance, the initial consonant of words such as 'thirsty', 'thing' or 'thick' is pronounced in at least three ways: the place '33rd Street' may be pronounced 'thirty-third street' (using the sound /θ/), 'toity-toid street' (using the sound /t/), or with a version that comes half way between the two (/tθ/). In casual unself-conscious speech the use of one or other of these alternatives is strongly influenced by the speaker's social class position: the most affluent New Yorkers are most likely to use /θ/; the least affluent New Yorkers are most likely to use /t/; and those towards the middle of the social scale are most likely to gravitate in the direction of /tθ/. The alternative pronunciations are thus clearly socially strati-fied.

Comparable phenomena are easy to find in the British Isles. In the city of Norwich, for example, (and in many other parts of Britain) the presence or absence of /h/ as the initial sound of such words as 'house', 'horse', 'heavy' is socially stratified in a similar way: the more middle class the speaker, the more likely s/he is to pronounce the /h/ even in casual speech and, conversely, the more working class the speaker the less likely s/he is to do so.

In each case – both in Norwich and in New York – the indi-vidual sound, whether it be /h/ or /θ/, is only one amongst a range of sounds that are particularly sensitive to social stratification in their pronunciation. In New York, for example, the initial sound (/δ/) of words such as 'these', 'them', and 'those' can be pronounced /d/ as in 'dese, dem and dose guys'. In Norwich, on the other hand, the phenomenon of the audible or absent /h/ interlinks with the presence or absence of /ŋ/ as the final sound of items such a 'flying', 'drinking', 'working' and with the behaviour of the /t/ sound in words such as 'bottle', 'letter', 'better', 'butter' and so on: so that a working-class speaker from Norwich would be more likely in casual speech to say 'Yer si'in' on me 'ot wa'er bo'el' than 'You're sitting on my hot water bottle'. Even quite close-knit groups will display social differentiation in their pronunciation. London Jamaicans with manual jobs, for instance, are more likely to drop the final /d/ on 'wild' or the final /t/ on 'first' than London Jamaicans with non-manual jobs.

Shifts in pronunciation according to situation

The social stratification of pronunciation has a curious twist to it, inasmuch as it will vary not only from speaker to speaker according to their respective positions within the overall social structure: it also varies for any one speaker from situation to situation. A New York street cleaner, for example, might well pronounce '33rd' as 'toity-toid' in casual speech, with an overall preference for /t/ as opposed to /θ/. But that same cleaner will shift towards /θ/ as contexts become more formal and allow for more self-conscious control of speech patterns. In reading a prose passage aloud, for example, /θ/ will begin to replace /t/. And if asked to read aloud a list of words including contrasting pairs of items such as 'true/through', 'three/tree', then we may find little to distinguish the street cleaner from the Wall Street financial consultant. The shift, in fact, is towards the speech habits of the dominant social group and it is their forms that become the prestige forms for a society.

Uniform attitudes to pronunciation within the speech community

The surprising thing is that whatever the variation, even within one locality such as a city, there seems to be a marked degree of unanimity in reaction and attitude to the differences. In Canada during the late 1960s, for example, a negative attitude towards Canadian French was not only quite uniform in the English-speaking community but was almost as unanimously held by the French speakers themselves. This uniformity in terms of attitudes to language is in part borne out by the fact that we consistently tend to overestimate the degree to which we produce the prestige form. Our own subjective impressions of the way we speak are in any case highly unreliable, as anyone can testify on first hearing a recording of themselves on audiotape. More specifically, it appears that as many as 62 per cent of New Yorkers who in casual speech rarely pronounced the prestige form /r/ in words such as 'far', 'card', etc., believed in fact that they did. In reporting their own usage, therefore, they were subconsciously reflecting a supposed norm of correctness: they were reporting, not what they actually did, but what they thought they ought to do.

Exploring our attitudes to the speech of others is equally revealing. Most New Yorkers, when asked to rate on a job-suitability scale a speaker who used a preponderance of the local prestige forms, rated him highly – irrespective of their own patterns of pronunciation and social background. And conversely most of them rated the same speaker badly on a 'fight' or 'toughness' scale.

Working-class loyalty to non-prestige forms

Behind this apparent uniformity of attitudes, however, lies a significant split. The reactions of New Yorkers to prestige forms as expressed on a 'job suitability' and 'fight' scale may be fairly uniform. But on another scale their attitudes show a noticeable tendency to diverge. When asked 'If you knew the speaker for a long time, how likely would he be to become a good friend of yours?', the middle class and upper working class thought friendship likely; but straight working-class respondents considered there to be little likelihood of friendship with the speaker. In fact, there was as much chance of their becoming friends with the speaker as of his coming out on top in a street fight.

This contradiction beneath the smooth surface of apparently uniform attitudes is important because it helps to explain why all people don't speak in the way they apparently believe that they should. There is after all considerable pressure in the direction of uniform standards of speech in modern societies; partly through the media, partly through education and partly through a tendency towards increased social mobility. But for certain groups – especially the more marginal groups of a society – behind their apparent allegiance to the generalized norms of the speech community lies a countervailing set of attitudes that revolves around strong identification and affiliation with the distinctive patterns of their own locality.

'Hypercorrection' in the lower middle class

Whilst sections of the working class may have a strong sense of loyalty to the speech patterns of their own locality, other strata of the population display in certain settings an exaggerated preference for the prestige forms. It has been discovered, for example, that in both Norwich and New York the lower middle class produce relatively more of the prestige forms when reading aloud from word lists than do members of the social group immediately above them on the social scale, even though they produce less than this group in ordinary casual speech. In settings that allow for more careful pronunciation they tend, as it were, to 'overproduce' the prestige forms. This tendency, sometimes known as 'hypercorrection', turns out to be particularly noticeable amongst women of the lower middle class, a trait that can be interpreted in a variety of ways.

It may be precisely the enactment of stereotypical expectations of women's speech. (Women, for example, are supposedly thought to use more 'politeness' forms in speech and less obscenity.) Sometimes it is seen as indicative of a more widespread linguistic insecurity amongst this social group, the members of which are poised uneasily half-way up the social hierarchy and who identify with the patterns of the group they aspire to join. It could also be interpreted as implying a heightened awareness on the part of women as a subordinate group to the socially sensitive nuances of pronunciation. (A fuller discussion of this question may be found in ch. 8, pp. 152–9.)

How do some patterns of pronunciation become the prestige forms?

It is often presumed that certain patterns of pronunciation become preferred within a speech community because they are inherently more correct, or because they are intrinsically more pleasing to listen to. Available evidence, however, points in a quite contrary direction and suggests that there is nothing in a sound itself that can guarantee a prestige status for it. Instead it is social evaluation solely that confers prestige or stigma upon certain patterns of pronunciation. For one thing the prestige form of one language area can turn out to be the stigmatized form of another. The prestige form of pronunciation in New York may well include an audible /r/ sound after a vowel in words such as 'car', 'north', 'guard', but in Britain the audible inclusion of this sound in this position can merely sound rustic or even comic, being primarily associated with the patterns of pronunciation of rural south-west England. For another thing, speakers unfamiliar with the language in question often have the greatest difficulty discriminating between one form of pronunciation and another, never mind identifying the prestige pattern. Among French speakers, for instance, Parisian French is generally held to be more prestigious than French Canadian. Non-French speakers, however, cannot even tell the difference between them, let alone display a consistent preference for one or the other. So there are no purely linguistic grounds for preferring one form of pronunciation to another. It is primarily a matter of social attitude: the speech patterns of the dominant social group come to be regarded as the norm for the whole society, though this normative pressure may often be rationalized in terms of aesthetic appeal or by reference to false notions of linguistic propriety.

Accents as a residue of earlier dialect differences

What we have been considering, in effect, is the accent aspect of dialect differences, where 'accent' as a term is exclusively reserved for whole patterns of pronunciation typical of a particular region or social group. The term 'dialect' covers a broader range of differences, including not only matters of pronunciation, but also distinctions in vocabulary and sentence structure. The extension of a language (say, English) through space and through time allows for quite fundamental differences to emerge and exist side by side within the whole, as its speakers move and settle, shape it to express new experiences, and it comes into contact with other languages. It will be changing continuously, but at differing rates within the sub-communities of the English speech community. Some of these changes will be instigated locally but many of them will spread out in waves from centres of power and influence, moving probably from city to city first, and then only later and more slowly encompassing the intervening rural areas. It is the varying and uneven rates of change actually 'on the ground', so to speak, that make dialect differences inevitable. None the less, if the hold of the centre on the periphery is strong (through, for example, uniform legal, administrative, educational and writing systems) then, despite the fact of language change, there will be strong pressures in the direction of linguistic conformity. Thus, within the British Isles many of the more fundamental differences of vocabulary and sentence structure between the English dialects have become eroded (not to mention, of course, the drastic decline – sometimes active suppression – of Welsh and Gaelic). Often, all that remains as a kind of historical residue of the original dialect is its distinctive mode of pronunciation – its accent. For this reason, we now have a situation in which the standard dialect is spoken with many differing regional accents.

Factors underlying the survival of accents

How is it that English accents have survived the merging of dialects? One important factor is probably mutual intelligibility. Groups who use different dialects but have some degree of contact with each other will find ways of erasing the linguistic obstacles to mutual understanding, if they want to communicate with each other and if they have need to do so. In this respect, accents are much less of an obstacle to mutual understanding than basic differences in vocabulary and sentence structure. A further factor that underpins the continuing vitality of accents is mentioned in the previous discussion of split reactions to prestige forms. Basically, a large proportion of the working class, while recognizing the prestige value of certain forms, none the less identifies strongly with the speech patterns of its own locality. In terms of accent this leads to a cone- or pyramid-like distribution of various forms, a situation that for the British Isles can be summed up in the following way.

The prestige accent, known as Received Pronunciation (RP), had its historical origins in a dialect of English associated particularly with the region stretching south-east from the Midlands down towards London, but including the historic university cities of Cambridge and Oxford. It survived because of its association with centres of power and influence. It was spoken by the merchant classes of London in the fourteenth century, for example, and would have been familiar to students attending the universities of Oxford and Cambridge in the middle ages. Its status as an important dialect was enhanced by its use in government and official documents from about 1430 onwards. More recently, its association since the nineteenth century with the public schools helped to achieve special pre-eminence for its distinctive patterns of pronunciation. Consequently, it is, for instance, the preferred form of pronunciation for reading BBC news bulletins and for teaching English as a second language; and this for the simple reason that, having lost its former regional affiliations, it is now the most widely understood and spoken of all the accents within the British Isles. Its wide dispersal and its typical use by members of the middle and upper classes guarantee it a prestige and status denied to the more regionally marked accents. These latter forms have survived amongst those

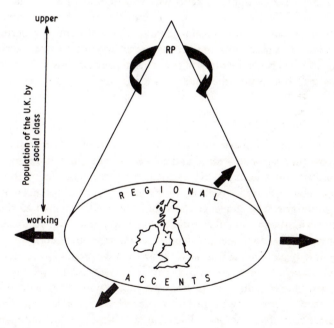

Figure 1

groups historically less mobile, with less access to higher education and to jobs that entail permanent moves away from their place of origin. Hence the conical nature of accent distribution: the 'higher' up the social scale, the more likely one is to find the single accent – RP; the 'lower' down the social scale, the more likely one is to find regional variation.

The survival of regional accents does not of course preclude quite sharp judgements upon and reactions to the forms that endure, often rationalized by reference to the way they sound. Thus, the Birmingham accent, associated as it is with a large industrial conurbation, is often disliked (even by a proportion of those who actually use it), and this negative reaction will be couched in terms of a dislike of its 'nasal whine'. On the other hand a much more positive reaction will commonly be registered for the Southern Irish accent which will be praised for sounding 'soft' and 'warm'. Other accents with similar ethnic or rural associations such as the Welsh, Scots and West Country accents will likewise evoke positive judgements – the South Wales accent, for example, often being regarded as 'lilting' and 'musical'. But despite the 'colourful' properties considered to reside in some of the regional accents, the only accent that speakers generally think of as having absolute claims to 'correctness', whether or not they like it, is RP.

Reactions to accents

Indeed, work by social psychologists in experimental settings has uncovered a surprising range and subtlety in our ordinary reactions to accents. For example, RP speakers are rated more highly than regionally accented speakers in terms of general competence (e.g. 'ambition', 'intelligence', 'self-confidence', 'determination', and 'industriousness'). But they emerge less favourably than regionally accented speakers in terms of personal integrity and social attractiveness (e.g. their 'seriousness', 'talkativeness', 'good-naturedness', and 'sense of humour'). Furthermore, some evidence seems to suggest that accents vary in their persuasive power. In one study four similar groups were played a tape recording of an argument against capital punishment. Each group heard the same argument but in a slightly different guise from the others: one group heard an RP version, one heard it in a South Wales accent, one in a Somerset accent and one in a Birmingham accent. A fifth group had the argument presented to them in written rather than spoken form. The RP spoken version was, perhaps not surprisingly, rated highest in terms of the quality of argument. In spite of this, however, it was in the groups which had heard the regionally accented versions that most shift in opinion on the issue was registered, so that regional accents rather than RP seemed to be most effective in changing people's minds. It may be concluded, therefore, that the sense of integrity associated with the lower-prestige accents counted for more with listeners than the apparent competence and expertise of the RP speaker.

Accents in television advertisements

Advertising agencies in their preparation of nationally broadcast television commercials display a developed aptitude for trading on these conflicting cross currents of prejudice. Advertisements for pharmaceutical products or for consumer durables (such as cars, televisions, washing machines, hi-fi equipment, vacuum cleaners, etc.), where the emphasis may well be on presenting a commodity that embodies expertise, will typically take an RP accent or perhaps an American one. But for products, especially food, where natural ingredients are to be emphasized (e.g. cottage cheese, frozen turkey, pork sausages, brown bread, 'dairy' butter) regional – especially rural – accents are more likely to be used. Much more rare is an accent associated with Asian or Jamaican ethnic minorities or one associated with a large industrial conurbation such as London, Liverpool or Birmingham – unless used for comic effect or for merchandise where the marketing strategy is more likely to be aimed at the working class (e.g. do-it-yourself car maintenance products or beer).

Changing attitudes to accents

The relative status of accents with respect to each other is, of course, not totally fixed and static. Just as the alignment of the various groups and formations in society in relation to each other is in a constant process of change, so with patterns of pronunciation and our attitudes towards them. The range and role of accents in the media probably provide quite sensitive indicators of more far-reaching changes taking place in the wider society. For example, until the 1960s it was relatively unusual in British broadcasting for any accent except RP to be used by 'institutional' voices such as presenters, quiz-masters, introducers, newsreaders, link persons, interviewers, etc. (Hence, of course, the currency of the term 'BBC English'.) Since that time there have been structural changes within broadcasting itself that have allowed access to a wider range of accent-types (not to mention minority languages) through the development of regional networks (BBC Wales, for instance, was established in 1964). This in itself reflects a certain sensitivity on the part of the state to separate regional identities within the larger society. But other kinds of sociocultural and linguistic change have filtered through into the overall composition of broadcasting even at a national level. For instance, the transformation of popular music in the 1960s – its partial alignment with, and expression of, a distinctive 'youth' or 'counter' culture, the popularity of the pirate radio stations – all had fundamental consequences for what had been known previously as the 'music and light entertainment' sections of broadcasting. The emergence of performers with some claim to working-class roots in large cities such as Liverpool and London (e.g. The Beatles and The Who), carrying with them in their speech clear marks of their origins, conferred a limited respectability on accents which had hitherto thrived only as the hall-mark of individual comics or of comedy as a genre. Disc jockeys with working-class accents began to fill radio time and these same accents began to be heard more frequently in drama and soap opera (e.g. 'Z Cars' and 'Coronation Street'). The accents of the Celtic minorities had always been minimally represented, but it is interesting to note the gradual elevation of both Northern English (e.g. Yorkshire) and Southern Irish accents to the relatively prestigious position of chat show host and interviewer: Southern Irish in the persons of Henry Kelly, Frank Delaney, and Terry Wogan; Northern English in the persons of Michael Parkinson, Russell Harty and Melvyn Bragg. Only in the extreme conditions of wartime radio broadcasting did the BBC use a regional accent for presenting the news. In the early years of the war, when it looked as if the Germans might invade, Wilfrid Pickles – who spoke with a strong Yorkshire accent – was moved south to London to read the news. It was considered that the Germans might successfully mimic an RP accented speaker for propaganda purposes, but that Wilfrid's Yorkshire accent would defy imitation. Audience reaction was mixed and the innovation only lasted as long as the fear of invasion. In peacetime the last bastions of BBC TV to fall to regional accents will no doubt be 'Panorama' and the Nine o'clock News; but then to a Scots, Irish, Welsh or Yorkshire accent rather than one associated unambiguously with one of the major industrial conurbations.

Surviving dialect differences

Local accents may be more resistant to erosion than the other features of dialect, for the reasons described above (see p. 70). But the other kinds of dialect feature have not, of course, died out altogether. There still remains throughout the British Isles quite distinct variation in matters of vocabulary and sentence structure. 'Sports shoes', for example, are referred to variously as 'daps', 'plimsolls', 'sandies' and 'pumps' in different parts of the country. Similarly, the passage or alleyway between terraced houses leading from the street to the yards or gardens behind, is variously referred to as 'ginnel', 'snicket', 'jettie', 'entry' and 'alley'. The very practices for naming persons may vary from region to region (as well, of course, as socially). In the American south, for example, double first names such as Billy Jean (or Gene), Larry Leroy, and Mary Fred are not uncommon; and some of these names may refer to persons of either gender, so that Billy, Jimmy and Bobby are used for both boys and girls, a situation unusual in English-speaking communities where until recently first names have been strictly gendered. (The present practice among the women's movement of adopting male-marked, short-form first names such as Bobby, Les, Stevie, and Chris is in many cases a much more self-conscious, deliberate attempt to side-step or actively undermine such gender marking than the southern American practice. It is noticeable in this respect that the shift tends only to work in one direction – from male to female.)

Over and beyond matters of vocabulary, differences still exist between standard and non-standard dialects in the form and construction of utterances, of which the following are fairly typical examples:

Non-standard dialect	Standard dialect
'Being on *me* own had never gone through *me* head.'	'Being on my own had never gone through my head.'
'We *was* forever having arguments.'	'We were forever having arguments.'
'Anyway they *done* it for me.'	'Anyway they did it for me.'
'I had*n't* got *nothing* to fall back on.'	'I had nothing to fall back on.'
'Go to the pub *is it?*'	'Let's go to the pub shall we?'
'Where's it *by?*'	'Where is it?'
'Over *by* here.'	'Over here.'

Variation between dialects – particularly standard and nonstandard – tends to be particularly noticeable when it comes to pronouns (e.g. 'me' versus 'my'), forms of negation (e.g. 'I couldn't buy none nowhere'), ways of handling the verb to register differences in time and duration (e.g. 'they done it') and in the use of tags. Within any one dialect, however, such differences will be handled systematically as rule-governed patterns – an intrinsic part of the way that dialect operates. In some cases the features will be highly specific to a particular region: for instance, features which seem to be exclusive to South Wales English are the common use of twin prepositions ('down by here', 'over by there') for locational expressions, and the 'is it' tag formation for suggesting a joint course of action ('Go to the pub, is it?'). In other cases, however, the feature may be much more widely dispersed. Multiple negation is a case in point: this feature is shared by many non-standard dialects and in this respect at least the standard dialect is out of step with many of the others. Indeed, at earlier periods multiple negation can be found in all dialects, including the English of Chaucer and of Shakespeare, so neither in numerical nor in historical terms would the standard seem 'more correct' than the non-standard. That the standard dialect should come to seem 'more correct' is merely the outcome of an historical evolution that has placed it in ascendancy over other dialects. It is the dialect of socially privileged groups and of written documents, of law, education and the media. Its preferred patterns of construction thus come to seem 'inevitably' and 'naturally' right in ways denied to those of less advantaged groups. Here again – as in the case of pronunciation – socially engendered reactions of approval or disapproval are at stake rather than anything to do with the inherent linguistic 'rightness' of particular linguistic forms. The features themselves may be of little consequence in terms of mutual intelligibility. Their real importance lies in their capacity to become charged with social significance.

Background sources and further reading

The social stratification of pronunciation (and other dialect features)

The American sociolinguist William Labov is the prime mover behind a whole tradition of work that meticulously correlates variations in speech patterns with social class and social context, as well as with locality. Seminal papers by him may be found in:

Labov, W. (1966) *The Social Stratification of English in New York City*, Washington, D.C.: Centre for Applied Linguistics.
Labov, W. (1972) *Sociolinguistic Patterns*, Philadelphia: University of Pennsylvania Press.

For similar important work in the British context see:

Trudgill, P. (1974) *The Social Differentiation of English in Norwich,* Cambridge: Cambridge University Press.
Trudgill, P. (ed.) (1978) *Sociolinguistic Patterns in British English,* London: Edward Arnold.

Accent variation and attitudes to it

An extremely comprehensive account in three volumes of the different accents of English may be found in:

Wells, J.C. (1982) *Accents of English,* vols 1–3, Cambridge: Cambridge University Press.

Volume 1 consists of an introduction. Volumes 2 and 3 deal with the British Isles and beyond the British Isles respectively.

The sociolinguistic approach of Labov, Trudgill and Wells includes discussions of speakers' reactions to differing forms of pronunciation. There is also a large body of work by social psychologists that focuses more exclusively on attitudes to accent and speech patterns generally. See, for example:

Giles, H. and Powesland, P.F. (1975) *Speech Style and Social Evaluation*, London: Academic Press.

Ryan, E. and Giles, H. (eds) (1982) *Attitudes towards Language Variation*, London: Edward Arnold.

The formation of the standard

A useful, sociolinguistically informed account of the development of modern English is:

Leith, D. (1983) *A Social History of English,* London: Routledge & Kegan Paul.

See also:

Milroy, J. and Milroy, L. (1985[1991]) *Authority in Language: Investigating Language Prescription and Standardization*, London: Routledge.

For an interesting discussion of the BBC's policy on the spoken word in the early days of sound broadcasting see:

Scannell, P. and Cardiff, D. (1977) *The Social Foundations of British Broadcasting*, Open University Course: *Mass Communication and Society*, 1–6.

Fieldwork projects

(1) Record or make notes on as many TV commercials as you can. Identify for each one, where possible:

(a) the broad accent type of the voice-over or salesperson – RP, American, ethnic, urban, rural, and then, where relevant, the subtype – e.g. Scottish, Welsh; London, Birmingham; North Country; West Country; if you can be more specific all the better;

(b) the product type – white goods (e.g. washing machines, dishwashers, cookers); hi-fi, television and radio; cars; pharmaceuticals; alcoholic drinks; food; financial services, etc.

(c) whether the advert is nationally or regionally networked.

On the basis of your classification of this material, consider some of the following issues:

(i) Do certain product types and accent types go together fairly consistently? For example, do pharmaceutical products (e.g. aspirin, cough mixtures, etc.) and financial services take the RP accent (or equivalent prestige form) whereas food products tend to take accents of a broadly rural character?

(ii) Do identifiable urban–industrial accents figure in any of your adverts? Which ones? What might this indicate about the intended audience?

(iii) What explanation can you offer for any regularities that you detect in your material?

(2) Systematically studying the social stratification of speech patterns in your own locality requires careful preparation. Asking people (in interview or by questionnaire) how they talk is not always a reliable guide to what they actually do. People tend to report what they think they ought to do, not necessarily how they actually do speak. But trying to record completely spontaneous speech in everyday situations also has its difficulties, since the presence of recording equipment can make people self-conscious (in much the same way as an obvious observer can). Allowing for these difficulties, however, here are two relatively simple examples of small-scale enquiries worth undertaking:

(a) (i) Try and identify some of the local non-standard dialect patterns. If you have difficulty isolating them, then the following is a useful reference book:

Hughes, A. and Trudgill, P. (1979) *English Accents and Dialects*, London: Edward Arnold.

(ii) Incorporating material from (i), construct pairs of sentences that involve standard versus non-standard variants, along the lines of p. 76 above.

(iii) Build them into a questionnaire (either as pairs or randomly distributed) which asks people, for instance, to tick for each example whether or not they would use the sentence, whether their family would use it, whether their close friends would use it, and so on. If none of the foregoing are thought to use it, leave a space for respondents to specify who they think might use it. At the same time collect basic information on the social identities of respondents. You need to try and balance out factors such as age, length of residence, gender and social class position. There is no easy way of deciding the latter. Many researchers do so on the basis of a respondent's occupation, income and years in formal education, which at best amounts to a handy rule of thumb. In addition, you can always try asking them what class they would identify themselves as belonging to.

(iv) See if your data confirm or disprove the hypothesis that the more working class the respondents, the more likely they are to attest and accept local vernacular forms. Is there any discrepancy between what they say they do themselves, and what they say their friends do?

(b) A similar enquiry into pronunciation can be built on to the previous project by asking people to read aloud a carefully selected prose passage. Choosing something in a relatively informal style may help to offset the formality of the task. Inspect performance on selected features of pronunciation – for example:

(i) presence or absence of word initial /h/ (e.g. in 'British Home Stores');

(ii) pronouncing the medial sound of words such as 'letter', 'bitter', 'bottle', 'better' either at the front of the mouth with the tip of the tongue or at the back of mouth (the glottal stop);

(iii) other features distinctive to the locality.

Score for occurrence of the prestige form (e.g. /h/, /t/, etc.) and see if you can confirm or disprove the hypothesis that the higher the score, the more likely the respondent is to be upper class. Do men and women of equivalent social class position gain equivalent scores?

4 LANGUAGE AND ETHNIC IDENTITY: BRITISH BLACK ENGLISH

Language and ethnic identity

Strong dialect differences may – in Britain – be a thing of the past. And the accent differences that remain do not normally hinder mutual intelligibility to any great degree. To some extent, then, the picture is one of gradually increasing uniformity and homogeneity. However, even in a highly centralized society such as Britain some very marked kinds of linguistic diversity remain. Most commonly these are bound up with promoting or preserving distinct ethnic identities. We can see this in the case of indigenous ethnic minorities in their deliberate attempts to reverse the decline of separate languages such as Gaelic and Welsh. To many Welsh people an important even crucial aspect of their 'Welshness' would be lost if their language failed to survive as a living means of everyday communication. The more recently settled ethnic groups, of course, have often brought their own distinctive mother tongue with them. Many children of the Asian communities in Britain, for instance, are likely to grow up speaking two languages – using Punjabi, Hindi, or Gujarati at home and English at school or work. The situation is complex, however, since some children of Asian communities find themselves identifying strongly enough with speech patterns and norms of the locality to resist continued use of the mother tongue. For others, the fluent command of both languages engenders a sense of dual ethnic identity and cultural ambiguity. Ultimately, the survival of the minority language is closely bound up with the preservation or affirmation of a distinct ethnic identity and culture. By and large the sharpest and most discrete forms of linguistic difference in Britain today fall into place around the boundaries that distinguish one ethnic group from another.

Linguistic markers of Afro-Caribbean identity

Maintaining a separate ethnic identity does not, however, depend necessarily on maintaining a totally distinct language. The situation of Afro-Caribbean Black Britishers provides a case in point: as a group, they probably have a more marked sense of ethnic separateness than at any time since the 1950s. Where this is marked linguistically, it is not necessarily by using a distinct language but by a denser use of Creole forms with Caribbean origins. Indeed, many Black Britishers, including those a generation or so removed from original migrants, control a linguistic repertoire that ranges from forms of Caribbean (principally Jamaican) Creole on the one hand to forms of Standard English (spoken with perhaps a London, Liverpool, Bristol or Birmingham accent) on the other. For some younger Blacks there was, by the 1980s, also a remodelled variety, Rastafarian talk, which was hardly intelligible at all to the English speaker restricted to the standard dialect. The emergence of Rasta talk and the continuance of Creole forms in the British context is probably best understood as bound up with the rediscovery and assertion of a distinctively Afro-Caribbean identity.

Origins and emergence of Caribbean Creole

To clarify how Creole forms such as those used in Jamaica can come to serve in the British context as markers of ethnic identity, it may help to outline briefly the history of Jamaican Creole. Although its precise origins and form are difficult to reconstruct, it must date back to at least the late seventeenth century and the colonization of Jamaica by white settlers from Britain. These settlers established plantations for the growth of agricultural staples such as sugar. The profits of these plantations (as elsewhere in the West Indies and in the southern parts of North America) were built on the use of slave labour imported forcibly from the west coast of Africa. Communication between white master and black slave was conducted by means of a simplified language – a pidgin. The vocabulary items were almost all drawn from English and used within a highly simplified grammar typical of pidgin grammars everywhere. The total construct would have reflected African influences mostly in its phonology (pronunciation), but also in a small proportion (perhaps 10 per cent) of the vocabulary and some elements of the grammar. This pidgin language would have remained fairly rudimentary as long as it served only for contact between master and slave. However, although many African languages were current on the West African coast, these apparently failed to survive the passage into slavery, probably because in the course of the journey to the 'New World' and subsequently on the plantations, speakers of the same African language were often separated from each other, thereby reducing the likelihood of there being a common African language amongst any one group of slaves. The pidgin language thus had to evolve not only as a way of communicating between white master and black slave but also as the principal means of communication amongst the slaves themselves. For subsequent generations of slaves it was learnt as their first language and became the main linguistic medium for sustaining their communal life, developing in the service of song, ritual, oral recollections of the past, celebration and resistance. In this process the original pidgin would be rapidly transformed into a much more complex and flexible language called a creole (defined technically as a pidgin which becomes the first language of a group). This kind of transformation took place throughout the Caribbean and, depending on the nationality of the colonial power, gave rise to French, Dutch and Portuguese related Creoles as well as to the English related Creole of Jamaica and other territories dominated by the British.

Some linguistic differences between Jamaican Creole and Standard English

The main difference between the Jamaican Creole and Standard English – apart from matters of pronunciation – is in the way distinctions of time, duration, number and person are indicated. In broad Jamaican Creole these distinctions are less likely to be signalled by a change in word shape as by word order and context or the use of an explicit function word. English itself, in its transition from Anglo-Saxon, has lost many of its word endings and other inflections: Creole has taken this process a stage further, as can be seen in the following examples:

	Standard English	Jamaican Creole
Plurals	the other girls	di addah girl dem
	with those other girls	wid dem addah girl
Past time	I went yesterday	mi go yeside
	I told you so already	mi tel yu so aredi
	I had already walked home	mi ben waak huom aredi
	I have finished sleeping	mi don sliip
Present	what are you doing out there?	whey you a dhu out yah?
	where are you going?	whey you a go?
Possession	the man's hat	di man hat
	the man's woman didn't like this	di man woman noh like dis

These represent just some of the differences between Jamaican Creole and Standard English. The last example above illustrates, in fact, another type of difference where the negative is formed merely by inserting 'no' before the verb as in:

JC   she decide seh she noh want it any more
SE   she decided that she didn't want it any more

and multiple negation can be used for extra emphasis as in:

JC   she decide seh she noh want none no more

Social situation and the use of Creole

Even in Jamaica, however, the sheer density of Creole forms (their relative frequency) will vary for any one speaker, depending on

84

situation. It is comparatively rare for speakers to restrict themselves continuously to broadest Creole. More usually, even where broadest Creole is available, a speaker will select forms that are some way along the continuum towards Standard English Dialect. Amongst Blacks of Afro-Caribbean descent in Britain the situation is much the same. They tend to vary the strength of Creole according to communicative circumstances (although British-born Blacks will probably have an additional choice between Afro-Caribbean accent and local British accent). Thus, for a job interview or a visit to the doctor they are likely to select forms nearer the Standard end of the continuum (though probably with the appropriate local accent), whereas in play or argument with younger members of the family or with a black peer group they are likely to select forms nearer the Creole end of the continuum.

The range of repertoire available to individual Blacks does, of course, vary according to age, generation, length of time in Britain and degree of exposure to standard forms. Three hypothetical Blacks of Afro-Caribbean descent might have repertoires that range along the continuum from Creole to Standard in the following way:

Creole   *Standard*

1. _____

2.   _____

3.   _____

Speaker 1 commands a broader repertoire than either 2 or 3.

The notion of the continuum from 'Black' Creole to 'White' English was felt to provide an adequate explanation of perceived features in Afro-Caribbean linguistic performance until fairly recently. More recently, however, a growing body of opinion (see Edwards, 1979; Sutcliffe, 1982) has claimed that Black English speakers move not along a continuum but between two discrete and separate linguistic systems, and are able to switch at will from one to the other, the switch being marked by significant alteration of voice set. This may happen from one sentence to another, or even in mid-sentence. The switch is still likely to be motivated by situational features (including, for instance, topic) but its very rapidity makes precise specification of the determining situational features difficult.

Asymmetrical selection of Creole forms within the Black community

While it is basically the kind of social relationship that influences what point on the continuum (or which discrete system) a speaker will select, it is worth noting that in certain circumstances the selection will not be symmetrical. It seems to be the case, for example, that broad Creole may well be adopted by parents towards children (perhaps as a sign of closeness and familiarity) but none the less they expect standard dialect forms in return (as a sign of deference and respect). This asymmetry may be seen at work in the following story composed and written in Jamaican Creole by Jennifer Johnson, a Black Britisher. Her story concerns four girls – British, but of Afro-Caribbean descent – who become involved in a fracas outside a party with a rival group. The fight is interrupted by an older Black woman from a nearby house. The woman stands on her doorstep and looks down on them.

Di woman stan' up pan she door step ina her dressing gown a look pan dem. Di addah gal dem a struggle up off di groun'.

'But wait, Lorna, is you dat,' di woman shout.

'But kiss mi daag a yard,' a noh eleven o'clock you goh a you bed an' now mi see you a road a fight.'

Now, dis woman was big an' hefty an when she come wizzing pass, everybody stan' still. She grab her daughter: 'Whey you a dhu out yah? Is whey you deh?'

'I was at the party, mommy, oh please don't beat me.'

di addah gal dem/ other girls
is you dat/ is that you? **daag/** dog
a yard/ at home
a noh/ it wasn't
a you/ to your
a road a fight/ in the road fighting

whey . . . yah?/ what are you doing out here?
is whey you deh/ where were you?

noh beat you noh/ please don't beat you?	'Noh beat you noh. Is what you was fighting ovah gal?'
is what/what	
whey/away	'Dem trying to teck whey my boyfriend. '
man/a man, men	'You what? Man? You have man? Gal, you can't even wash you draws good an'
fi deh a/to be in	a fight over man when you suppose fi deh a you bed. You have man. Well I going show you 'bout man you see, love.'
	Well, by now all di people from di
a watch/watching	party outside a watch while dis woman
lick/blow	teck off her slipper an' plant a lick ina dis gal head.

Source: Sutcliffe (1982).

The reported speech of the older woman employs a broader Creole than the narrative voice of the story. For instance, just prior to the quoted extract she interrupts the mêlée with 'Oonu young girl of today, all oonu know is fi fight.' The item 'oonu', used here in place of the second person plural pronoun 'you', is in fact a word of West African origin. It appears only in the reported speech of the older woman and not elsewhere in the story. In complete contrast to this, we find that her daughter, Lorna, replies initially not with Creole but with Standard English Dialect ('I was at the party, Mommy'), presumably as a mark of respect – Creole and Standard thus being selected in asymmetrical fashion. By this token, Lorna's subsequent switch to Creole ('Dem trying to teck whey my boyfriend') indicates a loss of proper deference on her part towards her mother. It may also at the same time be seen as an illustration of the rapid switch from one system to another discussed above (see p. 85).

The continuance of Creole

It might be thought that this kind of asymmetry among Black Britons – with parents using more Creole to their children than their children are expected to use in return – would lead to a gradual dying out of Creole forms (or Patois as it is often known), but this seems not to be the case. For while young Jamaicans may use Creole at home less than their parents, within the peer group they seem almost to be reinventing it. Recent estimates suggest that upwards of 70 per cent of young Blacks are regularly using Patois. This may, in part, be due to the simple fact of their increasing isolation. They suffer disproportionate levels of unemployment, which in turn restricts their access to the wider community and increases their reliance upon predominantly Black networks of social contacts. At the same time, however, competence in Patois – or the ability to 'chat bad' as it may be colloquially referred to – is an important badge of group membership, and for some young Blacks at least this may actually entail developing Creole forms that they hitherto lacked: 'Before she buck head wid [met up with] dem addah gal she couldn't chat a word a bad English; now she pass CSE ina it.' (As with Black dialects of the United States 'bad' can also mean 'very good', 'daring'.) Within the group 'talking Black' affirms special relations of solidarity between the members and also provides a way of 'freezing off' or excluding unwanted outsiders. This way of defining the boundaries of the group can also reinforce a loose, informal hierarchy within it: those most verbally adept with the Creole will most likely constitute the nucleus of the group; those less adept are likely to be relegated to the margins or to less prestigious positions within the hierarchy.

Creole, Black youth, and Black identity

At the same time, however, use of Creole or Patois is closely tied in with distinctively Black subcultural interests and activities. At this level the recourse to Creole by teenagers, many of whom have had perhaps no first-hand experience of the Caribbean, constitutes an assertion of ethnic identity: it is a way of identifying with an ancestral homeland and of conjuring up in language a Caribbean country of the mind as an alternative to the grim reality of their present circumstances. Indeed, in all likelihood it is precisely *because* Creole forms have historically a somewhat indirect relationship with Standard English, one mediated through generations of plantation slavery, beyond which lies a dimly sensed substratum of African forms, that they can be used appropriately to register social, ethnic, and linguistic differences from the surrounding contemporary British speech community. Within Rastafarianism, of course, this whole tendency is made more explicit and self-conscious: the ancestral homeland becomes Africa and the present reality becomes in an extended Biblical metaphor 'exile in Babylon':

> We nah get justice inna dis yah
> Babylon,
> We h'affee seek ah justice outta
> Babylon,
> We mus' return to Africa our
> righteous blessed land.

(Written by Julie Roberts, then a third-year pupil at Vauxhall Manor School, London. Cited in Sutcliffe, 1982.)

Rastafarianism, indeed, adopts a deliberate position on matters of language:

> It was the whites who took our culture away from us in the first place. I an I [we] thought Jah [Jahweh, God] gave each an every race their own language so no other than that race can overstan [understand] them but it is through [because] we were taken into slavery and now in a Babylon that we speak the white tongue.

(Sis Zuleika Moore, letter in *Voice of Rasta*, no. 18, cited in Sutcliffe, 1982.)

Strong use of Creole is here reduced by the use of the written mode. None the less this very statement of Rastafarian beliefs illustrates how such forms can become overlaid with a distinctive Rastafarian idiom and vocabulary (e.g. 'I an I' for 'we', and 'overstan' for 'understand') as a way of forging a distinctive consciousness by attempting to connect with lost cultural roots. It is as if the sense of lost ancestral tongues generates a pressure to coin new linguistic forms which will accentuate the linguistic distance between Rastafarians and the larger speech community.

Background sources and further reading

General background to pidgins and Creoles

Hall, R.A. Jr (1966) *Pidgin and Creole Languages,* Ithaca and London: Cornell University Press.

Hymes, D. (ed.) (1971) *Pidginization and Creolization of Languages,* Cambridge: Cambridge University Press.

Todd, L. (1974) *Pidgins and Creoles,* London: Routledge & Kegan Paul.

Black British English

A good overview of sociolinguistic and sociocultural issues relating to British Black English, from which many of the examples in this chapter are drawn, is provided by:

Sutcliffe, D. (1982) *British Black English,* Oxford: Basil Blackwell.

For an equally good overview but with special reference to educational issues see:

Edwards, V.K. (1979) *The West Indian Language Issue in British Schools,* London: Routledge & Kegan Paul.

A short but excellent pamphlet, intended for teachers but of wider relevance, detailing Caribbean sources of British Black English is:

Le Page, R.B. (1981) *Caribbean Connections in the Classroom,* York: Mary Glasgow Language Trust.

Some of the examples of Jamaican Creole sentence structure were drawn from here. It is available from Institute of Linguists, 24a Highbury Grove, London N5 2EA.

The classic study of Black English in the United States is:

Labov, W. (1972) *Language in the Inner City: Studies in the Black English Vernacular,* Philadelphia: University of Pennsylvania Press.

Language and ethnicity

Giles, H. and Saint-Jacques, B. (eds) (1979) *Language and Ethnic Relations,* Oxford: Pergamon Press.

Giles, H. (1979) 'Ethnicity markers in speech' in Scherer, K.R. and Giles, H. (eds) (1979) *Social Markers in Speech,* Cambridge: Cambridge University Press.

A searching and careful discussion of the role played by Creole in youth subcultures in Britain is:

Hewitt, R. (1986) *White Talk Black Talk: Inter-racial Friendship and Communication amongst Adolescents*, Cambridge: Cambridge University Press.

A comprehensive account of the status and extent of minority languages within Britian from Welsh and Gaelic through to Punjabi and Gujarati is:

Safder, A. and Edwards, V. (eds) (1991) *Multilingualism in the British Isles Vols 1 & 2*, London: Longman.

Fieldwork projects

Here is the opening of Jennifer Johnson's story 'Ballad for you', cited earlier in this chapter. (The complete version is given in Sutcliffe, 1982.) Try and provide a continuous and complete translation for someone unfamiliar with Black English and with no access to the marginal glossary given below. What sorts of things do you find difficult to carry over in translation?

BALLAD FOR YOU
Jennifer Johnson
Chalice and her four college friends are friendly but definitely 'high-spirited'. Trouble seems to follow them around. When they go to a party one Saturday night they soon take over; certain other girls at the party object to this but they are put firmly in their place.

	There is five gal I want to tell you 'bout.
dem lick head/	Dem lick head from different part a
they met up	London; but is one t'ing dough, dem is

one an' di same but individual in every sense. Mek a tek dem one by one.

Lightening hail from Guyana an' is a soul-head. Before she buck head wid dem addah gal she couldn't chat a word a bad English; now she pass CSE ina it. Why dem call she Lightening is because when dem sit down ina corner a chat people business, she always miss everyt'ing an' a confuse di issue. She live up ina bush Lan', according to di addah four gal, Thornton Heath, Surrey.

Chalice come from Guyana too, but she come in jus' like a Jamaican to di addah gal dem. She can chat bad an' love a gossip. She better dan any newspaper or radio. She live a North London an', out a all a dem, dis is di Top Bitch.

Nex' come Charlie. She is a bwoy in every sense but wid looks. She love a trouble an' always deh in di thick of it. She hate all di soul-head dem, excep' fi Lightening, because she t'ink dem mad. Trouble is she noh know seh she mad too! I mean if you a goh mash up six chair an' set dem a fire ina de middle a di common room dat pack up wid people, somet'ing wrong some where: I wonder is soh all Peckham people stay?

Granny Roach is jus' four feet an' mash-mash, but, bwoy she have di biggest mout' in di world. She live a Dulwich an' fi she family is di only black family pan di road. She is an only chile (thank God, him know whey him a dhu) but, Lord, she have dem whites pan she road

---

mek a tek/let me take
soul-head/soul music fan **buck head**/met up
dem addah/those other
a chat/discussing

come in/seems
gal dem/girls
a gossip/gossiping
a/in **a**/of

bwoy/boy

deh/is
soul-head dem/soul fans **fi**/for
noh know seh/doesn't know that
a goh mash up/are going to smash up
I . . . stay?/I wonder if all Peckham people are like that?
an' mash-mash/'odd'; small change
fi she/her
pan/on
whey him a dhu/what he was doing

undah manners/ showing respect
fi/for
pan/on
Front Line/ Railton Road
seh/say

seh/that
aint/don't (general negative)
ah did seh/I said
yah soh/here
ina/in **dem/**their
Jam-Down/Jamaica
fi dem pickney/ *their* children
seh/that **you woulda . . . a run it/**you would have thought *they* had discovered Jamaica and were running it
yah soh/here
ina dem/in their

is man/it is men
a labrish/are gossiping
renkest/most cheeky, impudent
buck up/run into
anywhey/anywhere

undah manners. An' fi a person no bigger dan a cockroach, she have many people walking in fear, because of her mout'.

Squeakey is di last pan di list. She live right pan di Front Line a Brixton. So everybody kinda cagey 'bout she (so we wont seh no more 'bout she for mi noh want any contract out pan mi life).

Now di five a dem togeddah is not really looking fi trouble; dem is jus' high-spirited. Soh dem seh. But trouble love dem. Now I certain seh you mus' know dis certain set a gal, because if you noh know dem, you aint know anybody. Like ah did seh, two a dem come from Guyana; di addah three born right yah soh ina Inglan' but dem parents come from Jam-Down. (Mind you, if you ask dem parents if dem is fi dem pickney, dem will let you know seh dem never seen dem before ina dem life.) But di way dem get on you woulda' t'ink seh is dem discover JA an' a run it!

Back to story now. Right yah soh ina dem college there is a common room known as di gossip corner, because dem gal will sit ina corner an' a laugh an' smile wid you but a chat you same time. But most of di time is man, food an' music dem a labrish 'bout. Now dem is di renkest an' most bold-face set a gal you will buck up anywhey.

one big queue deh/
there certainly was
(**deh**) a queue!
dem noh business/
they didn't care
fi full up/to fill up
naw pay/weren't
paying **fi**/for
dem a wait/ they
were waiting
fi/to **decide seh/**
decided that
whey/what (do . . .)
in a/in **fi**/to
a check up/was
working out
price dem/prices
drink off/drank up
full up/filled up
fi/to **dem bold**
face/they are bold-
faced **noh di vicar!/**
the vicar! **have di**
mine/wanted **whey/**
what **t'ief**/stole
a mek . . . four/
making *their* eyes and
his eyes 'make four'
(met his gaze directly)
start pap/began to
'pop', i.e. to come out
with

a have/was having
gal dem/girls
a plan/were planning
whey/what **a goh/**

One morning, it was 'bout tea-break
time an' dem fly upstairs to di canteen.
One big queue deh in front a dem but
dem noh business 'bout dat. Dem jus'
walk up to di front and start fi full up
dem pocket wid biscuits an cheese.
Dem naw pay fi doze but dem will pay
fi dem buns an' sandwich. Well, while
dem a wait fi pay, Granny decide fi start
eat she buns; but when she tek a bite
she decide seh she noh want it any
more. Soh whey you t'ink she dhu wid
it? She fling it back in a di tray an' get
somet'ing else! Dem reach up fi pay now
an' while di woman a check up di price
dem, Squeakey stan' up in front a di
woman, drink off a glass a orange drink,
full up di glass again an' seh she only
paying fi one. Dis is fi show you how
dem bold-face. When dem ready fi move
off now, who you t'ink a stan'-up
behind dem? Noh di vicar! An' not one
a dem a have di mine fi put back whey
dem t'ief. Dem jus' carry on walking no
an' a the look ina di vicar eye, a mek fi
dem an' fi him eye mek four. When
dem reach back ina di common room
dem start pap big laugh 'bout it.

Well, it so happened dat one a di gal
ina di college a have party pan di satdey
nite an' she invite di gal dem. From
di time dem hear 'bout party, dem all
a plan whey dem a goh wear, because

were going to

is nothin . . . deh/
it as going to be
nothing but *fashion*
that night (more
literally: nothing but
only (**pure**) style was
going to (be) cut that
night)

is . . . gwaan/it all
happened!

did dey deh fi/have
been there to

I a goh/I am going to

is nothing but pure style a goh cut dah
nite deh.

Well di satdey nite come an' is one
piece a t'ing gwaan. Man, you shoulda
did dey deh fi see it, but seen as you
wasn't, I a goh tell you 'bout it.

5 LANGUAGE AND SUBCULTURES: ANTI-LANGUAGE

Anti-language

Anti-languages may be understood as extreme versions of social dialects. They tend to arise among subcultures and groups that occupy a marginal or precarious position in society, especially where central activities of the group place them outside the law. Often the subculture or group (the 'anti-society') has an antagonistic relationship with society at large and their natural suspicion of outsiders makes it difficult to study their language; but some examples have been documented – notably the language of Polish prison life (*grypserka*) and that of the Calcutta underworld. In addition to these relatively contemporary cases, some historical records survive of a variety known as 'pelting speech' – an argot employed by roving bands of vagabonds in Elizabethan England.

Linguistic features of an anti-language

Anti-languages are basically created by a process of *relexicalization* – the substitution of new words for old. The grammar of the parent language may be preserved, but a distinctive vocabulary develops, particularly – but not solely – in activities and areas that are central to the subculture and that help to set it off most sharply from the established society. Accounts of 'pelting speech', for example, contain over twenty terms for the classes of vagabond including 'rogue', 'wild rogue', 'prigger of prancers' (horse thief), 'counterfeit crank', 'bawdy basket' and so on. Similarly, the language of the Calcutta underworld contains over forty words for the police and over twenty words for bomb.

Making up new words is continuous within the anti-language (another factor that makes them difficult to document – they very quickly go out of date); but often very simple strategies underly the relexicalization process. An argot in use among bar girls in Addis Ababa included many items formed by regularly substituting /ay/ in place of the first vowel of the original and inserting /ə/ before repetition of the final consonant. Thus:

sım ('name')	becomes	sayməm
bırr ('dollar')	becomes	bayrər
hedə ('go')	becomes	haydəd
bədda ('copulate')	becomes	baydəd

Source: Demisse and Bender (1983).

Other forms of innovation include using items from the parent language in metaphorical ways and borrowing items from non-native languages, both of which processes are evident in the following examples from the Calcutta underworld:

Table 4

Item	Original/literal meaning	New/metaphorical sense
kācā-kalā	'unripe banana'	'young girl'
dabal-dekār	'double decker' (from English)	'plump woman'
sāinbord-olā	'signboard' (from English) 'ola' = owner' (reference to vermilion mark on forehead of married woman)	'married woman'

Source: based on Halliday (1978).

To some extent, the innovations in vocabulary and the proliferation of terms in certain key areas make possible finer distinctions in meaning than are found necessary in the parent language. It is also the case, however, that some of the new items are actually synonymous with each other and virtually interchangeable. In this respect therefore it is not just relexicalization (same grammar, different vocabulary) that is at work, but a process of *over*-lexicalization, particularly in certain key areas. This has two main consequences: it enhances the possibility for verbal play and display within the anti-society; and it makes the anti-language especially impenetrable to outsiders. The sense of solidarity between members of the subculture is heightened and maintained; and their frequently illicit dealings can remain semi-confidential, even when conducted in relatively public places such as the club, bar or street.

CB radio slang as anti-language

The broad slang at one time used for Citizens' Band (CB) radio transmission has some similarities with an anti-language. In a glossary published around the time of the legalization of CB in Britain there were clearly certain areas of experience which were heavily lexicalized in metaphoric ways. In addition to a vast array of terms concerned with handling the transmission, its quality and the type of rig involved, also listed were several items for 'police', many interchangeable, including 'bear', and 'smokey'. As extensions of such expressions there were several for police-related objects and activities, typified by the following:

police station	–	'bear cage', 'bear cave'
police helicopter	–	'bear in the air'
police using radar	–	'smokey with a camera',
		'portrait painter',
		'kojak with a kodak'
police car	–	'smokey on rubber',
		'jam sandwich',
		'bubble-gum machine'

When a police vehicle is using flashing lights and a siren, it is 'advertising'. When attempting to be inconspicuous it is 'sitting under the leaves'. Many expressions existed for diverse types of vehicle, including:

lorry without trailer	–	'bobtail'
flat-fronted lorry	–	'cabover'
ambulance	–	'blood wagon', 'meat wagon'
breakdown truck	–	'dragging wagon'

There were also several expressions for 'prostitute', including 'pavement princess', 'dress for sale', and 'goldilocks'. The generic term for women (with pejorative connotations) was 'beaver', hence 'beaver breaker' ('woman CB user'), 'beaver hunt' ('searching for women').

The particular way in which expressions proliferate along metaphorical pathways (e.g. bear → mama bear → lady bear → bear in the air → bear cave → feed the bears; and blood wagon → meat wagon → dragging wagon) is reminiscent of, for instance, Elizabethan pelting speech, in which similar strings of items occur, e.g.:

teeth	–	'crashing-cheats'
nose	–	'smelling-cheat'
apron	–	'belly-cheat' (where 'cheat' means 'thing-to-do-with')

Often the particular vocabulary of an anti-language and the metaphorical links within it embody and suggest a distinctive world-view for its users. In the case of CB slang it had distinctly masculine overtones, and otherwise it was as if the users were on a trip through a National Park which slides into the fairy tale of the Three Bears: hence, smokey bear, bear cave, mama bear, goldilocks, bobtail, bear, beaver, beaver hunt, sitting under the leaves, feed the bears, and so on. Although this was only one strand within CB slang, it gave it a curious Disneyland quality. Whilst in several respects CB slang shared important linguistic features with anti-languages, its comic-strip quality set it apart. For the image of the world that typically emerges in a hard-edged anti-language such as *grypserka* is much more in opposition to that of established society. Admittedly CB users did constitute something of an oppositional – if apparently slightly eccentric – minority, until

CB transmission in Britain was legalized (and it is interesting to note that, after legalization, a good deal of CB transmission proceeded with little use of the esoteric expressions listed above). Granted that the camaraderie of CB users was probably enlivened and reinforced by the issue of illegality, none the less their relation to the norms and values of established society was sensitive on only one point, which did not in any case involve the breach of fundamental taboos.

Anti-language and social structure

In more extreme and hard-edged cases of anti-language, the anti-society that provides the conditions for its generation tends to be much more marginalized and at the same time both more insulated from the wider society and under greater pressure to conform to its norms. The 'second life' of Polish prisons, for example, involves an elaborate caste system of 'people' and 'suckers' which is partially constituted by reference to type of offence, length of stay, and so on, but also in part by the degree of facility displayed by members of the anti-society in their anti-language – *grypserka.* Movement within the hierarchy is dependent on adhering to the rules of an elaborate game in which *grypserka* plays a crucial role. One of the ways in which an inmate can be downgraded to the level of 'sucker' in the social hierarchy is by breaking the rules of verbal contest and another is by selling the secret language to the police. Under conditions such as these, the view of the world constructed in and by the anti-language is much more likely to be totally oppositional in character and its role in determining the speaker's place within the anti-society much more crucial.

On balance, therefore, the language of CB transmission – even before legalization – probably did not constitute an anti-language in the fullest sense of the term. Applying the notion of anti-language to such a variety, however, does help to highlight some of its more salient features. Indeed it is in precisely this kind of exercise that the usefulness of the term lies: not as an absolute category to which particular varieties must conform on an all-or-nothing basis, but as an idea to which given instances approximate more or less closely.

The idea of an anti-language can, perhaps, cast some light on the complicated social significance of 'talking Black' in the British speech community. Linguistically, Black English has identifiable origins in Caribbean (principally Jamaican) Creole. But in the British context its precise point of geographical origin is not immediately at issue. As far as is known to date, Patois in Britain does not vary much from region to region. On the contrary it belongs not so much to a locality but to a particular, ethnically defined social group. At the simplest level, close integration with the Black community entails the frequent use of Patois and the consequent likelihood of a high degree of competence in it. But this fact of use based on networks of particular kinds of relationship can take on a larger social significance. In 'Black' settings its use conveys solidarity between speakers. It is the easiest way to be on the same wavelength. But in 'White' or mixed settings use of Patois inevitably comes to symbolize social distance from mainstream society and to count as an assertion of ethnic identity. Its significance in this respect is all the more marked if as a variety it is perceived as very distinct from local English norms. The more linguistically distinct it sounds, the more it can come to symbolize social distance. From this perspective the African traces in Patois – in voice-set and intonation in particular – can clearly play a crucial role: so that, for at least some Black speakers some of the time in some situations, 'talking Black' can provide a mode of resistance on the linguistic level to the dominant social order. In its potential for articulating a form of symbolic resistance Patois has some resemblance to anti-language.

Anti-language and the speech community

The notion of an anti-language, therefore, can be used to illuminate certain kinds of social dialect. It can also be used, however, to clarify the notion of speech community. It is not just that a speech community is likely to embrace and include a range of different forms of speech. Nor is it just a question of these differing forms of speech all being linguistically equal and equivalent. Nor even is it a question of a speech community consistently attaching a higher value to some varieties over others, despite their linguistic equality.

101

In the final analysis, viewed from the perspective of anti-language, the speech community emerges as an arena of competing affiliations and antagonistic differences.

Background sources and further reading

Halliday, M.A.K. (1976) 'Antilanguages', in *American Anthropologist*, 78 (3).

A shortened version appears in:

Halliday, M.A.K. (1978) *Language as Social Semiotic; the Social Interpretation of Language and Meaning*, London: Edward Arnold.

Halliday's work is notable for its sustained attempt to theorize the nature of language in a way that reveals and clarifies its relationship to social structure. *Language as Social Semiotic* is crucial in this respect, especially section IV, 'Language and Social Structure'.

Demisse, T. and Bender, M.L. (1983) 'An argot of Addis Ababa unattached girls', in *Language and Society*, 12, 339–47.

This reports in some detail the linguistic characteristics of an argot adopted by a group of women described by the authors as 'freelance prostitutes'. The argot shares many characteristics of the varieties discussed by Halliday as 'anti-language'.

Fieldwork projects

Secret languages

Demisse and Bender (1983) say of the argot used by bar girls in Addis Ababa that it originally developed amongst a cohort of schoolboys around the former Haile Sillase I Day School. It was used for:

> calling out secret messages in football (soccer) games, or in conflicts with other gangs, such as the one from the Piazza (old

town center) area. Besides sports (losers of contests often started fights), a source of conflict was competition in collecting film and show advertisements. Details of how the argot moved on to the night clubs is not known, though it is natural to guess that aging gang members would have taken it with them when they moved on from the schoolyard to such entertainment areas. (340)

Boarding schools in Britain quite often feature an argot or secret language of this type, which depends on 'scrambling' in a regular fashion the pronunciation of words. Another setting in which they can feature is fish markets of the north-east of England. Here a slang is adopted that works by regular reversal of normal pronunciation so that 'fish' is referred to as 'shiff', 'woman' as 'namow' and so on. Try and document in detail the form and function of an argot such as these. To what extent do they correspond to the notion of anti-language?

Teenage subcultures and slang

Here is a sample of some vocabulary current among teenage boys in Glasgow during the mid-1990s. Some of it seems to be quite specific to this age range (16–18), locale, and gender, some of it has a wider currency than this particular group.

STATE OF ALCOHOLIC INEBRIATION
steaming; blootered; swallied; rockered; jaiked; slappered; pished; oot'yer face

CANNABIS/MARIJUANA
hash; shit; grass; pot; weed; ganja; doobie; wacky-backy; mauwee-wauwee; a wee toke; spliff; joint; blaw; soap bar; skunk; skunk weed; Thai stick; black rock; rocky; gold seal; red seal; golf-ball black

LSD
flying kiwi; strawberry dips; penguins; batmans; cids; trips; tabs

YOUNG WOMEN
dolls; babes; honey

In addition, the following expressions are all synonymous:

spanking the monkey; polishing the rocket; choking the chicken; knobbing; tugging

(1) To what extent and in what ways does this data reveal aspects of an anti-language at work?
(2) What further kinds of data would you need to collect in order to confirm that an anti-language is involved?
(3) Are you aware of similar kinds of linguistic innovation at work in your own locality amongst people that you know? Design a study to explore whether your local data display characteristics of an anti-language.

6 LANGUAGE AND SITUATION: REGISTER

Language is sensitive to its context of situation

We have seen that any speech community is likely to be composed of different groups, groups which may operate with differing versions of the same language or even with discrete and separate languages. In this sense different varieties are 'owned' by different groups, and speech will vary according to the primary group affiliation of the speaker around crucial reference points such as class, region, ethnicity, gender and also age. Such reference points heavily shape our speech so that we inevitably signal much about our social identity in producing even (or especially) the most banal utterance.

There is, however, a further crucial dimension along which language varies: it varies not just according to who we are, but also according to the situation in which we find ourselves. This latter type of variation is traditionally approached through the concept of *register,* sometimes also being referred to as *stylistic variation.* The basic notion is that any given instance of language is inextricably bound up with its context of situation and that different types of situation require us to handle the language differently. The sensitivity of language to its context of situation is so strong that we can often recover features of the context from very small – almost trivial – examples. For instance, many readers will feel confident that they can reconstruct the different contexts of situation for the following utterances:

(1) 'I'm going to give you a prescription for the pain.'
(2) 'Cream together butter, sugar and beaten yolks until smooth.'
(3) 'New Tubifast. The tubular dressing retention bandage. No sticking. No tying. No pinning.'
(4) 'Beauty of Velvet at truly Budget Prices. In 16 colours. Send now for full details and actual fabric samples.'

It will come as no surprise to learn that (1) comes from a doctor–patient interview; (2) from a recipe; and both (3) and (4) from magazine advertising. Our capacity to distinguish between these different examples and our ability to identify different contexts for them suggests that there are, in fact, distinctive varieties of language use associated with particular contexts of situation.

It might seem that the distinguishing trait for the examples above is their actual vocabulary, so that mention of 'prescription' automatically evokes the doctor's surgery, and 'cream', 'butter' and 'sugar' bring to mind cookery settings. To a certain extent this is true – that specialized vocabularies do develop for certain contexts of situation – but it is only part of the total picture. 'Prescription' after all could as easily occur in a chemist's; 'cream' and 'butter' could occur as signs in a hypermarket; and 'bandage', of course, could be associated with a hospital casualty department. The sensitivity of language to context is registered by more than the individual words themselves: what seems to be more crucial is the way in which particular vocabulary is articulated together into utterances and what types of utterances can then result.

For instance, in example (2) above it is the co-occurrence of 'yolks' with 'beaten' that is symptomatic of recipe text. Furthermore 'cream' is used here to describe not an object but an action, one which the utterance requests the reader to perform in the completion of the task. Example (3) on the other hand displays two prevalent features of advertising text. First of all, there is the unusual sentence structure, in which (despite its origins in a piece of written text) certain elements are left unstated. The distinctiveness of this pattern can be illustrated if we compare it with a hypothetical journalistic account of the same material:

(5) 'Tubifast this week announced a new product. It is a tubular dressing retention bandage which requires no sticking, tying or pinning. '

Secondly, it deploys a common device of magazine advertising – namely the triple repetition in close succession of an identical structure, in this case 'no ——ing' as in 'No sticking. No tying. No pinning.' It is the presence of patterns such as these – over and beyond the use of particular vocabulary items – that signals the contextual origins of the examples and makes them easy to identify: it is through such features that individual utterances carry the imprint of their context of situation.

Register

The notion of *register* helps to clarify the interrelationship of language with context by handling it under three basic headings – *field, tenor* and *mode*.

Field

Where utterances are embedded in an ongoing activity so that they help to sustain and shape it, then the notion of *field* refers to the activity itself. An utterance such as:

(6) 'scalpel . . . clips . . . swab here' would have as its field the activity of a surgical operation; whereas an utterance such as:

(7) 'This is alpha romeo tango requesting clearance to proceed to runway one, over' would have as its field the activity of taxi-ing an aircraft.

Not all instances of language are so closely embedded in an ongoing set of actions, since utterances (spoken or written) may be concerned with a topic or subject matter (ranging from 'last night's TV programme' to 'sub-atomic physics') quite remote from the immediate circumstances in which they are produced. In such cases the notion of *field* refers not so much to an ongoing activity but to the subject matter of the text. In the following piece of newspaper text the *field* may be summed up as 'party politics in the United Kingdom':

(8) 'With Tory divisions over Europe so deep, any new leader could split the party still further.'

The *field*, therefore, may vary from being *intrinsic* to the text, as in the last example, or *extrinsic* to the text as in the case of examples of activity-based talk ((6)–(7), above).

TECHNICAL, SPECIALIZED AND FIELD-SPECIFIC VOCABULARIES

The particular aspect of language most affected by the *field* is probably the lexis or vocabulary. As pointed out above, specialized vocabularies do emerge for certain specific *fields*, so that items such as 'software', 'disk-drive', 'peripherals', 'data-storage', 'floppy-disk', are probably exclusive to *fields* related to computing. Individual items, which in themselves may not be specialized, can, none the less, cluster into expressions which have relatively restricted domains of application. The following expressions, for example, are unlikely to have currency outside a *field* concerned with motorcycles: 'shaft drive', 'water-cooled inline middleweight V twin', 'air-adjustable front forks', 'rising rate monoshock rear suspension'.

Items and expressions of this kind are often referred to as 'technical vocabulary'. The term, however, is somewhat misleading, since it suggests modern science or technology as the major domain requiring such vocabularies. Yet specialized items and expressions develop for a wide range of *fields,* including knitting or, as in the following, high fashion: 'boned, strapless bodices', 'black crêpe dress with satin godet inset', 'draped *décolleté'* backs', 'thigh-high side split'. Since such expressions, whether topic-oriented or activity-based, are likely to be exclusive to a particular *field*, then it would seem appropriate to refer to them as *field-specific vocabularies.*

Finally, it must be stressed, of course, that a high proportion of vocabulary items are potentially capable of registering many diverse types of *field.* Even so it is surprising how certain pairings of apparently non-specialized vocabulary items become suggestive of a particular, highly restricted *field:* 'bijou residence', 'town house', 'character farmhouse', 'period villa' are fairly specific to residential property advertising, especially when premodified with positively evaluating adjectives to give expressions such as 'enchanting character farmhouse', 'delightful period villa', 'imposing town house', 'desirable bijou residence'. It is difficult to envisage any but the most ironic use of such expressions outside the domain of property advertising.

Tenor

Whereas the *field* corresponds loosely to what a text is about, *tenor* refers to the kind of social relationship enacted in or by the text. The notion of *tenor*, therefore, highlights the way in which linguistic choices are affected not just by the topic or subject matter of communication but also by the kind of social relationship within which communication is taking place. Assume for a moment a situation in which one person (A) needs someone else (B) to open a door: A might address B in any of the following ways:

1 'Could you possibly open the door?'
2 'You couldn't open the door, could you?'
3 'I don't suppose you could open the door for me, could you?'
4 'Please open the door.'
5 'Open the door, will you.'
6 'Open the door.'
7 'The door!'
8 'Why don't you open the door?'
9 'Aren't you going to open the door, then?'

All these utterances give verbal expression to the same basic need on A's part, but they clearly do so in subtly different ways. They differ along various dimensions related to the kind of social relationship obtaining between A and B. Some versions are more polite than others: for instance, (1), (2), (3) and (4) are more polite than either (5) or (6). Some versions imply more power or status on A's part relative to B, e.g. (7) compared with (1). Some versions imply a greater degree of assumed obligation on B's part to perform the action, e.g. (8) or (9) compared with (1) or (2).

The examples, therefore, express different forms of social relationship between A and B. The aspects of social relationship most crucial under the heading of *tenor* include politeness, degrees of formality, and the relative statuses of participants; and these dimensions of interpersonal relations affect a whole range of linguistic choices. The use of modal auxiliary verbs such as 'might', 'may', 'can', 'could', 'would', especially in utterances that request action, is often related to politeness (see, for example, (1), (2) and (3) above, where they cushion A's request by apparently allowing B some discretion in response).

FORMS OF PERSONAL ADDRESS

The use of different forms of personal address is also related to *tenor*. Some languages carry a distinction between singular and plural addressees embodied in the pronoun system: French, for example, has *tu* ('you', singular) versus *vous* ('you', plural) and similar distinctions may be found in German and Russian. English used to carry the distinction in terms of the opposition between *thou* and *you*. On closer inspection, however, we find that the distinction is not a simple one between singular and plural, since both forms can be used to a singular addressee. The choice of one or other form is motivated not just by how many people are being addressed, but also by a sense of personal familiarity versus social distance, the singular form being used to invoke intimacy and the plural form being used to register a sense of formality and distance. Thus, the *tenor* of the social relationship is reflected in the choice of personal pronouns.

Although English no longer uses the distinction between *thou* and *you* in the personal pronoun system, there are still, of course, many ways of registering intimacy versus distance in forms of personal address. Mr Jonathan Crisp, aged 20, may be called 'Crispie' by his workmates, 'Jonathan' by his mother-in-law, 'Jonnie' by his wife, 'Crisp' when answering the attendance register on his day-release course, 'sir' when being measured for a new suit, and so on. There is still the option of plain 'you', of course, or even no specific form at all. Indeed, English is interesting in its capacity for avoiding reference within an utterance to features of the recipient for whom it is intended: basically we can 'no-name'. This is done particularly in settings where there is some uncertainty over the exact relationship that exists between participants: how, for instance, should a prospective or actual father-in-law be addressed? Should he be called 'Mr Brown', 'Bill', or possibly 'Dad'? Until the appropriate form has been settled, perhaps by explicit negotiation, either plain 'you' or 'no-name' provides a way out of the difficulty.

Some settings, of course, have more or less explicit instructions concerning how key participants should be addressed. British law courts, for example, may include exchanges such as

'I must ask counsel for the defence to limit his cross-examination to questions of fact.' 'Yes, m'lud.'

Parliamentary proceedings in the House of Commons will include reference to 'The Right Honourable Lady' or 'The Right Honourable Gentleman'. The incumbent of the White House is addressed by journalists at press conferences as 'Mr President'. In such cases the selection of address terms (and other linguistic options) seems merely to reflect the nature of the social relation involved and the pre-established positions of participants. However, in settings that are not clearly status marked in this way, linguistic choices may be used to establish, shift, negotiate and manipulate the nature of the relationship. Consider, for example, the following interchange between a policeman (white) and a member of the public (black) on an American street:

W: What's your name, boy?
B: Dr Poussaint. I'm a physician.
W: What's your first name, boy?
B: Alvin.

Source: Ervin-Tripp (1972).

The use of 'boy' by the policeman to address an adult male is insulting, but the insult is heightened by reselecting it when he knows his interlocutor to be a doctor. It also, of course, has racial overtones and the combined effect of the policeman's utterances is to imply that a black man is only a black, whatever other claims to status he might possess. More can be said about this interchange (why, for instance, elicit his first name, when initials suffice for most official purposes) but the important point remains that through specific linguistic selections the doctor is symbolically stripped of all social identity but 'blackness'. The language here works to define the relationship of the two participants in a particularly active manner.

In addition to considerations of topic and social relationship, language is also sensitive to the means adopted for communication. These have varied in an astonishing variety of ways across different cultures and between different historical periods, ranging from tablets of stone and marks on papyri to smoke signals and drum beats. The principal distinction within *mode* is between those channels of communication that entail immediate contact and those that allow for deferred contact between participants. The prime instance of this distinction in our own culture is that between speech and writing.

Despite the fact that even the most literate amongst us spend much more of our time engaging with the spoken medium, it tends to be the written medium that conditions our view of language. This is because control of the two *modes* is achieved in very different ways. We develop the capacity to speak very early in life with little conscious awareness of the processes involved and with little explicit instruction. Writing, on the other hand, is rarely acquired except by explicit instruction and as the focus of conscious attention. Indeed it is a prime component of the initial school curriculum and in this context relative success or failure in handling the *mode* attracts praise or censure. The very act of judging the written *mode* is easier, of course, because of its relative permanence in contrast to the transitory nature of speech. Because speech is all-pervasive, it is taken for granted. Because engagement with the written *mode* is always something of a struggle, it can unjustifiably come to stand as a tangible though partial sign of overall linguistic competence.

FEATURES OF SPONTANEOUS SPEECH
We are so rarely self-conscious about speech in the way we are about writing that it is interesting to scrutinize closely transcribed passages of spontaneous talk because, captured in this fashion, its distinctive features emerge most starkly and dramatically:

EXAMPLE 6.1

A: What about erm Stephen do you s
B: └he comes to Aikido with
    me now (A:oh yea) I try to er encourage him to do it (.)

I I've tried the painting a bit on 'em all (A:yea) painting I've tried you know (A:yea) tried to find if there's anything there you know anything that's been passed on (.) Sally's quite good (.) for her age like you know (A:mm) (.) erm she seems to be able to put things in the right place (.) which is something (.) which is the main thing really . . and er (.) I try and get them to do the things you know but (.) you know they sort of go their own way (.) you know

Several features of unrehearsed talk displayed here can be briefly summarized as follows:

(i) *Pauses* – these are indicated by full stops in parentheses in the transcript but their distribution does not correspond to punctuation points in writing. Sometimes they may occur at a point roughly equivalent to a sentence or clause boundary, but this is not always the case ('Sally's quite good (.) for her age like you know'). They are commonly understood to derive from the problems of planning speech simultaneously with producing it, so that speakers need intermittently to take 'time off' to work out the next piece of their utterance. In interactive settings, however, where turns at talk are constantly exchanged between speakers, a pause may indicate a possible completion point of an utterance, so much so that it may be heard as an invitation to another participant to contribute. The way in which pausing generates a potential ambiguity for participants to a speech event ('Is this pause, at this moment, part of the current speaker's turn, or a signal of its termination?') is resolved in part by the next feature.

(ii) *Ers/erms* – these are usually referred to as *fillers* and tend to occur in place of, or in conjunction with, pauses. They have a characteristic intonation contour, taking a level tone rather than a rise or a fall. The intonation in particular distinguishes them from, for instance, the checking 'eh?', spoken with a rising tone, since the level tone generally signifies incompleteness. In this way they fill potential or actual gaps in the flow of speech and indicate to participants that the current turn is to be continued. This is especially so when they occur at a possible completion point in the turn such as:

113

'Sally's quite good (.) for her age like you know (A:mm) (.) *erm* (.) she seems to be able to put', etc.

(iii) *Back-channel behaviour* – speech is rarely, if ever, projected into a social void. More usually it is shaped in such a way as to prompt immediate and ongoing responses from other participants. Indeed, someone talking aloud but addressing no one in particular, especially in public places, runs the risk of being considered mentally ill. In face-to-face settings where talk is the prime focus of the interaction, participants will tend to show their alignment with it in a variety of ways; by posture, by gesture and by gaze direction. From these are drawn the non-vocal forms of back-channel behaviour – indications by non-speaking participants of their reactions to what is being said. These are supplemented by (and in certain situations – for example, on the telephone – altogether replaced by) vocal forms of back-channel behaviour – expressions such as 'mm', 'mmhum', 'yea', 'wow', laughter and so on. An interesting characteristic of such vocalizations is that they often do not constitute a turn in themselves, and in fact can be used to support the current speaker in the turn s/he is engaged upon. In the transcribed passage above, A seems to be using them at possible completion points of B's turn as an invitation to him to continue:

B: I I've tried the painting bit on 'em all (*A:yea*) painting I've tried you know (*A:yea*) tried to find if there's anything there you know anything that's been passed on (.) Sally's quite good (.) for her age like you know (*A:mm*) (.) erm

(iv) *Markers of sympathetic circularity* – so called because they invite the listener to assume the speaker's point of view. They are typified by expressions such as 'like', 'you know', 'sort of', 'ain't it', 'that sort of thing'. They allow speakers a degree of imprecision or verbal inexplicitness in what they are saying, on the grounds that not everything needs to be, or even can be, exactly spelt out in so many words. Indeed, extreme verbal explicitness and exactitude in speech would merely sound pedantic. Markers of sympathetic circularity, therefore, function in part as an appeal to a framework of shared understanding which makes absolute explicitness unnecessary. They are particularly prominent towards the end of A's turn: 'I try and get them to do the things *you know* but (.) *you know* they *sort of* go their own way (.) *you know*'

(v) *Repetitions* – speech tends to be more repetitious than writing for a variety of reasons, one of them being the constraint of making it up as we go along. The repetitions of 'painting', 'tried', and 'anything' in the transcribed passage seem to be related to this consideration: it is as if successive portions of the turn provide a platform for its subsequent development:

> *I try* to er encourage him to do it (.) I I've *tried* the *painting* a bit on em all (A:yea) *painting* I've *tried* you know (A:yea) *tried* to find if there's *anything* there you know *anything* that's been passed on

(vi) *False starts and self corrections* – these are rather crude terms to cover the various ways in which utterances are reworked in the act of speaking them. Sometimes an utterance or part of an utterance is begun, only for what has just been enunciated to be left unfinished and immediately replaced by something else. Sometimes what has just been said comes under erasure by the speaker and is explicitly corrected. Both these processes can be seen at work in the following example:

EXAMPLE 6.2

C: well I was going to put that phone out *in the workshop* but I er *not in the workshop in the cottage*

D: well you see (.) I'm sure it would I'm sure it would have been possible if they'd known anyone who was a (.) er post office engineer to instal (.) a um er (.) rig *so that the the* (.) where you can actually dial from the from the from that phone (.) er *and if you* (.) but that could be locked away and *the er* something like that (.) so you could actually dial from that one bypass the coin mechanism

The general impression gained from closer scrutiny of the properties of speech may be one of sloppiness. This, however, would be a mistaken conclusion to reach, deriving in part from the actual procedure involved, which entails transferring the product of one mode (speech) by transcription to another mode (writing) for which it was not originally shaped. This helps to highlight the actual differences between the two modes, but we should be careful not to judge one in terms of the other. The hesitancies and apparent disfluencies that emerge in transcription are not necessarily at all noticeable or in any way a problem for the actual participants in the original context of situation. On the contrary, they form an inextricable component of the medium, so that the two media are best understood as semi-independent modes of expression for language, each systematic in its own way, each with its own intrinsic logic.

GENERAL DIFFERENCES BETWEEN SPEECH AND WRITING
The features of speech that have been discussed above fundamentally stem from the dynamic and interactive aspect of the mode. Particularly in face-to-face settings of an informal type, speech is both an instantaneous and collaborative engagement of one participant with another with the separate actions of each finely meshed together. The process of composing and planning speech goes hand in hand with the act of speaking itself: and the process of interpretation has to be just as instantaneous, because the product is not recoverable. We have to make it up as we go along, and make sense of it as it is said.

Whereas speech is a relatively transitory and impermanent medium, writing yields a relatively fixed and permanent product. This enables the separation of participants in time and in space. The process of composition may be lengthy, involving several stages and many revisions as the final product takes shape. And because the final product is relatively fixed, the process of interpretation may be extended, deferred and interrupted, involving several readings and re-readings. Writing tends also to be more self-contained as a medium, in contrast with speech where the meaning of an utterance is often supplemented by the context and by paralinguistic behaviour.

MIXED MODES
It is for reasons such as these that the two *modes* appear so different from one another when close comparisons are made between them. It would be wrong, of course, to insist on an absolute dividing line

between all writing on the one hand and all speech on the other. There do exist intermediate cases such as the prepared lecture or dramatic dialogue, written in advance, but to be spoken aloud; or conversely, the recorded interview or discussion which is subsequently transcribed for publication. In fact the electronic media are probably beginning to erode the distinction between the two. Telephone-answering machines, for example, place the speaker in the unusual position of composing a spoken product for deferred contact with an absent audience and thereby involves using one *mode* under constraints usually attendant upon the other.

Indeed, the development, dissemination and adoption of alternative modes of communication within a speech community will tend to have repercussions for whatever modes were already in use and ultimately of course on the culture itself. The emergence and widespread use of a written mode within a speech community is a potent force for the standardization of linguistic norms within the spoken mode. In the history of English, for example, the adoption of the south-east Midlands dialect as the norm for written documents was an important contributory factor in its subsequent adoption as the standard dialect in 'educated' speech. And the prestige accruing to the standard dialect is reinforced by its capacity to facilitate access to the written mode and the material advantages that ensue. Thus, within a speech community as a whole the two modes are not totally separated off from each other.

None the less, when considering the use of language within situation, the adoption of one mode rather than another has clear repercussions for the kinds of linguistic choices that are made. *Mode,* then, (alongside *field* and *tenor*) is the final term of the three that help to articulate the relationships between a given instance of language in use and its context of situation. Taken together, the terms comprise the notion of *register.*

Register: an example

The following text is a letter which was sent by a bank to its customer after service charges have been levied on his account when it had briefly become overdrawn.

Carradale Bank PLC
East Bay Branch
10 Tarbert Street
Glasgow G16

Our ref VJR/AE
Date 12 February 1993

Dr M Smith
15 Montgomery Road
Glasgow G16

Dear Dr Smith

You will recently have received an advice note from the Bank providing details of the Service Charge due to be applied to your account on 16th February 1993.

On examining the details of the charge due at this time I have discovered that the advice note is in fact incorrect. Due to the fact that your account became overdrawn on only one occasion and in view of the other accounts held at the Branch, I would advise that the net charge has been reversed.

Unfortunately, our desire to give you sufficient advance warning of any forthcoming service charges means that there is insufficient time to take corrective action on the very few occasions where the charge is found to be incorrect and I apologise for any inconvenience or confusion this may cause.

If you wish to discuss this further, please do not hesitate to contact me.

Yours sincerely

William Andrews

William Andrews
Office Manager

It is easy to recognize this as an example of official language: the writer in his role of office manager communicates not so much as an individual in his own right but as a member of a large institution in order to explain or interpret that institution's operations for a member of the public. As with any text, the letter is made up of a continuous series of linguistic choices, both of vocabulary and of grammatical structure. By using the notion of register – and the concepts of *field, mode* and *tenor* – we can inspect these choices in terms of how they exhibit and implement aspects of the context of situation. As we saw above, *field, mode* and *tenor* may be considered as 'lines of linguistic force' connecting the text to its context of situation. As such, they each operate relatively independently; but as we shall see in the following discussion of the bank's letter, we shall also need to recognize that these lines of force overlap.

MODE

The mode, obviously, is written. What effect does this choice of mode have on the choices of the text? Generally it displays several features of considered and self-conscious prose composition. A large proportion of the vocabulary, for instance, is derived from Latin roots: *receive, advice, provide, examine, discover, incorrect, occasion, reverse, desire, insufficient, corrective action, discuss, hesitate, contact.* Furthermore, the structure of the sentences is complex, especially in the way that one sentence is embedded inside another. A good example of this structural complexity comes at the beginning of the letter, where the recipient is told that 'the service charge is due to be applied to your account'. This sentence is embedded inside another that tells us that 'the bank provided details of the service charge'. This in turn is embedded inside another sentence that asserts that 'you will recently have received an advice note from the bank'. Complex structures of this type are more likely to occur in written rather than in spoken texts.

Another kind of sentence pattern more typical of written than spoken texts is the adoption of passive rather than active structures: for instance, 'your account became overdrawn' (rather than 'you overdrew on your account'). There is also a tendency to nominalize – i.e. to use complex noun phrases for verb phrases, as in: 'our desire to give you sufficient advance warning of forthcoming service

119

charges' (rather than, 'because we wanted to warn you in enough time that we were going to charge you for services'). Note here how the act of someone '*charging* for services' becomes nominalized in the expression 'forthcoming service charges'; the act of '*warning* someone in time' becomes nominalized in the expression 'sufficient advance warning'; and the act of someone '*wanting* something' becomes 'our desire'. Nominalization can, it is true, be a more economical way of expressing an idea – partly because, when nouns (or noun phrases) are used instead of verbs (or verb phrases), it is possible to leave the participants in processes unspecified. At the same time, however, the processes themselves become 'thing-like objects', rather than 'personal events'. Compare, for example, 'Service charges will be forthcoming' with 'I will charge you for services'. The latter version makes it clearer that one person is acting upon another. In the former version, by contrast, the process is much less personal and is further depersonalized in the phrase 'forthcoming service charges'. Nominalization is common in bureaucratic *written* communication; it also has consequences for the *tenor*, as we discuss later.

FIELD

The *field* of the letter may broadly be described as that of 'personal banking' of 'financial services'. Vocabulary items and expressions particularly associated with this field are:

'bank'
'service charge' (×2);
'net charge' (×1);
'charge' (×2);
'account(s)' (×3);
'overdrawn'.

The last item in this list is the clearest example of field-specific vocabulary in the text since it rarely occurs in contexts other than those related to personal banking. (It is more field-specific in this way than 'service charge', which might apply equally in service encounters in hotels and restaurants.)

Field may refer not just to topic but also to activity – in this case advising the customer about bank charges. Here the writer clearly has a problem. The customer has previously been notified that he will have to pay bank charges. How can this decision be reversed without making it look as if a silly mistake has been made? One strategy is to treat what has happened as if it were the outcome of a purely abstract, impersonal process. This is helped by the choice of the passive that we noted above, as in:

'the Service Charge due to be applied to your account' (not the Service Charge which I was going to apply to your account');
'your account became overdrawn' (not 'you overdrew on your account');
'the very few occasions where the charge is found to be incorrect' (not 'the very few occasions where I find the charge to be incorrect').

In this way, the text seeks to avoid finding actual individuals (including the customer) responsible for any of the events which it refers to. Where responsibility *is* claimed, it is for the discovery of the mistake: 'I have discovered that the advice note is in fact incorrect'.

TENOR
Linguistic choices that occur as part of the field and the mode also have repercussions for the *tenor*, i.e. the kind of social relationship brought into play by the text. In various ways the relationship is formal. The use of the Latinate vocabulary, which we noted above in discussing *mode*, helps to contribute to the formal quality of the relationship, partly by virtue of emphasizing strongly that the *mode* is written rather than spoken and therefore potentially less personal.

It is also noticeable, as we pointed out above, that the relationship presupposed by the letter is not so much between individuals in their own right, but between a member of the organization (the bank) and a member of the public (a customer). We can see this in the form of self identification adopted at the end of the letter – *First Name + Last Name* ('William Andrews'). On the face of it, this is slightly less formal than the method used to identify the recipient at the beginning of the letter which uses the status-marked *Title + Last Name* ('Dear Dr Smith'). The letter-writer's use of *First Name + Last Name* goes a small way to establish him as an individual, but this is quickly balanced by his designation of himself as 'Office Manager'. Part of his role is to act as a functionary of the organisation; at the same time, however, customers need to feel that they are being attended to by an individual person who will bear their interest in mind. In this respect, then, 'William Andrews, Office Manager' is at one and the same time functional-within-the-organization and individual.

We should also note that the letter is very polite. What do we mean by this? Most crucially, it involves not imposing constraints on others, preserving their room to manoeuvre socially, and not threatening their face or dignity by implying that they have behaved badly or incorrectly. In encounters where there is an uneven distribution of power between participants, considerations of politeness would seek to minimize or disguise the power differential. In seeking to be polite, for instance, a speaker even in a position of power is much more likely to select a request than a command. In the case of the letter, the relations of power are complex. At one level the office manager has power over the customer in various ways including in this case the power to impose bank charges. At another level, however, the customer exercises a certain power over the bank through the possibility of taking his or her money elsewhere.

Several features of the language of the letter can be understood in terms of these contradictory lines of power and the adoption of strategies of politeness so as to negotiate them. In general, the whole burden of the letter is to suggest that whatever was done was in the best interests of the customer. An '*advice* note', for instance, sounds as if the bank was being helpful to the customer (although in this case, of course, it 'advises' him of what the bank will deduct from the account because it was overdrawn). It was pointed out above in the discussion of *field* how certain aspects of the language of the letter tend to treat the events described as if they were abstract impersonal processes. It is interesting to note, therefore, some of those sentences where persons enter unambiguously into the processes:

I apologise for any inconvenience or confusion this may cause.

Making apologies downgrades the power of the speaker or writer – for one thing it is an implicit admission of guilt or blameworthiness. In this case, however, the writer avoids some loss of face by apologizing for what is presented as a possible rather than an actual inconvenience or confusion.

I would advise that the net charge has been reversed.

All the writer needs to say, in fact, is that the net charge has been reversed: 'I would advise that' is strictly speaking redundant. It seems to be designed primarily to foreground the role of the writer in an act that is of benefit to the customer (along the lines of 'I have discovered that the advice note is in fact incorrect' commented on previously).

Please do not hesitate to contact me.

Such invitations have something of a ritual role in official letters but the wording itself is significant. It could be argued that the most elementary form of this invitation would be

Contact me.

The remaining parts of the sentence do various kinds of softening work to increase the politeness of the sentence by making the action very much at the discretion of the addressee. Thus

Do not hesitate to contact me

implies that the addressee might view contacting the writer as an imposition on the latter but invites the addressee to go ahead anyway.

Please do not hesitate to contact me

further softens the invitation by the introduction of the politeness marker 'please'.

If you wish to discuss the matter further, please do not hesitate to contact me

increases the politeness yet further by making the act of contacting conditional primarily upon the addressee's desire. The positioning of this item at the end of the letter is in itself significant, since it helps to cushion any possible abruptness of closure by suggesting that the recipient may resume or reopen communication whenever they choose.

The register of the letter, therefore, is the outcome of a whole series of significant choices in wording – not just the choice of specific items of vocabulary but also of whole patterns of placement and structure. The overall effect of these may be highlighted by comparing the actual letter with a possible alternative. The office manager could have written:

Dear Mike

We sent you a note recently telling you that we were going to make you pay for services because you were overdrawn.

But when we checked our records we realized that you are a valued customer with other accounts at this branch and that anyway your over-draft only lasted for a couple of days. So the note about charges was a mistake.

We send out these notes to give customers early warning of the charges that we're going to impose. Every now and then we get it wrong – as happened in your case.

Sorry about the misunderstanding. Do get in touch if you want to talk about it some more.

All the best,

Bill

Bill (Office boss)

While this version covers more or less the same points dealt with in the original letter, the overall effect is very different – a difference based primarily on changes in register. Indeed, given what we know about the original context, this alternative letter sounds mildly incongruous – it is perhaps too chatty and informal for its context. This kind of incongruity, or register clash, is often exploited by comedians for humorous effect. In this particular case, our constructed example helps to highlight to specific appropriacy of the linguistic choices in the original and, in so doing, gives further support for the general claim concerning the dependency of language on its context which the notion of register is designed to systematize.

Conclusion

We speak a particular kind of English depending, for instance, upon which region of the country we come from or upon which class we are most strongly affiliated with. But we also use a particular kind of English if we are giving evidence in a law court or writing to the bank or choosing make-up or playing darts in the pub. This chapter has focused on the latter dimension of linguistic variation: language varies not just according to who we are but also according to the situations in which we find ourselves. We have seen in some detail how closely language is tied to its social context, so that certain linguistic choices – of grammar as well as vocabulary – seem naturally appropriate to certain contexts, while others do not. Contexts have associated with them, we might say, repertoires of linguistic choice. This is not just an elaborate way of saying that we have to choose the right word to match the occasion. For what the notion of register implies is that contexts of situation consist of options for meaning. The fact that some wordings are more appropriate than others in particular contexts reflects a deeper underlying difference: that contexts differ fundamentally in the kinds of meanings that they allow.

Background sources and further reading

Register

Halliday, M.A.K. (1978) *Language as Social Semiotic: the Social Interpretation of Language and Meaning*, London: Edward Arnold.
Halliday, M.A.K. and Hasan, R. (1989) *Language, Context and Text: Aspects of Language in a Social-Semiotic Perspective*, Oxford: Oxford University Press.

Both of these contain important discussions and developments of the concept of register, including in the case of Halliday and Hasan detailed application to text.

For a general introduction to the notion of register with many examples, see:

Gregory, M. and Carroll, S. (1978) *Language and Situation,* London: Routledge & Kegan Paul.

For a detailed analysis of one kind of register, see:

Cook, G. (1992) *The Discourse of Advertising,* London: Routledge.
Leech, G.N. (1966) *English in Advertising: a Linguistic Study of Advertising in Great Britain,* London: Longman.

For analyses of a range of registers, see:

Crystal, D. and Davy, D. (1969) *Investigating English Style,* London: Longman.
Fairclough, N. (1988) 'Register power and socio-semantic change', in Birch, D. and O'Toole, M. *Functions of Style*, London: Pinter Publishers.

For an alternative approach to the relationship of language to situation, see:

Hymes, D. (1972) 'Models of the interaction of language and social life' in Gumperz, J. and Hymes, D. (eds) *Directions in Sociolinguistics,* New York: Holt, Rinehart & Winston.

Forms of social relationship and forms of language

Basic sources for material on address terms are:

Ervin-Tripp, S. (1972) 'Sociolinguistic rules of address', in Pride, J.B. and Holmes, J. (eds) *Sociolinguistics,* Harmondsworth: Penguin.
Friedrich, P. (1972) 'Social context and semantic feature: the Russian pronominal usage', in Gumperz, J. and Hymes, D. (eds) *Directions in Sociolinguistics,* New York: Holt, Rinehart & Winston.

For an important discussion of the relationship between social structure, interactional structure, and forms of address, see:

Brown, P. and Levinson, S. (1979) 'Social structure, groups and interaction', in Scherer, K.R. and Giles, H. (eds) *Social Markers in Speech,* Cambridge: Cambridge University Press.

See also:

Brown, P. and Levinson, S. (1978) 'Universals in language usage: politeness phenomena', in Goody, E.N. (ed.) *Questions and Politeness: strategies in social interaction,* Cambridge: Cambridge University Press.

Modes of linguistic expression: speech and writing

There are many features of speech not addressed in the account given above. For further work see, for example:

Brown, G. and Yule, G. (1983) *Discourse Analysis,* Cambridge: Cambridge University Press.

Schenkein, J. (ed.) (1978) *Studies in the Organization of Conversational Interaction*, New York: Academic Press.

For further material on writing as a mode of expression:

Stubbs, M. (1980) *Language and Literacy: the Sociolinguistics of Reading and Writing,* London: Routledge & Kegan Paul.

For cultural consequences of the shift to literacy:

Goody, J. and Watt, I. (1972) 'The consequences of literacy', excerpted in Giglioli, P.P. (ed.) (1972) *Language and Social Context,* Harmondsworth: Penguin.

For a wide-ranging and scholarly comparison of the two modes see:

Ong, W.J. (1982) *Orality and Literacy: the Technologizing of the Word*, London: Methuen.

Fieldwork projects

(1) (a) Record a conversation in circumstances that are likely to make it as spontaneous and uncontrived as possible.

    (b) Transcribe it as carefully as possible. (See notes on transcription conventions, pp. xix–xx.)

(c) Which features of the spoken mode does your recording display?

(d) Do you agree with the characterization of these features given on pp. 112–16?

(2) On pp. 129–30 are two adverts from the magazine *Company*:

(a) Comment on the *tenor, mode,* and *field* of the adverts in relation to the specific linguistic features that they employ.

(b) In discussion of the *mode,* you may find it useful to refer to the following diagram.

Suggested distinctions along the dimension of situation variation categorized as user's medium relationship

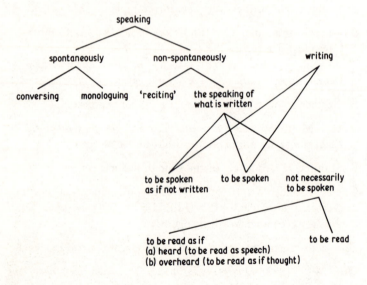

Figure 2

Source: Gregory and Carroll (1978).

Of some significance here are features of typography and layout. Why, for instance, punctuate a phrase such as 'Superlative cleansers for super skins' as if it were a sentence? And how usual is it in the written mode to have paragraphs composed of a single sentence such as 'It leaves it soft, shiny and in great condition, too'?

clean..
cleaner..
cleanest...

Why are the cleanest skins Anne French clean?

You see, your skin is not just a superficial covering. It's really very simple. You need a cleanser that does much more than simply skate over the surface. It is actually many layers deep. So you need a cleanser that does the deep down cleansing care covering. Anne French Deep Cleansing cotton on to the deep down cleansing care for a cleaner skin, Anne French. Anne French Deep Cleansing Cream achieves the same that you get when you use a cream. Both have Milk is a light lotion Deep Cleansing Cream achieves the same Anne French Deep Cleansing Cream to use a cream. Both have results, for those who prefer to get your skin clean—been specially formulated to get your skin clean—deep down.

Try Anne French for yourself.

Superlative cleansers for super skins.

ANNE FRENCH
DEEP CLEANSERS*

first choice for faces

*Trade Mark

129

It only takes 10 minutes to wake up your hair.

Wake up your hair's natural highlights and let your colour come alive.

All it takes is a few minutes and a tube of Harmony.

Just use it like a shampoo. Leave it on for anything from ten to twenty minutes, depending on how rich you want the colour to b Then rinse it out.

Harmony washes and colours your hair in one go.

It leaves it soft, shiny and in great condition, to Over about seven shampoos, the Harmony colour gradually washes out.

So the next time yo can either try another of the fourteen shades o

use the same again.

With Harmony, livel hair is all so simple, quic and easy.

Wake up your hair with Harmony colour.

130

(c) In discussion of the *tenor* note the following features that seem designed to secure active engagement on the part of the reader:

    (i) Explicit pronominal reference to the reader:

> '*You* can meditate, *you* can listen to music or *you* can cat nap.'
>
> *You* see, *your* skin is not just a superficial covering.'
>
> 'Harmony washes and colours *your* hair in one go.'
>
> 'A number on the window tells *you* how many of the 5 blades *you*'ve used.'

    (ii) Questions:

> 'Why are the cleanest skins Anne French clean?'
>
> 'A pretty close shave?'

    (iii) Direct commands:

> 'Don't get all cut up about it.'
>
> 'Try Anne French for yourself.'
>
> 'Wake up your hair with Harmony colour.'

How common do you think it is to find features such as these in written text? What does it suggest about the way this text is operating?

(d) In considering *field*, you may find it useful to refer to Dyer, G. (1982) *Advertising as Communication,* London: Methuen, and Cook (1992) *The Discourse of Advertising*, London: Routledge, both of which include discussion of the vocabulary of advertising. How specialized is the vocabulary? How much repetition is there and of what kinds of items?

(3) The following letter has some similarities to the letter from the bank manager discussed above (see pp. 119–25). The *field*, for instance, is financial services and the *mode* is written. The *tenor*, however, is very different.

(a) What linguistic choices can you identify that contribute to this very different *tenor*?

(b) Does the difference in *tenor* also have consequences for the coding of *field* and *mode*?

(c) What explanations can you offer for the differences in the register of the two letters?

THE BARNSLEY

Mr M Smith   March 1994
Top Flat
Montgomery Street
Glasgow
G16

'USE THE VALUE IN YOUR HOME TO IMPROVE IT'

Dear Mr Smith

Don't wait any longer to turn your dreams into reality

We recently wrote to tell you about a very sensible way to increase the enjoyment of your home without the hassles of moving – a Home Improvement Loan.

If you've already contacted us, your arrangements should be progressing smoothly, but if you haven't don't forget that the sooner you make an appointment to discuss your loan, the sooner the details can be arranged. And that means your home improvements can begin virtually straight away.

It's easy to apply

Your first step is either to ring or call in at your local branch and make an appointment. You'll find the telephone number below. If, however, this branch is not convenient, you can of course use any branch of the Barnsley. The Home Arranger or one of our Loan Specialists can then help you sort out the details.

Barnsley Permanent Building Society

123 Barnsley Street

Glasgow G1

Tel: 09 20 03

A loan to suit your lifestyle

A Home Improvement Loan uses your home as security, so you pay a competitive rate of interest and can spread the repayments over any period up to 25 years.

If you aren't planning to improve your home, a Lifestyle Loan may suit you. You can use this for almost any purpose – a new car, a holiday, carpets or a caravan for instance. Yet because, like your mortgage, it is secured against your home, it also offers a competitive rate of interest.

The Home Arranger or one of our Loan Specialists will make sure that you obtain the loan that's right for you – and that your monthly repayments are affordable. And for real peace of mind, we can arrange cover to protect your repayments against accident, sickness or involuntary unemployment.

We won't delay if you don't

We'll do all we can to help you turn your dreams into reality as quickly as possible.

We'll work out the details with you and then give you a decision in principle right away. And we'll do our best to ensure that your money is ready as soon as you need it.

So don't wait any longer. Contact your branch to make an appointment.

Yours sincerely

Charles Wylie

Charles Wylie
Head of Lending

P.S.   If you need a quick answer, we've made arrangements to process your loan quickly.

YOUR HOME IS AT RISK IF YOU DO NOT KEEP UP
REPAYMENTS ON A MORTGAGE OR OTHER LOAN
SECURED ON IT.

---

7 LANGUAGE AND SOCIAL CLASS: RESTRICTED AND ELABORATED SPEECH VARIANTS

Language and social class

We have in a sense already touched upon the relationship of language to social class. Accent and dialect, we noted, have more than a purely regional basis: they have come to act as indicators not only of one's relationship to a locality but also of one's social class position. In signalling such information, features of pronunciation and sentence structure have assumed obvious social significance. Considered in strictly linguistic terms, however, the differences remain relatively inconsequential. The fact that some dialects use 'we was' rather than 'we were' or 'we never done nothing' rather than 'we didn't do anything' is no sign of deficiency or even eccentricity on their part. After all, the double negative, for example, was common in the English of Shakespeare and is a normal construction in contemporary French. These features have no intrinsic consequences for our capacity to communicate with each other, in the sense, for example, of restricting the range of meanings we can express.

However, some accounts of the relationship of language to class go some way further than this. It has been claimed, for instance, that members of the middle class have access to ways of organizing their speech that are fundamentally different from the ways habitually adopted by the working class, and that these two modes of utterance organization involve contrasting orientations to the production of meaning in language. This, in somewhat oversimplified outline, is the central claim of a body of work produced by Basil Bernstein and colleagues at the London University Sociological Research Unit. The differing principles of utterance-organization are referred to as the *restricted* and *elaborated codes* which give rise respectively to *restricted* and *elaborated speech variants;* the speech variants are thus the result of having adopted either a restricted or elaborated coding orientation. Use of either coding orientation is influenced partly by situational circumstances (somewhat in the manner of *register* above) and partly by social class position (somewhat like *accent* and *dialect*). The claim is, therefore, complicated – all the more so because of two central difficulties; the first, how to specify precisely the difference between the two codes (and associated speech variants), and the second the difficulty of tracing exactly the relationship between social class position and adoption of one code rather than the other. The argument is not only complicated; it has also been an area of continuing controversy. We shall begin by attempting to clarify the difference between the two speech variants, and will then work outwards towards social class.

Restricted and elaborated speech variants

The best way of approaching the issue of restricted versus elaborated speech variants is by way of example. The two extracts given below each come from interviews with married men in their late thirties to early forties. They were both being prompted in a relatively unstructured way to talk about their roles as husband, father and worker:

DATA EXTRACT 7.1

INTERVIEWER: . . . did you enjoy it there?

A: what? the insurance industry?

INTERVIEWER: yea

A: er (.) to a degree (.) erm (.) I think originally a lot (.) erm (.) my father was in the insurance industry also (Int:yea) so I sort of grew up with erm this insurance background (.) (Int:yea) but er gradually I got more and more disillusioned I think with the whole set up of commerce and insurance in particular (.) erm this was probably influenced by things you've read about in the press (Int: yeh yeh)

INTERVIEWER: (.) what d' you think makes for job satisfaction?

A: (laughter) erm (.) I think that's always an impossible question to answer because it all depends very much on the individual (.) what the individual wants (Int:yeh) out of life (Int:yeh) (.) erm but I think (.) there's got to be a vital interest (.) erm (.) the job's got to be interesting enough to (.) maintain your interest in the job (Int:yeh) you've got to feel it's worth while coming in at nine o'clock every morning and doing whatever it is you do (.) if you do that and you're also reasonably well paid because (.) you often get family responsibilities and so on (Int:yeh) and you want a bit of the good life (.) er this is probably essential (.) company

This extract has many of the features of the spoken mode that were discussed above, such as hesitations, fillers, back-channel behaviour, and so on. It may usefully be contrasted with the following extract from a different interview:

DATA EXTRACT 7.2

INTERVIEWER: Erm (.) have any of your (   ) attitudes changed since you've been married (   ) about er what you think about your your job and . .

B: yea (.) well erm (.) things have changed a bit (.) although I don't feel it's right (.) er (.) I always felt that if you put your back into anything (.) worked hard (.) you'd be all right (.)

but it's not really the case and I think well (.) if you erm (.) if you take no notice and don't bother so much you still get on the same anyway (Int:really?) I think that's true (.) I think that's tr— I'll tell you a little tale (.) erm when I was on the furniture (.) on the furniture removals (.) I was a foreman (.) I – over all the lads chaps there (.) anyway erm (.) things were going along smashing you know er (.) the firm started to erm build up you know and erm (.) he wanted to break into the shipping you know (.) business you know that was shipping immigrants abroad you know (.) so I said oh I know about that

I said er

if you want to have a go have a go

so er (.) we started that and I started doing all these jobs and everything you know (.) and er (.) I got on well with the gaffer and everything you know (Int:yeh) (.) and all this business you know (.) so er I was steaming along quite happily (.) and he used to manage the fu–firm hisself (.) and he says to me one day he said erm (.) erm (.) its getting a bit too much for him to manage he said erm (.)

I think I'll have to get a manager in (.)

I said

oh aye great idea

you know I said

leave you more time to er (.) sort things out you know on the erm (.)

he used to like going round to see the customers you know and things like that (.) so erm (.) he got a manager.

The story continues by recounting how the new manager took away responsibilities from the speaker (B) and gave them to a newly appointed younger man who was eventually promoted in B's place. B quits his job and it transpires that the new manager and appointee were running a small racket between them. All this changes B's attitude: 'I still work hard now but * * * only if it's doing meself any good you know.'

Now in many ways this extract is similar to the first: as in the first passage we find many features of the spoken mode, such as hesitations, fillers and back-channel behaviour. There are, however, some important differences. Extract 7.1, for example, tends to operate with generalized and semi-abstract statements: 'it all depends very much on the individual'; 'there's got to be a vital interest'. When personal reference is used it is frequently towards an abstract figure, not a particular individual: 'you've got to feel it's worth while coming in at nine o'clock every morning and doing whatever it is you do'; 'you often get family responsibilities and so on'. Many of the statements are framed by, or include, a reference to the individual point of view of the speaker: 'I think originally a lot'; 'I got more and more disillusioned I think'; 'I think that's always an impossible question to answer'. Consequently, although the speaker is continuously proposing fairly generalized accounts of affairs (even when they involve himself), he simultaneously constrains their absolute applicability by stressing that they are his own personal points of view.

Extract 7.2 on the other hand, while it does admittedly contain one or two statements of general principle ('if you take no notice and don't bother so much you still get on the same anyway . . . I think that's true'), is predominantly focused on a particular piece of the speaker's experience which seems to support the general statement. Indeed the major point of contrast between the two extracts is the way B slips into the narrative of personal experience ('I'll tell you a little tale'). Within the narrative personal pronouns are inevitably used frequently (*'he* says to *me* one day *he* said'), especially the third person ('he'). But the initial use of 'he' is somewhat ambiguous: it only subsequently becomes clear that 'he' must refer to 'the gaffer'. At the same time, whereas extract 7.1 relies heavily on 'I think', extract 7.2 – by the use of phrases such as 'you know', 'and everything you know', 'and all this business you know', 'you know and things like that' – constantly invites the listener to complete for him/herself the sense of what has been said.

The basic difference in the styles of the texts could be summed up in terms of a universalizing tendency in text 7.1 in contrast to a particularizing tendency in text 7.2: as a partial consequence of these differences, text 7.1 would seem to be more explicit in its meaning than text 7.2 which arguably depends more on a shared framework of experience and values for its understanding. Significantly, the sociocentric sequences of text 7.2 ('you know') contrast sharply with the egocentric sequences ('I think') of text 7.1.

The two texts, therefore, could be seen as exemplifying two contrasting speech variants, the two variants being the product of two subtly different 'codes' or ways of communicating – a restricted code and an elaborated code.

Two kinds of social formation

Bernstein, of course, sought not merely to identify and establish the existence of two speech variants and their associated codes; his ultimate aim was to explain their emergence. The argument here runs something like the following. Assume for a moment a society which displays two major types of social formation. In the first type of social formation there are strong bonds between members and their social roles are clear and well defined. An individual's social identity is here given on the basis of relatively set and stable characteristics such as age and sex; so that, if we consider within this social formation the inner workings of the family (an important unit for most societies in so far as it provides a significant arena for the reproduction of basic norms and values), we find that its members make sense of who they are and how to behave in relation to each other fundamentally on the basis of distinctions such as 'male' or 'female', and 'older' or 'younger'. In the distribution of domestic tasks, for example, it may be men exclusively who work the allotment and keep things generally serviceable; women who prepare and serve food and keep garments wearable. And, of course, there will in all likelihood be further task distinctions dependent upon age differences. In this way members of the social formation have their roles ascribed to them on relatively public and fixed criteria. Indeed, the characteristic kind of role system associated with this type of social formation is, in Bernstein's terms, *positional* or *closed;* that is, it reduces role discretion to comparatively fixed 'positions', but at the same time 'closes off' potential role ambiguities. Given a social formation of this type, shared knowledge and assumptions between members of the subculture are likely to be high, so that communication goes on against a dense background of meanings held in common which rarely need to be stated explicitly.

The second type of social formation is rather different from the first. The bonds between members and their relative social positions are less well defined. In this kind of social formation persons achieve a social role and identity, not so much on the basis of publicly obvious and self-evident criteria, but more on the basis of individual disposition and temperament. If we consider a family within this social formation there may be no obvious division of labour and behaviour on the basis of age and sex: we may find a man working in the kitchen, because he likes preparing food; and a woman doing the oil change on the car because she likes playing around with motors. Generally, within this social formation members negotiate and achieve their roles rather than have them there ready-made in advance to step into. In this way, who they are and where they stand within the social formation is subject to constant definition and redefinition. The characteristic kind of role system arising within this social formation is, in Bernstein's terms, of the *open* or *personal* type. Communication plays an important part in this negotiation and renegotiation of roles, because within this social formation meanings and definitions cannot be so readily assumed in advance. The individual intentions and viewpoints of speakers need to be spelt out and made explicit. The contrast between the two social formations could be summed up in terms of the relative bias of each toward the collectivity or the individual. The first raises the 'we' over the 'I'; the second raises the 'I' over the 'we'. In so doing, each formation – with its characteristic role systems – develops a distinctive orientation towards communication.

Role systems and codes

Within a *positional* or *closed* role system language will typically be used to affirm solidarity and to invoke shared understandings. In consequence the meanings of utterances are often not explicit but implied, taken for granted. Forms of speech within the positional role system can afford to be ready-made and predictable, (i.e. there will be a high likelihood that listeners will be able to guess what's coming next). Indeed, they may be invited to do so by expressions such as 'ain't it?', 'sort of', 'you know'.

Within the *personal* or *open* role system language is used to explore and construct individual identities. There is a consequent pressure on the language to be more explicit. The forms of speech tend to be less predictable (i.e. it will be more difficult to guess what's coming next), because the meanings expressed can less often be taken for granted.

The two role systems thus give rise to characteristically differing orientations towards language – the positional role system giving rise to what Bernstein termed the *restricted code;* and the personal role system giving rise to what he termed the *elaborated code.* The restricted code orients and sensitizes its users towards 'particularistic' orders of meaning in which principles and operations are relatively linguistically implicit and meaning is tied to particular and immediate contexts of situation and to the ongoing social relationship. The elaborated code, on the other hand, orients and sensitizes its users towards 'universalistic' orders of meaning in which principles and operations are relatively explicit and meanings are less tied to an immediate context of situation.

Codes and social class

Now, in principle – and Bernstein himself is at pains to point this out – such role systems may arise in a variety of social circumstances: the positional, for example, may be typical of the armed forces, monasteries, prisons and it would, in consequence, not be surprising to find the restricted code as a feature of such settings. Indeed there is an intuitively plausible correspondence between the two contrasting codes and the two contrasting role systems, and between these in turn and the two contrasting social formations. But these latter elements of the argument – the role systems and the social formations – have a hypothetical or ideal typical status; and difficulties do arise in linking them into the real and actual texture of contemporary British class structure. In essence Bernstein has to divide British society into two classes – 'working' and 'middle' – corresponding to the two hypothetical social formations, in such a way that the working class becomes the terrain for the positional role system and the middle class becomes the terrain for the personal role system. Ultimately, this runs the danger of becoming at one and the same time overly schematic and somewhat stereotypical. The gradations and the fractions within the British class system become collapsed into a basic twofold division – one in which the working class as a whole comes to seem like a stereotype of the close-knit, traditional (and declining) working-class communities of South Wales or north-east England; and the middle class comes to seem like trendily progressive city-dwellers. Neither version, of course, fully exhausts the gradations of the class system as a whole.

Admittedly, Bernstein attempted to overcome the somewhat rigid polarities of his analysis by allowing cross-over points so that both types of role system could emerge within the major class formations. Thus, the earliest version of his thesis – that the restricted code would emerge within the working class, and the elaborated code would emerge primarily as the product of middle-class social relations – was later modified and replaced by the claim that, whereas the middle class was likely to have access to both the restricted *and* the elaborated code, *some* sections of the working class were likely to have access *only* to the restricted code. This claim remained a key element in Bernstein's account, one which – were it proved to be true – would have important implications. For, if – as Bernstein believed – certain key institutions of society (e.g. schools, law courts) worked in terms of the elaborated code, then anyone limited to a restricted code would be denied complete and full participation within them.

Bernstein's argument was undoubtedly motivated by libertarian and emancipatory impulses: he clearly believed that differences in language had become the ground on which systematically to deny large portions of the working class success within education. This would have been relatively innocuous, if all that was being claimed were relatively superficial surface linguistic differences of the dialect type. When he presented his argument in its starkest terms, however, he seemed to imply (a) that the restricted code was inferior to the elaborated code, in as much as – whatever its delicacy, subtlety and imaginative potential – its symbolism was ultimately of a 'low order of generality', orienting its users to a 'low level of causality': all this in contrast to the elaborated code which with its complex conceptual hierarchy gave its users access to 'the grounds of their experience' and hence the capacity to 'change the grounds'. And he further seemed to imply (b) that certain people were 'limited to a restricted code', in the sense that they would be able to use or understand the elaborated code only with great difficulty, or not at all.

Reactions

These claims provoked various kinds of reaction. They were, for example, susceptible to a highly anti-libertarian twist: some commentators actually used them to justify a view of the working class as inherently ineducable, according to which its members required at worst remedial or compensatory forms of education or at best a more practical and technical education than that received by the middle class. This may have been a travesty of what Bernstein intended, but the fact that he was susceptible to such interpretation provoked a long line of critical attacks on his basic position. And there are in fact many points of difficulty in Bernstein's argument. Throughout his work there is a tendency to operate with pairs of contrasting terms: 'restricted' versus 'elaborated', 'positional' versus 'personal', 'closed' versus 'open', 'object' versus 'person', and so on. These can be very useful for organizing ideas and insights in a conjectural and hypothetical fashion ('let's assume for a moment two codes; let's assume for a moment two types of role system'). But they seem to provide rather blunt instruments for the description of actual linguistic and social reality. There is, for example, in the final analysis hardly any linguistic evidence to support the division of speech into two mutually exclusive codes or speech variants. And by the same token, Bernstein's treatment of social structure looks with hindsight somewhat rigid and schematic.

But it was precisely that schematic mode of thought that enabled Bernstein to raise important theoretical issues about the relationship of the social system to the symbolic system, about the role of language in socialization, about the relationship between language and educational failure. Most of all he tried to explain *why* language was the way he thought it was. He has also always been extremely sensitive to actual features of language usage. After all, extracts 7.1 and 7.2, with which we began this discussion of elaborated and restricted variants, *are* actual instances of language. And they *are* amenable to description in the terms that Bernstein used to describe the variants. From this, however, it does not follow that the two variants are necessarily mutually exclusive; or that one variant is necessarily better than the other; or, indeed, that either speaker is necessarily trapped inside the variant he is currently using.

An alternative hypothesis

An equally plausible hypothesis would be that speakers adopt a *degree* of 'restrictedness' or 'elaboratedness' depending on situational factors – how much common ground can be assumed, how much solidarity exists, how much explicitness is required, and so on – in a way comparable to the continuum proposed earlier for users of Creole forms (see chapter 4, p. 85). In the case of speech variants (restricted versus elaborated), not all speakers may be comfortable operating at one or other end of the continuum. There are very few of us, in fact, who are equally sociolinguistically proficient and at home in all the situations that require the use of language. And, indeed, there may well be tendencies for certain groups of speakers habitually to prefer one or other end of the continuum. This, however, is a much more elastic kind of hypothesis than that commonly associated with the 'codes – class' position. For that very reason, of course, it would be all the more difficult to establish as fact – or not, as the case may be.

Background sources and further reading

The historical development of Bernstein's own work on (social) class-related fashions of speaking can best be traced in a collection of papers:

Bernstein, B. (1971) *Class, Codes and Control,* vol. 1, *Theoretical Studies Towards a Sociology of Language*, London: Routledge & Kegan Paul.

The first paper dates from 1958 and the last from the year the volume was published so they cover a thirteen-year period, during which time Bernstein substantially revised and developed his original position. The codes, for instance, are defined first in linguistic terms, then in psychological and finally in sociological terms. His later writings still use the notion of codes but rarely to refer to linguistic systems. Some people have criticized Bernstein for 'not being consistent'. But it seems churlish to judge him adversely for changing his mind and developing his ideas. None the less, he is a thinker whose work is very difficult to summarize succinctly and accurately. You should take anyone's account of Bernstein with a pinch of salt. It's probably a strategic distortion (including the one above). Celebrated, sometimes highly polemical, critiques of Bernstein are:

Labov, W. (1972) 'The logic of non-standard English', in *Language in the Inner City: Studies in the Black English Vernacular*, Philadelphia: University of Pennsylvania Press.

Rosen, H. (1972) *Language and Class: a Critical Look at the Theories of Basil Bernstein*, Bristol: Falling Wall Press.

A year later Bernstein replied to some of these criticisms in his post-script to the Paladin paperback edition of *Class, Codes and Control*. His chapter, 'A critique of the concept of compensatory education', is in any case a strong rebuttal of accounts of working-class speech that assume it to be in some way deficient. A more recent reaction to Rosen's criticisms may be found in:

Adlam, D. and Salfield, A. (1980) 'Sociolinguistics and "linguistic diversity"', in *Screen Education*, 34, Spring, 71–87.

Other reactions to Bernstein and to issues of language and class may be found in:

Dittmar, N. (1976) *Sociolinguistics*, London: Edward Arnold.

Edwards, A.D. (1976) *Language in Culture and Class*, London: Heinemann.

Stubbs, M. (1976) *Language, Schools and Classrooms*, London: Methuen.

For an interesting discussion of anecdotes in working-class speech see:

Tolson, A. (1976) 'The semiotics of working class speech', in *Working Papers in Cultural Studies*, 9, University of Birmingham: Centre for Contemporary Cultural Studies.

145

For an important comparison of concepts of code, register and social dialect see:

Hasan, R. (1973) 'Code, register and social dialect', in Bernstein, B. (ed.) *Class, Codes and Control*, vol. 2, *Applied Studies Towards a Sociology of Language*, London: Routledge & Kegan Paul.

Fieldwork project

One of Bernstein's early pieces of empirical work on language and class involved comparing the speech of messenger boys attending a day-release course with the speech of boys from one of the major public schools. They were recorded in relatively informal, undirected small group discussion on a common topic – capital punishment. One of many differences that Bernstein reported was in the use of sympathetic circularity markers ('sort of', 'like', 'you know', 'ain't it?', etc.). The working-class boys were found to use significantly more of them than the middle-class boys. The middle-class boys used more egocentric sequences ('I think', 'I suppose', etc.).

(1) How might you gather further evidence about these pheno-
    mena, perhaps using different types of group, in a different
    situation, but still exploring class-based differences in speech?
(2) Whom would you record, and for how long?
(3) How would you ensure rough comparability of data?
(4) How would you identify sympathetic circularity markers and
    egocentric sequences?
(5) How would you measure them? As a proportion of the total
    number of words? Or as an average number per sentence?
    Or . . .?
(6) If a difference did emerge, how would you explain it?

8 LANGUAGE AND GENDER

Speech is an act of identity: when we speak, one of the things we do is identify ourselves as male or female.

(Coates, 1986, 161)

Introduction

This chapter is concerned with differences between women and men in the way that they use language. It will also be concerned with why these differences arise. It is possible that some differences between the language of men and women stem from differences in anatomy and physiology. The view taken here, however, is that the more significant differences are socially constructed. For that reason the term 'gender' rather than 'sex' has been adopted to discuss the linguistic differences between men and women.

This whole area, of course, has aroused and continues to arouse a fair deal of controversy, in which positions have been fluid and changing as debate has developed. For this reason, it is an area that is difficult to sum up neatly in an overview and it has been necessary to cite more explicitly proponents of particular viewpoints.

'Gender' versus 'sex'

Arriving at any mixed social gathering we identify those already present in various ways – as strangers or friends, young or old, and as male and female. We make these judgements continuously, if unconsciously, in most social settings. We may typify others (i.e. sort them according to type) as male and female partly on the basis of physiological and anatomical cues (e.g. this person looks pregnant, that person has a beard); but our typifications are primarily informed by our tacit knowledge of the codes of social behaviour appropriate to the sexes – particularly the codes of dress and demeanour. Thus, while physiology undoubtedly informs the fundamental distinction between male and female, what we attend to, and conform to, on an everyday basis are socially constrained patterns of behaviour. The genetic code may determine our sex; but social codes provide us with a repertoire of behaviour which defines our gender.

The distinction between gender and sex is important because although all documented societies find the basic differences between the male body and the female body important, there remains a great deal of variation over what is deemed appropriate behaviour for women and men from one society to another and from one historical period to another. These changing patterns of difference between male and female are, in effect, gender differences – social and cultural impositions on the 'natural' categories of sex. In recognizing this additional level of gender, we allow for the possibility of change – even of a deliberate kind; and perhaps, to some extent, the possibility of choice. And these gender differences include not just features of observable behaviour but extend to our whole way of regarding ourselves as male and female, i.e. they include questions both of gender role (ways of behaving) and also of gender identity (ways of relating, to ourselves and others).

Accordingly, when the new-born child is identified on the basis of anatomy as either a girl or a boy, it is only the beginning of a long process of induction in which it will learn quite contrasting kinds of gender role and identity. In this process language has an important part to play. For language comprises not only a significant element in behaviour, signalling a great deal about our social origins; it also provides us with concepts for thinking with and with ways of meaning that are crucial to the construction of our identity. If obvious gender differences are signalled in part by surface contrasts in dress and demeanour, it is likely that even more profound differences of gender role and identity are carried by language.

Voice pitch: a difference of sex or gender?

The implications of making the distinction between sex and gender, nature and culture, may be shown by considering one of the most obvious differences between the speech of women and men, namely that they have distinctly different voice qualities. In the majority of cases most people can easily tell whether a voice belongs to a man or a woman: men's voices are commonly thought to be lower-pitched and more resonant than women's voices. The obvious explanations for this usually draw upon the evident differences of physiology. The pitch of the voice, for instance, is produced by vibration of the vocal cords in the larynx (the 'voice box', as it is sometimes known) which is situated at the top of the wind pipe. As breath from the lungs passes through the larynx the vocal cords can be set to vibrate. Thick, heavy vocal cords vibrate more slowly than lighter ones; and, since men tend to develop a larger larynx than women, their voices tend to be pitched lower. In addition, the rate of vibration is also affected by patterns of hormonal secretion. Indeed, the evidence suggests that the size of the larynx in men depends to a great extent on the release of those hormones which give rise to male secondary sexual charac-teristics in adolescence. Conversely, it has also been suggested that women experience changes in voice quality during menstruation and pregnancy, again as a result of hormonal changes. And so there is a strong case for treating the differences in pitch between men's and women's voices simply as sex differences rooted directly in the facts of physiology.

Physiological factors, however, only provide part of the picture. For one thing, although the average pitch of men's voices tends to be lower than the average pitch of women's voices, all speakers use a range of pitch above and below their average. And comparisons of the pitch *ranges* of men and women cast some doubt on physi-ology as the single determinant of a speaker's voice pitch. In effect, no-one, male or female, speaks on an absolute monotone. Early mechanical voice synthesizers may have done so, but human speakers vary the pitch of their voice quite systematically as they talk. They need to do so for particular communicative purposes – signalling the end of an utterance by dropping in pitch, for instance, or using other aspects of pitch variation for asking questions or for selecting out parts of the utterance for contrastive purposes. These communicative uses of pitch variation are known as *intonation* and the deployment of pitch for intonation means that speakers inevitably range upwards and downwards in pitch as they talk. This happens for the most part quite unconsciously; but individuals, male or female, may additionally and quite deliberately attempt to adjust their whole pitch range upwards or downwards; as did the actor Dustin Hoffman (upwards) in playing the part of a woman in the film *Tootsie*, or as the then Mrs Thatcher did (downwards) after becoming Prime Minister.

In fact, when we compare the average *range* of women's voices with the average *range* of men's voices, a considerable degree of overlap is discovered, which leads Graddol and Swann (1989) to remark that:

> men and women could, if they wished, use similar pitch ranges and hence adopt a similar average speaking pitch. To do this, men would have to restrict themselves to the upper part of their ranges, while women would have to avoid their upper ranges.
> (Graddol and Swann, 1983, 19–20)

Reporting on an earlier study of their own, they comment:

> people can place their voice ranges somewhat flexibly. For some reason, the men and women in our study were adopting different strategies. Men's voices reflected their physical size because they used the lower limits of their pitch range and adopted intonation patterns which were more monotonous than women's; women by contrast, were more variable in their use of voice, both in the sense of using more expressive intonation and in differences between individual women. Such differences seem to indicate that pitch of voice carries social meanings and that men and women try to communicate different social images.
> (Graddol and Swann, 1983, 20)

What emerges, therefore, is the influence of social factors, of culture, even upon something as physiologically rooted as the pitch of the voice. In the first place, the pitch of the voice would seem simply to reflect differences of sex; on further consideration, however, it emerges just as much as the expression of gender differences. For, while physiology establishes a certain basic potential pitch range, the cultural context of language learning and language use leads us to refine or adapt this potential so as to mark and signal the gender difference. We will now turn to consider further claims and evidence for gender differences in language use.

Do men and women talk differently?: the claims and the evidence

One important way in which language interacts with aspects of gender role and identity is through the commonsense beliefs and stereotypes that are held about the basic differences between the language of men and women. Women, it is said, are less assertive (more tentative) in their speech than men; it is said that they use fewer taboo forms and more euphemisms than men, that they talk more than men, or conversely that they talk less than men; that they are inclined to gossip; that they are more conservative in their speech and at the same time, more sensitive to matters of correctness; that their speech is more polite, and so on. These may be described as folk-linguistic beliefs – widely held, grounded in anecdote and cursory observation, but not necessarily supported by systematic research.

It is only in the last decade or so, and primarily due to the impact of the women's movement, that these claims have been subjected to close scrutiny. Until then most socio-linguistic research was carried out by men, who tended to focus upon male speakers – especially when studying marginal or subordinate groups such as adolescent peer groups, prisoners, or ethnic subcultures. Male linguistic behaviour was often assumed implicitly to be the norm; and when the linguistic behaviour of women was noted this was often treated as a departure from a norm centred on male behaviour. In some ways, then, until women researchers began to reshape the field of study and to pay more attention to the speech of women, socio-linguistics was prone to confirm gender stereotypes rather than to question them.

Gender is now generally recognized as the most widely salient dimension of social difference, and has become the focus for a great deal of recent discussion within socio-linguistics as a result of the burgeoning of feminist scholarship. In the light of the accumulating evidence, it has become easier to distinguish between fact and stereotype.

Do women tend to speak 'more correctly' than men?

We already noted in chapter 3 that studies of social class differences in pronunciation in both the US and the UK had observed a tendency amongst lower-middle-class speakers to produce relatively more prestige forms when reading aloud from word lists than do members of the social group immediately above them on the social scale, even though they produce less than them in ordinary casual speech: in effect, they overproduce the prestige form (the socially favoured pattern of pronunciation) in formal settings, a phenomenon sometimes referred to as 'hypercorrection'. Women, especially those from the lower middle class, seem to be more prone to this

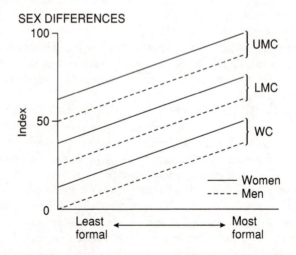

Figure 3 A diagrammatic representation of stratification according to social class and sex.

Source: Coates (1986, 63).

152

tendency than men. Thus, in data from Macaulay's study (1977) of Glasgow speech we find the greatest contrast in group scores for vernacular versus prestige forms emerging between lower-middle-class men and lower-middle-class women. In choosing between the form /t/ and its stigmatized or vernacular alternative, the glottal stop/?/, in places such as the middle sound of the word 'letter' (versus 'le'er'), or 'butter (versus bu'er), it was found that women avoided the glottal stop 40 per cent more than men did. This kind of finding emerges fairly predictably in a wide range of studies. Indeed on social class measurements of pronunciation women generally score higher for prestige forms than men do right up and down the social scale. A generalized diagram for what typically emerges might be as follows:

The detailed picture turns out to be more complicated than this diagram suggests. In South Carolina, USA, for instance, Black speakers operate on a continuum which can be represented as on a line (see Fig. 2 below) ranging from Gullah – an English Creole – at one end, to a variety of Black English in the centre, to a regionally standard variety of English at the other end, with this last variety being the one with most prestige. (See chapter 4 for a discussion of similar continuum involving Creole.)

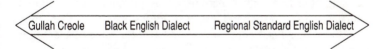

Figure 4

And yet Nichols (1983) in her study of two South Carolina Black communities found that it was older mainland women whose speech was most firmly positioned at the Creole end of the continuum. It was they who most consistently adopted Gullah forms, using them to a greater extend even than men of the same age. Among *older* speakers, therefore, her findings give no support to the claim that women always gravitate in their speech towards the prestige form. By contrast, *younger* women do use the standard

English variety and use it more consistently than any other group. Indeed, the speech of older and younger women is more different from each other than it is from men. Older and younger women occupy opposite ends of the continuum of speech variation with men coming in between – a situation that we might represent thus:

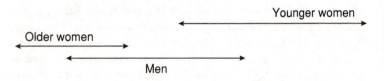

Figure 5 Three separate groups on the dialect continuum.

The reasons for this are deceptively simple but profoundly important for understanding speech differences. Not only are patterns of employment among these communities very different for men and women but there is an even greater contrast between older and younger women. Men of all ages tend to hold manual and semi-skilled jobs such as carpenting and brick-laying. However, whereas older women have tended to work in farm-labouring and domestic jobs, younger women have been finding work increasingly in white collar and service jobs such as sales, nursing, and elementary school teaching. This changing pattern of employment has required younger women to spend longer in education than any other group within the local Black community and has at the same time brought them into contact with a wider range of varieties outside their own communities, with more exposure to the use of the prestige standard forms.

It is clearly not the case, therefore, that all women in these communities of South Carolina gravitate to the prestige forms and varieties. Some women do; but equally some women do not. So the deciding influence on linguistic behaviour in this case is not simply gender alone. Equally as crucial are the changing kinds of social relationship that the labour market requires of women in South Carolina. It is these changes which determine the differences between older woman and younger women.

Milroy's study (1980) of working-class communities in Belfast also supplies evidence of contrasting linguistic loyalties in different groups of women. It had long been recognized that speech communities can operate with opposing sets of norms. When a standard variety exists (often associated with the speech patterns of the economically and socially dominant group) its norms tend to exert pressure on speakers throughout the community, especially when they are interacting in formal contexts. Alternative norms, however, based on locally specific patterns of speech, usually persist alongside those of the standard variety; and speakers from less dominant groups with strong roots in the local community orient to them, especially in informal contexts, even while maintaining a belief in the superior correctness of the standard variety. Vernacular speech, with its regional distinctiveness rooted in the everyday life of a particular locality, is precisely the expression of these covert norms continuing to defy downward pressure from the overt norms of the standard variety (see chapter 3).

In studies, men tend to be identified as the principal users of vernacular, non-standard, speech. Some of the richest examples have come from studies of Black male adolescent peer groups in the United States (see Labov, 1972c). Such studies, by implication, seemed to confirm the view that it was women who were more sensitive to the norms of the standard. But Milroy's study, rather like Nichols's in South Carolina, showed an interesting contrast between two groups of working-class women. One group came from a traditional respectable working-class community (Ballymacarrett) where the men worked mostly in ship-building. The other group of women came from a working-class community (Clonard) badly affected by high rates of unemployment (around 35 per cent at the time of the research). For some speech sounds, expected differences in pronunciation were found between men and women, with men more frequently resorting to the vernacular, local patterns of speech than women, and with younger men using the most.

These tendencies were especially noticeable in the case of the more fixed and stable features of the vernacular. But vernacular varieties, no less than any other, are subject to change and innovation. In Belfast a particular example of vernacular change in process could be found in the pronunciation of the middle sound of words like 'back', 'hat', 'man'. Here the vowel sound in question would

155

normally be pronounced in standard English low and to the front of the mouth. But in vernacular speech in Belfast the sound was gradually being raised higher and to the back of the mouth, so that 'man' as pronounced in the vernacular was becoming a near rhyme with 'don'. While the speech of Ballymacarrett women lagged behind the men in the use of this feature, in Clonard the situation was reversed. There the younger women tended to score highly on this vernacular innovation, higher even than the young men of the area. Their speech was at the forefront of this change and, indeed, could be seen as actively promoting it.

Once again, therefore, as in the case of South Carolina, not all women from the same region are behaving in the same way: younger women are behaving differently than older women. But whereas in South Carolina we noted younger women leading change in the direction of the standard, in Belfast we can observe some younger women – those from the Clonard district – playing a leading role in implementing a vernacular innovation. Although the explanation in each case of why particular groups of women are leading the direction of change is rather similar, Milroy's account of social and regional variations in Belfast speech draws upon an important additional explanatory concept, the notion of social network, which has become influential in subsequent socio-linguistic studies.

SOCIAL NETWORKS AND THEIR INFLUENCE ON LINGUISTIC BEHAVIOUR

Milroy's fieldwork in Belfast involved close study of three separate working-class communities altogether, core members of which she was introduced to as a 'friend of a friend'. She was able to maintain contact with these groups over a period of time during which she was able to gather vernacular speech data (including tape-recordings) in a variety of informal settings. Most significantly, she was able to incorporate into her analysis a description of the types of social networks to which her speakers belonged.

Broadly, the notion of social network allows comparisons to be made between groups based on the density or looseness of group ties. An open network is one in which the number of reciprocal ties in the network is low: not everyone knows everyone else. A closed network, on the other hand, is one in which each member of the network has several ties with other members of the network. Diagrammatically we can represent the difference between open and closed networks as follows, where the arrowed lines represent reciprocal relationships between members of the network (Fig. 6).

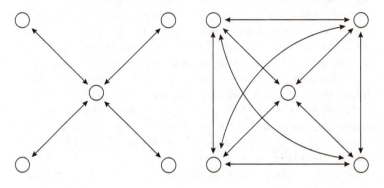

Figure 6 An open network   A closed network
Source: After Milroy (1980).

In addition to the numbers of ties within a network it is also possible to take account of the nature of the ties of work, kinship, friendship, recreation and so on. A closed network, for instance, may itself be of two types – uniplex or multiplex – so that in the latter case the ties are not only many and reciprocal, but also of multiple types. The workplace, for example, may give rise to closed networks but these will not necessarily be of the multiplex type, unless members of the networks are also connected by other ties, for instance, those of kinship and shared recreational pursuits.

The notion of social network proved particularly useful to Milroy in explaining her findings in Belfast. Vernacular culture and speech tends to be underpinned by high density, multiplex networks. In Ballymacarrett, where ship-building provided reasonable employment opportunities, the men participated in precisely such high-density, many-sided networks. Their speech, in consequence, tended to be more focused on vernacular norms than that of the women from the same area whose networks were less tight knit. In

Clonard, however, where male unemployment levels were high, the situation for the younger age group was reversed. The young Clonard women belonged to a dense multiplex network: they lived close together, worked in the same place, and spent leisure time with each other. This was by contrast with the men who found work, where they could, outside the area; and who shared more in domestic tasks with a consequent blurring of traditional sex roles. The young men, therefore, participated in less dense networks than the young women. The fact that the speech of the young women of Clonard exhibited, at least in some respects, more commitment to certain vernacular features owes much to the strength and variety of the ties that constituted their network.

Generally, therefore, the claim that women as such are more sensitive to norms of correct speech than men is not borne out by precise studies of concrete groups of women. From Clonard to South Carolina it depends upon which women are being considered (older versus younger, for instance) and most fundamentally upon what kinds of relationships shape their everyday lives. Certainly, there is no simple, direct link between the sex of the speaker and tendency to use the vernacular or the standard. Instead, adoption of, and allegiance to, vernacular norms of speech seems to be associated broadly with membership of high density, multiplex networks with strong roots in a territorially-bounded, local community: membership of such groups goes hand in hand with use of the vernacular. While networks of this type tend to be more characteristic of traditional male working-class culture, they are not an exclusively male phenomenon. Where women belong to such close-knit social networks they exhibit similar degrees of vernacular loyalty.

This is not to claim, of course, that there are no differences between the speech of men and women. But, in the same way that we noted in the discussion of pitch above, these differences tend to be relative rather than absolute. And in the area of allegiance to overt versus covert norms of usage – standard versus vernacular – those differences that do obtain tend to be matters of degree and are not consistently in one direction with women always adopting overt norms more than men. Even in cases where equivalent groups of male and female speakers display adherence to vernacular norms they do not necessarily support precisely the same features. Cheshire's (1982) study of adolescent peer groups from Reading, for instance, showed different ways of marking allegiance to the vernacular in girls and boys. While there was undoubtedly some degree of overlap in vernacular usage between adolescent male and female peer groups in Reading, some features tended to be markers of vernacular loyalty for boys and others for girls. Thus, girls with a strong allegiance to the vernacular culture and values would be more likely than boys to use non-standard 'come' as in 'I come down here yesterday'; and, conversely, boys with a strong commitment to vernacular culture proved more likely than girls to use non-standard 'what' as in 'Are you the little bastards what hit Billy over the head?' So, although the boys and girls in Cheshire's study speak substantially the same non-standard dialect and have similar degrees of loyalty to the vernacular, they still manage to mark this loyalty in gender-specific ways.

Is women's speech more polite, less direct, and less assertive than that of men?

This question goes to the heart of the way we use words to make our social relationships. In order to answer it we have to focus upon quite specific and discrete ways of doing things with words, such as using them to command or question or interrupt. When talk between men and women is examined in these terms we do find evidence to support the view that female speakers are more polite than males, but care needs to be taken over how we interpret such findings. It is important always to take the context of situation into account (see chapter 6 above) and to consider whether it involves talk to the same or the other sex, or more generally whether it involves relationships of power or solidarity. An utterance may sound polite and unassertive in one context but not in another. For instance, if one pupil says to another in the course of planning an issue of the school paper, 'Let's ask the head what she thinks, shall we?' it carries potentially quite different politeness values than if a pupil addresses the same words to a class teacher in the course of an altercation (see also chapter 10). Bearing these factors in mind, let us consider more closely some of the evidence for gendered differences in commands, questions, and interruptions.

COMMANDS

If we define a command loosely as an utterance designed to get someone else to do something, then Goodwin's study (1980) of street play in Philadelphia showed interesting differences in the ways boys and girls phrased them. Boys tended to rely upon simple, direct commands such as:

'Gimme the pliers.'
'Get off my steps.'
'Look man, gimme the wire.'

Girls on the other hand tended to couch their commands as inclusive suggestions for action such as:

'Let's go round the corner.'
'Let's ask her for some more bottles.'
'We could go round looking for more bottles'.

These examples illustrate habits of speech within their respective peer groups, which tend to be single sex; boys play with boys and girls with girls. And on the face of it the girls' utterances look more polite.

Commands by boys are primarily other-directed, focusing exclusively on the actions of the person being addressed, whereas in the girls' peer group the speaker includes herself in the proposed course of action. According to Goodwin, these different kinds of commands seem to reflect differing types of peer group organization, one based on power, the other on solidarity. The boys' group tended to be more leader-dominated and hierarchical in its organization. The girls tended to rely more on negotiation to reach decisions among themselves. These examples, however, characterize talk within same-sex peer groups. And Goodwin notes that it is not the case that girls are incapable of forceful commands, especially if the context demands it, as, for example, in arguments with the boys.

QUESTIONS

Many studies of male and female speech have found women using more questions than men especially when the addressee is a man. For instance, women were found to ask more questions than men when buying tickets at Central Station in Amsterdam, especially when the ticket seller was male (Brouwer *et al.* 1979). And in a detailed study of three separate heterosexual couples based on 52 hours of tape-recorded conversation in their homes, Fishman (1983) found that the women asked a staggering two and a half times more questions than the men did. Fishman sees this as a practical measure of the work these women were doing to keep conversations going. Men, for instance, produced twice as many statements as women in the same conversations. If these tendencies are considered in relation to topic initiation it is easy to see why Fishman concludes, in a memorable phrase, that the women were doing most of the 'interactional shitwork'. Women made 62 per cent of all attempts to introduce topics but only 38 per cent of these attempts achieved joint development. Conversely, nearly all the topics initiated by men (usually in the form of a statement) received conversational uptake. Thus, on the one hand, women responded more positively to topics raised by men; and on the other hand they had to work harder to establish topics themselves, which required them to use more questions.

This kind of finding seems fairly clear-cut and can be used to support claims that women are more attentive in their talk to the needs and rights of others. However, Fishman makes no attempt to differentiate between various different types of question: her conclusions would have been all the more persuasive if she had discussed in more detail whether different types of question might not have been at work in her data and what criteria might be used to identify them. For questions are not all of a piece: not all of them need necessarily work to support and sustain topical development. Indeed, they can perform a range of interactional work. A questioner, for instance, may claim, confirm, or even challenge a power relation by their use, as the discussion in chapter 10 will show.

Other studies have attempted to address this difficulty by narrowing their focus quite specifically to a particular question-type. It has been claimed, for instance, that women use more tag questions than men, thereby signalling diffidence, tentativeness, or insecurity, since tags provide a convenient way of downgrading the strength of a statement or command into an utterance offered to the recipient for them to answer with 'yes' or 'no'. Thus,

'It's a nice day isn't it?'

looks like a less assertive observation than:

'It's a nice day.'

The evidence, however, is somewhat mixed. When Dubois and Crouch (1975) taped proceedings at a small academic conference, they found that the men actually used *more* tag questions than the women. Holmes (1984), on the other hand, discovered a roughly similar incidence of tags used by men and tags used by women in her matched samples of male and female speech. Part of the difficulty here is that there is more than one type of tag question; and so Holmes went on to distinguish between tags designed to check whether or not something is the case and tags used as conversational prompts designed principally to give the addressee a turn. The former type can be characterized as speaker-oriented (checking) tags and the latter as addressee-oriented (facilitating) tags, as in:

(a) 'You like living in Glasgow, do you?' [speaker-oriented, checking tag]
(b) 'That was a good film, wasn't it?' [addressee-oriented, facilitating tag]

When Holmes used this distinction to compare the tags used by women with those used by men, she found that the women used far more facilitating than checking tags, with the proportions being reversed for the men. The preponderance of facilitating tags in the speech of women seems to offer some support for Fishman's contention that women are carrying out, as she puts it, 'the interactional shitwork'.

None the less, the results once again need to be interpreted with some degree of caution. An attempt by Cameron *et al.* (1988) to replicate Holmes's findings on a different corpus of data arrived at somewhat different results: although women used three facilitating tags for every checking tag, the proportions were not reversed in the expected way for the men, who used three facilitating tags for every two checking tags. Thus, although there was still a difference between men and women, it was much smaller than the study by Holmes would have predicted. Part of the discrepancy between the two studies may be accounted for by the problem of distinguishing analytically between the two types of tags. Cameron *et al.* are very clear about their criteria but none the less observe that the distinction between the two types is not always straightforward in practice, so that different analytical decisions might produce different results, more in line perhaps with those of Holmes. Another source of discrepancy between the studies may be traced to the behaviour of two particular men in the data examined by Cameron *et al.*, who produced abnormally high scores for facilitative tags, a fact which led her and her colleagues to conclude that the use of facilitative tags could well be associated with conversational role rather than gender *per se*.

More fundamentally, however, they question whether utterances sharing the same construction as facilitating tags always function in the same way, as a conversational prompt which simply provides turn space for the addressee. This facilitating function may well be apparent in an example such as:

'It's a nice day, isn't it?'

But what about the following example:

'You still haven't put out the rubbish, have you?'

Indeed, in asymmetrical, status-marked settings, such as the classroom or the courtroom, tags similar in formal construction to those of the facilitative type seem to take on a different force. They quite typically operate to coerce agreement from the addressee in some negative assessment of their behaviour. Consider, for instance:

'This homework isn't very good, is it?' [Teacher to pupil]

or

'You're not making much of an effort to pay off these arrears, are you?' [Magistrate to defendant]

Thus, the same construction as that adopted for facilitative tags can well become coercive, even accusatory, in particular circumstances. Consequently, even if women use more constructions of this kind than men do, it is difficult to be sure that they are always signalling diffidence, insecurity, or lack of assertiveness. There is at least the possibility, as Cameron *et al.* point out, that women's more frequent use of facilitative tags could be a marker of control over conversation rather than one of responsibility for 'interactional shitwork', 'subordinate-groups do after all struggle against the conditions of their oppression' (Cameron *et al.*, 1988, 91–2).

TURN-TAKING, OVERLAPS, AND INTERRUPTIONS

Giving commands and asking questions are all examples of conversational acts, ways of doing things with words that are crucial to the conduct of social life. Examining the distribution of conversational acts – who uses which kind of act, when and to whom – can reveal much about the character of social relationships, including the expression of gender relations, at any particular point in society. Conversation as a process, however, depends not only upon these acts themselves but also upon a more general underlying mechanism of exchange called the turn-taking system, which provides the framework for these acts to be performed in.

Studies of the turn-taking system, notably that of Sacks *et al.* (1974), claim that it enables conversations to proceed without everyone talking at once. The tacit adherence of conversationalists to the rules of the turn-taking system is displayed in the way that turns at talk routinely succeed one another smoothly, without overlap on the one hand, or more than minimal gaps on the other. Sacks *et al.* (1974) argue that conversationalists manage the exchange of talk with such fluency by listening out for points in each turn where transition to another speaker has become relevant because the turn is (potentially) complete. These transition relevance points are signalled principally by grammatical completeness, but other supporting cues are provided by changes in the pace and pitch of the speech as well as by gesture and eye movement. The more the cues coincide, the more likely it is that the turn is complete. By relying on cues such as these (and some evidence suggests that infants of only a couple of months have learnt to attend to them, long before they can express themselves in words), conversationalists manage the exchange from one turn to another often with gaps of only a fraction of a second.

None the less, despite the availability of the turn-transition cues, departures from such smooth turn transitions do occur under

164

certain circumstances, particularly in asymmetrical relationships involving dominant and subordinate parties. The departures from normal fluency are of two main types: (a) interruptions, (b) delayed responses to a turn. Both types of departure from normal turn-taking were examined by West and Zimmerman in two studies (1975, 1983) of cross-sex talk. Interruptions were carefully distinguished from mere overlaps: in the latter case, the beginning of one turn momentarily coincides with the end of another and is a common rather than a disruptive feature of fluent talk. Interruptions, however, constitute a deeper incursion into a speaker's ongoing turn, penetrating well within the grammatical boundaries of a current speaker's utterance. In the following example the male speaker interrupts (rather than merely overlaps) with the female speaker.

FEMALE: Both really. it just strikes me as too 1984ish y'know
         to sow your seed or whatever. an' then have it
         develop miles away not caring if
MALE: Now:: it may be
         something uh quite different. you can't make
         judgements like that without all the facts being at
         your disposal

The first speaker has begun a new clause ('not caring if . . .') when the second speaker's turn begins, and the onset of his turn is thus classified as an interruption of hers. In single sex pairs Zimmerman and West (1975) found that interruptions were not particularly common and were distributed fairly evenly between speakers. In mixed sex pairs, however, interruptions were not only more frequent but also much more likely to come from the men: 96 per cent of the interruptions were made by males to females. In a more stringent follow-up study (West and Zimmerman, 1983) the proportion of male to female interruptions in cross-sex talk was not quite so high but still accounted for 75 per cent of the total, confirming the gross imbalance of their initial findings. In the latter study they used previously unacquainted pairs in a laboratory setting so that the frequency of interruptions cannot be explained, for instance, in terms of intimacy.

Zimmerman and West in their initial study also found that the average length of gaps between turns increased from 1.35 seconds in single sex pairs to 3.21 seconds in mixed sex pairs. The increased time lag seems to have been produced by two factors. On the one hand women would tend to fall silent after an interruption; and on the other hand men in cross-sex talk seemed to withhold minimal responses such as 'yeah' or 'mmhum'. The easiest way to interpret such delayed minimal responses is that they signalled a lack of interest in, or commitment to, the topic at hand on the part of the men. Paradoxically, therefore, when men were talking with women, they seemed to: (a) interrupt more on the one hand; and (b) on the other hand be less supportive of the previous (female) speaker's topic.

It is not difficult, therefore, to derive from West and Zimmerman's work some support for the claim that women are less assertive and more polite than men in cross-sex communication. Note, however, that this formulation takes male behaviour as its taken-for-granted reference point. An alternative formulation of the same point would be that men are more assertive and impolite than women when engaged in cross-sex conversation. After all, given the basic constraints of the turn-taking system, it is not women but men who seem to override them.

Conclusions: difference and dominance

What emerges from any review of work on speech differences between women and men is a complicated sense of variation affected by a range of factors. Two points in particular, one socio-logical and one linguistic, should be noted. First, speech differences between men and women are not clear-cut. The sex differences which stem from anatomy or physiology are filtered through the social construction of gender identity and gender relations which work differently in different societies, epochs and cultures. For this reason, we should not expect some set of universal differences in the language of men and women. Instead, we need to consider care-fully the ways in which gender as a dimension of difference between people interacts with other dimensions such as those of age, class, ethnic group, and so on. Nichols's work on speech communities in South Carolina makes this point well, demonstrating differences not only between women and men but also between older woman and

166

younger women. Milroy's work on Belfast speech helps to clarify some of the underlying factors involved in these differences by conceptualizing the role of social relationships in terms of social networks.

Second, from a linguistic perspective, we need to be very clear about what exactly is being identified as a difference between men and women. Generalized claims about assertiveness or politeness are difficult to substantiate unless they are translated into more specific statements involving identifiable linguistic behaviour – hence the focus on activities such as questions or interruptions. The systematic study of differences depends upon the accurate definition and identification of specific linguistic behaviour; but this is not always easy, as some of the work on questions, commands and interruptions, reviewed above, has shown. And there is always the additional complication that the formal construction of utterances is no consistent guide to what function they might be performing in a specific context, a point that will be discussed in more detail in chapter 10.

Despite these complications there seems to be growing evidence to suggest that, in the words of Coates,

> women and men do pursue different interactive styles: in mixed-sex conversations this means that men tend to interrupt women; they use this strategy to control topics of conversation and their interruptions tend to induce silence in women. Women make greater use of minimal responses to indicate support for the speaker. It also seems that women ask more questions, while men talk more, swear more and use imperative forms to get things done. Women use more linguistic forms associated with politeness. (Coates and Cameron, 1988, 117)

Underlying this felt sense of difference, and the growing body of evidence to support it, is a recurrent concern with power. Studies of language and gender have returned repeatedly to the question of how the language used by men and women reinforces their respective positions in society. Women are maintained in a subordinate position, it has been argued, because they are socialized to adopt powerless patterns of speech; and conversely men maintain their dominance by the use of verbal strategies associated with power. The propensity of men to interrupt women more than women

167

interrupt men may be seen in these terms. As West and Zimmerman maintain:

> the fact that females find themselves subject to interruption more frequently than males in cross-sex conversations is not merely an indicator of a power differential . . . it is . . . a way of 'doing' power in face-to-face interaction, and to the extent that power is implicated in doing what it means to be a man vis-à-vis a woman, it is a way of 'doing' gender as well (West and Zimmerman, 1983, 111).

However, an equally important theme that has emerged more recently is the focus on differences between men's and women's speech as the outcome of what are in effect two different subcultures with contrasting orientations towards relationships. In effect, women and men, it is claimed, grow up within different social worlds, as a result of which women are inclined to see relationships in terms of intimacy, connection and disclosure whereas men are inclined to see them in terms of hierarchy, status and independence. These subcultural differences are enacted in contrasting communicative styles.

Coates (1988) in a study of an all-female group of speakers notes particular tendencies which she feels are characteristic of women's style of speech with each other, including gradual topic development, frequent, and well placed, minimal responses, supportive overlaps between one speaker and another, and many markers of sympathetic circularity such as 'I mean', 'sort of', 'kind of'. The combination of such features amounts to a distinctive style of co-operative talk in which the joint working out of a group point of view takes precedence over individual assertions. This communicative style is not only characteristic of women in interaction with each other but, Coates believes, is in implicit contrast with men's communicative style which is likely to be more adversarial and competitive.

If the contrasting subcultures of men and women give rise to contrasting communicative styles, then these very differences provide ample grounds for misunderstanding between men and women: as Tannen (1992) argues, they end up talking at cross purposes. Women, she believes, tend to speak and hear a language of connection and intimacy, whereas men speak and hear a language of status and independence. Thus, men find that seeking advice (especially from men) is potentially demeaning; women may be less inhibited in doing so. Women talk about troubles to share them; men talk about troubles to solve them. In her book *You Just Don't Understand* Tannen draws upon everyday examples to explore the nature of the misunderstandings that arise when these two styles interact. The following case is fairly typical.

> Eve had a lump removed from her breast. Shortly after the operation, talking to her sister, she said that she found it upsetting to have been cut into, and that looking at the stitches was distressing because they left a seam that had changed the contour of her breast. Her sister said, 'I know. When I had my operation I felt the same way.' Eve made the same observation to her friend Karen, who said, 'I know. It's like your body has been violated.' But when she told her husband, Mark, how she felt, he said, 'You can have plastic surgery to cover up the scar and restore the shape of your breast.'
>
> Eve had been comforted by her sister and her friend, but she was not comforted by Mark's comment. Quite the contrary, it upset her more. Not only didn't she hear what she wanted, that he understood her feelings, but, far worse, she felt he was asking her to undergo more surgery just when she was telling him how much this operation had upset her. 'I'm not having any more surgery!' she protested. 'I'm sorry you don't like the way it looks.' Mark was hurt and puzzled. 'I don't care,' he protested. 'It didn't bother me at all.' She asked, 'Then why are you telling me to have plastic surgery?' He answered, 'Because you were saying you were upset about the way it looked.' (Tannen, 1992, 49–50)

Although Eve and Mark both speak the same language (inasmuch as they share a common vocabulary, grammar, and patterns of pronunciation), they use it for different interactive purposes and it is at this level that the most profound misunderstandings between men and women arise. As Tannen comments: Eve wanted the gift of understanding, but Mark gave her the gift of advice. He was taking the role of problem solver, whereas she simply wanted confirmation of her feelings (ibid., 50).

Many of the examples of gender differences in language discussed in this chapter have been identified in terms of specific features, tag questions, interruptions, and so on. While such features may be reasonably easy to identify in themselves and also easy to count because of their relative frequency, it is not always easy – as we have seen – to know precisely what they are doing in interaction, since their function may depend upon the particular context in which they occur. In consequence we are often faced with conflicting interpretations of the same or similar sets of data, relating to the occurrence of a feature such as, for example, tag questions which can be tentative in some contexts, coercive in others. Tannen's work sidesteps this problem by addressing directly the issue of function and purpose in interaction, irrespective of the features through which such functions are realized.

However, although gender differences in the *functions* of language within interaction are clearly a most important area of investigation, it has not been easy to gather systematic evidence concerning their relative occurrence. It is much easier, for instance, to study the incidence of interruptions in cross-sex talk than it is to study men offering solutions as if to a problem in contexts when a woman has anticipated a matching response to her feelings, like Eve and Mark above. For one thing, talk of this type tends by definition to be private and not easily available for the public scrutiny of research projects based upon tape-recordings and transcripts. For another thing, even when such recording techniques are used, the actual incidence of events of this type is relatively small: communicatively, of course, they may be of great significance but accumulating statistical evidence about them is difficult,

For this reason, Tannen relies for much of her evidence on her own and others' remembered experiences, which she renders in the forms of short scenarios, pen sketches, and anecdotes. In many ways she is like an anthropologist, although one doing work on her own rather than someone else's culture. In fact, many readers – men as well as women – find her account compelling since it seems to match their own experience while casting it in a new light. But this should not blind us to the possibilities of discrepancies between what we think we do as social beings and what we actually do: gender differences are an area where people are particularly prone to stereotypical judgements – to overestimate differences between men and women while underestimating differences within each category. There is no easy way round this problem; but it is certainly the case that Tannen has provided important and provocative hypotheses about what is going on when men and women are talking, ones on which more research needs to be done.

At the same time we have to recognize that Tannen's account effectively and quite deliberately sidelines questions of relations of power between the sexes in order to focus upon the cross-cultural component of misunderstandings. Hers is a study of differences rather than of dominance: misunderstandings arise, she argues, because of the different (even if overlapping) subcultures inhabited by men and women. Two criticisms may be made of this broad approach. First, the scale of cultural differences identified is ultimately rather narrow. Tannen assumes, for the most part, one common culture for women, and another for men, at least in the United States. And so we are faced with essentially two subcultures, neither of which is differentiated internally, by reference, for example, to ethnicity or class. To what extent, we might ask, do Asian working-class women from Bradford, for instance, occupy the same subculture as women from the affluent suburbs of Washington DC?

Second, the picture that emerges from Tannen's examples is of a somewhat idealized world in which the best intentions of men and women to understand each other are frustrated because of the cultural mismatch between them. Although this is a positive, even a therapeutic, approach, since it suggests that greater awareness on both sides can overcome these misunderstandings, it none the less leaves out of the account ways in which miscommunication arises because of, and is fuelled by, real conflicts of interest based upon asymmetries of power. Is it possible, one might ask, that men sometimes miss the point of what is said to them, because in order to find it they would have to understand the utterance from the position of a subordinate in a relation of power? One of the most important consequences of the work on language and gender is that even in those areas of investigation where the evidence remains inconclusive about the exact nature of the differences, there is still enough to make it possible to pose questions of this type on an everyday basis and in an analytically informed way that may help to expose the prevailing patterns of power.

Background sources and further reading

A major work by a British academic on language and gender, going far beyond the scope of this chapter, is:

Cameron, D. (1992, 2nd edn) *Feminism and Linguistic Theory*, London: Macmillan.

This is a critical account of two contrasting traditions of work: the theoretically informed work of French scholars, and the empirically rooted work in the Anglo-American tradition. Important collections of work in the latter tradition are represented by:

Coates, J. and Cameron, D. (eds) (1988) *Women in Their Speech Communities*, London: Longman.
Thorne, B. and Henley, N. (eds) (1975) *Language and Sex: Difference and Dominance*, Rowley, Mass.: Newbury House.
Thorne, B., Kramarae, C. and Henley, N. (eds) (1983) *Language Gender and Society*, Rowley, Mass.: Newbury House.

This latter title, besides including several frequently-referenced papers, also contains 180 pages of annotated bibliography, an invaluable research resource.

Another useful collection of classic papers is:

Cameron, D. (ed.) (1990) *The Feminist Critique of Language: a Reader*, London: Routledge

For a very well-written and clear overview of the issues relating to speech differences between men and women, see:

Coates, J. (1986) *Women, Men and Language*, London: Longman.

Also very useful, and broader in scope, including theoretically well-informed discussion of sexist discourses is:

Graddol, D. and Swann, J. (1989) *Gender Voices*, Oxford: Basil Blackwell.

Finally, a recent, and very popular, account of differences in communicative style between women and men, though not immune from criticism from other scholars working in the field of language and gender is:

Tannen, D. (1991) *You Just Don't Understand*, London: Virago.

Fieldwork project

It makes sense to start with material close at hand. If you are a student, then mixed-sex student seminars and tutorials provide wonderful opportunities for fieldwork. Various simple projects can be undertaken that rely in the first instance only on real-time coding:

(1) For groups of a reasonable size, a simple coding sheet such as that below can be used to gain a sense of which gender talks most. Enter every contribution made during the seminar against the name of the speaker using a tick.

Tutor		Females		Males	
Jane Whiteside	✓✓ ✓ ✓✓ ✓	Sara Brown Casey Miller Jean Armitage etc.	✓✓	John Swift Phil Bloom Ken Johnson etc.	✓ ✓ ✓✓ ✓

If there is an equal number of male and female students, then one would expect an equal number of contributions from both men and women. (If the numbers of speakers are not equal, then the numbers of contributions to the seminar should be proportionate to the balance of male to female. For instance, if there are four men and six women, then one would expect 40 per cent of the contributions to be from men and 60 per cent to be from women, not counting contributions from the tutor.) Are the contributions of male and female speakers proportionate? If not, why not?

(2) Of course, one of the problems with the above coding schedule is that it only gives raw scores for the number of contributions and tells us nothing about the length or indeed the nature of the contributions. Suggest how you would remedy this defect. What happens when you implement your revised coding technique? Do your new results confirm the previous ones or are they very different? Is there a gender imbalance?

(3) More detailed work on cross-sex talk ultimately requires tape-recordings and transcripts. (Always seek permission for recordings; and see pp. xix–xx for guidelines on transcription.) Transcripts take

a long time to prepare but enable the fine detail of talk to be studied. A transcript of a seminar enables you to study the kinds of turns which participants make and other features such as the distribution of interruptions (see the discussion of Zimmerman and West (1975) above). For some seminars it is worth considering the issue of speaker selection and the role of the tutor. How are speakers selected in the course of the seminar? Do they select themselves? Or are they selected by the tutor? In the latter case do men get selected proportionally more than women? Does the sex of the tutor make a difference?

Although the results from small-scale, fairly informal, fieldwork such as this need to be treated tentatively, they can often provide a stimulating basis for discussion of the everyday interconnections of gender roles, power and language. They may even provide a basis for interventions which seek to improve established patterns of interaction.

9 LINGUISTIC DIVERSITY AND THE SPEECH COMMUNITY: CONCLUSION

The speech community

The term 'speech community' has occurred a number of times in part two without being explicitly defined. As an idealized notion it refers to a group of people who share: (1) a language in common; (2) common ways of using language; (3) common reactions and attitudes to language; and (4) common social bonds (i.e. they tend to interact with each other or tend to be linked at least by some form of social organization).

In practice, however, the term is not without its difficulties. In particular it is difficult to find cases where all these conditions are fulfilled simultaneously. Throughout the foregoing section, for instance, we have considered for the most part aspects of what might be called the British speech community. What emerges is a wide diversity both of linguistic practice and of attitudes to language. We find a diversity ranging from the use of totally different languages, through Creole forms and regional variants of English, to situational varieties. Part of the difficulty lies with the notion of 'community', which – in the ideal, at least – frequently implies a high degree of common interest and cohesion between its members. If we are to identify the term with British society, however, then we have to recognize that beneath the surface forms of its cohesion, lie strong fault lines of internal division.

In addition to its apparent homogeneity, it is also highly differentiated – materially, culturally, politically, by employment, occupation, gender, age, and so on.

This recognition is important, because it is difficult to disentangle linguistic practices from the wider social processes in which they are embedded. And if the society displays internal differentiation, diversity and division, then verbal signification itself will be similarly differentiated and diverse. The term *speech community* is in this respect something of a misnomer: at the very least it has to be thought through in a way that includes, not only the notion of verbal practices held in common, but also of tension and conflict between them.

At the same time it would be a mistake to think of language merely as an adjunct to the social process. Society does not exist prior to and independent of language. The emergence and maintenance of even the simplest social group or formation is from its very outset predicated in the most fundamental fashion upon acts of signification. In this respect the diversity of language is not merely a reflection of the pre-existing fault lines within society: it is active in respect of them.

Diversity in language

Diversity of language within the overall speech community can be understood in two main ways. On the one hand, a distinct variety of (or even a variant within) language can be used to affirm social solidarity between those who use it. And, on the other hand, it can be used in a boundary-maintaining role to signal or impose distance between those who use it and those who don't. Thus, as we saw, for example, in chapter 4, to 'chat bad' by selecting a high proportion of Creole forms is used by some Black teenagers to affirm a common identity amongst themselves. At the same time, by virtue of the fact that these linguistic forms contrast sharply with those of the surrounding speech community, they can be used to emphasize a degree of social distance between Black youth and mainstream society.

Anti-languages (including cases such as CB slang) can be understood in this way. It is perhaps less obvious, though, that the workings of regional accents and dialects can also be understood in similar terms. Despite the widespread acceptance of one dialect as a standardized variety for the purposes of written communication and other key communicative functions (such as, for example, news broadcasting), regionally distinct forms of speech (particularly accents) still survive among sections of the population. They survive, not so much because people lack alternative models, but because they need and wish to go on affiliating themselves with localized social structures. For this reason local forms of pronunciation and utterance construction continue to be domains of active linguistic innovation.

The relationship of the standard dialect to other varieties

Any variety – whether it be a dialect, social dialect, anti-language, or whatever – as long as it is sustained by a group of speakers must, by that very fact, adequately serve their communicative needs. In this sense there is no inadequate, inferior or incorrect variety. (It is of course possible to select a variety inappropriate to the situation: to use the language of poetry in the supermarket wouldn't get you very far, unless perhaps you'd recognized your interlocutor to be a part-time poet.) If the communicative needs of a group evolve in some way, then the variety will also evolve to meet those needs. This is quite a generalized process, of which the rapid evolution from pidgin to Creole in the Caribbean is but a particular instance. (It is now considered likely that English itself emerged out of some kind of Creolization process involving Anglo-Saxon, Old Norse, and Norman French.) Thus, though varieties may differ in many particulars, they are all equal in their capacity to meet the communicative needs of their users.

The process whereby the south-east Midlands dialect, for example, evolved into the standard dialect of English was not determined by some kind of intrinsic linguistic superiority. It was underwritten by social and historical factors such as its use by sections of the mercantile class and by students at the two Universities. Its growing adoption from the fifteenth century onwards as the preferred variety for written communication, in education, in the conduct of the professions, etc. is a question of historical contingency rather than linguistic superiority. The establishment of a standard has clear advantages in terms of mutual intelligibility. But it also leads to a situation in which the standardized variety exerts normative pressure on other varieties – a pressure that stems in large part from its use by dominant groups within society for privileged forms of communication; but we should not be misled thereby into believing that it represents some absolute standard of correctness. Nor should we be misled into supposing that the language used by subordinate groups or in less status-marked settings is in some way inferior or deficient, merely because the patterns displayed therein are not identical to those of the standard.

Communicative styles, subcultures, and the speech community

It is not only differences of grammar, vocabulary, and pronunciation that make up the range of linguistic differences within the speech community. Just as crucial are differences within the speech community over the fundamental functions or purposes of language and how these might be interpreted. For example, to a Black American, especially a male teenager from New York, an utterance such as 'Your mother play dice with the midnight mice' will most probably be interpreted as a semi-humorous ritual insult. This is because, to an urban Black, it is part of an identifiable speech genre with its own name (e.g. 'sounding', 'signifying', or 'playing the dozens'); with its own rules of composition (e.g. the use of rhyme and the references to the recipient's mother); and with its own rules of use (e.g. the insult should be fictional rather than true, a condition often signalled through the use of outrageous assertions). (See chapter 10 below for further discussion.)

However, while some sections of the American speech community will be familiar with this genre, others will not: a white, middle-class American may well have difficulty seeing the point of an utterance such as 'Your mother play dice with the midnight mice', even though each word of it makes sense in itself. When speakers adopt a particular subset of the range of rules of use and rules of interpretation, it can be described as a communicative style; and there is clearly potential for serious misunderstandings. If 'sounding' or 'signifying', for instance, should occur between users of different communicative styles who do not share the same rules of use and norms of interpretation, then serious insult may result where only mock insult was intended.

How do such differences arise? One way of explaining the emergence of such differences in communicative styles within the speech community is in terms of the subcultures that underlie them. A subculture defines itself partly on the basis of internal norms but also by reference to what separates it from other groups. In all of this, language is a most powerful instrument both of group definition and of group cohesion: 'speaking the same language' is a crucial badge of group membership and subcultural identity. More is at stake here, however, than merely sounding alike. Speaking the same language or dialect may be a very visible badge of group membership, but even more important to the production and reinforcement of sub cultural variation are underlying differences in communicative style – in the uses and purposes of language.

It was this perspective (to some extent, at least) that informed Bernstein's approach to language and class. For him, as we saw in chapter 7, two different fashions of speaking – the restricted code and the elaborated code – could be traced to two contrasting subcultures. The restricted code is thought to favour implicit meanings and is based on a subculture which emphasizes common values and group solidarity. The elaborated code is considered to favour the expression of explicit meanings and individual rather than group values. Education, according to Bernstein, is closely identified with the latter code and its associated meanings. Consequently, children from more communally-based subcultures are likely to communicate within the restricted code and to find the experience of schooling to be one of socio-linguistic discontinuity and disadvantage.

These claims concerning language and class bear interesting comparison with those which have emerged around issues of language and gender. Men and women, it is claimed, develop within two different subcultures. Male subcultures are based on power; they are organized in terms of status and hierarchy; they tend to be competitive and to emphasize the values of individualism and independence. Female subcultures, by contrast, place a premium on solidarity; they are more oriented to intimacy and to connection

179

and they emphasize the values of interdependency and co-operation. According to (among others) Tannen, this gives rise to different ways of using and interpreting the language so that (as we saw in chapter 8) women, for example, talk about troubles to share them, whereas men prototypically talk about troubles to solve them.

Adopting a more specialized version of this argument, Coates concludes that men and women do not share the same communicative competence; their rule systems for the use and interpretation of utterances are actually different as a result of their different patterns of socialization into two contrasting subcultures. Women, accordingly, develop a co-operative repertoire of verbal behaviour, especially with other women, in contrast to men who are thought to interact more competitively. It is further claimed that these differences between male and female speech place women at a crucial disadvantage in key social institutions. In the educational system, for instance, language – as in many other institutions – operates not for intimacy and connection but indirectly to achieve status within the institutional hierarchy. The ethos of the institution is not, therefore, one which values the particular communicative competence of women – an analogous claim to Bernstein's hypothesis that part of the reason why working-class children find it more difficult to succeed within the education system is that they are less likely to have had access to the characteristic individualistic code of schooling – the elaborated code – than middle-class children.

In this respect, it seems that some of the arguments about gendered styles of interaction have come to resemble the debates which surrounded Bernstein's work on language, social class and education. In both cases the claims have attracted a great deal of interest and generated a certain amount of controversy. And yet, it has to be recognized that in neither case is the burden of proof overwhelming. In Bernstein's case (as noted in chapter 7) empirical support for the notion of two separate class-based codes, or fashions of speaking, has been difficult to establish. In addition to which his mode of argument can be criticized for being overly schematic, organized as it is around the pairs of opposite terms:

restricted v. elaborated codes
positional v. personal role systems
working class v. middle class.

His approach relies upon setting up idealized oppositions which exclude the space between them. Role systems, for instance, need to conform in his account to one or other of two broad types: they are either positional or personal. And, in spite of Bernstein's attempts to avoid it, one side or other of the oppositions implicitly receives more approval in his account than the other. It is hard, for instance, to read Bernstein without feeling that ultimately he identifies more positively with the nuanced negotiations of the elaborated code than with the supposed simplicity and directness of the restricted code. Notwithstanding the absence of clear empirical evidence to support the division into two mutually exclusive codes, once the terms have been set up in opposition to one another it is hard to avoid an implicit hierarchy of value where 'personal' is better than 'positional', 'open' better than 'closed', and so on. At the same time, with each of Bernstein's oppositions it is fair to ask to what extent they exhaust the range of possibilities and whether these might not better be dealt with in terms of continua.

Surprisingly similar reservations can be raised as regards the recent claims about subculturally shaped, gendered fashions of speaking. The work of Coates (1986), for instance, offers evidence that highly co-operative communicative styles can be found in the conversations of a women-only group and she further suggests that a distinction between co-operative and competitive styles may provide a basis for distinguishing between the communicative competence of women and men. However, her own empirical work on a group of women is not matched by comparative evidence from groups of men talking among themselves. Her claim, therefore, remains at the level of an intriguing, but empirically undemonstrated, hypothesis.

It is noticeable also that claims about men's and women's language, almost by definition, have to be couched around pairs of terms in simple opposition to each other: men, it is suggested, tend to adopt linguistic forms associated with power, women those of subordination; or women tend to adopt co-operative styles, men those of competition. In an early attempt to characterize speech differences between men and women, Lakoff (1975), for instance, suggested that women were less assertive in their speech than men. At the time when this claim was advanced, it was understood as pointing to a deficiency or a lack in women's speech that was both the cause and the effect of their subordination (not dissimilar to earlier claims of a linguistic deficit in the working class). This view may be contrasted with Coates's (1986) more recent work where the opposition between (female) co-operative and (male) competitive speech is presented as a difference between men and women rather than as a deficit on women's part.

For the moment, these claims remain at the level of an important hypothesis about possible differences between women's speech and men's speech, which still awaits the accumulation of decisive evidence. As a hypothesis, however, it is worth considering in greater detail. For one thing, it seems to exist in two forms – a strong form and a weak form. In its strong form the hypothesis would claim that the speech differences between women and men are the outcome of underlying differences in communicative competence: men and women apparently possess a different set of rules for the use and interpretation of speech. It might be argued, for instance, that women have access to the rules of gossiping, but men do not.

This approach, however, raises more questions than it answers. Are the rule systems followed by men and women actually discrete or are they overlapping? The answer presumably must be the latter, otherwise no communication between men and women would be possible. But, if the rule systems are overlapping, then in what particular ways are they different? Are they, for instance, different in their particulars, as in the example of gossiping above. Or are the rule systems similar in their particulars but different in their overall configuration: in other words, is it that men and women know how to do the same things communicatively but are subject to different contextual constraints? Men, it might be claimed, for instance, *do* know how to gossip but do it in different circumstances and under a different name.

In general the claim of the strong form of the hypothesis is not just that men and women communicate differently but that women know how to communicate like women but not like men; and vice versa. It is difficult, however, to see how the different competences are developed, sustained and kept distinct from one another, even as part of socialization. Although the construction of gender identity through socialization is by definition going to take different paths for girls and for boys, it is increasingly rare, none the less, in highly industrialized societies, for the two sexes to be rigidly segregated during childhood or adolescence. Consequently, the socialization process that shapes babies into girls and women, on the one hand, and into boys and men, on the other hand, is for the most part visible to both genders. It is difficult to see, therefore, how girls and boys should be completely incompetent at the communicative behaviour of the other gender. It is certainly difficult to see how in societies of this type the two contrasting subcultures can generate completely opposing competencies while occupying the same, or at least overlapping, social space. By the same token it is not easy to see how the opposing genders can have had access systematically denied to each others' subcultures to the extent of limiting access to each others' communicative competences – both receptively as well as productively.

Alternatively, the weak form of the hypothesis would claim that the difference between men and women is one of communicative style rather than competence: speakers, while subject to an unconscious gendered preference for a particular range of communicative options, are none the less capable of using more than their habitual range. In its weak form, then, the hypothesis would suggest that women can select those communicative options associated in some accounts with men – such as, for example, direct commands used to enforce or reinforce differences in status or power in hierarchical relations. It is just that they are more likely to opt for solidarity forms. According to this account, therefore, a sense of gender identity channels speakers into restricted sectors of the total communicative repertoire available in a speech community, while leaving them capable of selecting outside their habitual range. On the face of it this is a plausible hypothesis, but one which is not easy to test empirically. For, once this degree of flexibility is granted to speakers – allowing them to override their gender – it is difficult to know *which behaviour of which speakers* to use as empirical evidence of gendered styles of communication, without simply slipping into the trap of reproducing existing stereotypes.

Questions remain, therefore, about the precise form of the hypothesis relating to gendered differences in speech as well as questions concerning exactly how to prove it. None the less, the crucial insight which underlies all of this interest in communicative styles, repertoires or competence, is that different groups and subcultures within the overall speech community not only have access to different grammars and vocabularies; they may also use language differently for different purposes. Furthermore, all this diversity is both a source and an enactment of subcultural identity and difference. Selecting from the available repertoire of communicative styles is an act of identity in an even more fundamental fashion than choosing to wear jeans and a denim jacket as opposed to a twin-set and pearls.

Conclusions: language and community

In conclusion we may note that the idea of the speech community is important for highlighting the way in which language exists not just as an abstract system, codified in grammar books and dictionaries; it is integral to everyday social life and belongs ultimately to its community of users. It is they who make and remake it in their everyday encounters.

At the same time, as we noted at the beginning of this chapter, the term 'speech community' remains problematic. In the first place, the reference to *speech* recalls earlier societies based on face-to-face contact, and this seems inappropriate to societies where print and electronic means of communication have opened up a whole range of mediated transactions which do not rely upon the unmediated primacy of speech itself. In consequence, some linguists now prefer the expression *language community*. In the second place, the reference to *community* seems something of a misnomer under late capitalism. Modern societies tend to elaborate differences along many different lines – not just class and region – but also gender, age, ethnicity, and so on. And these become not only lines of difference but real social divisions around which material inequalities accrue. Given such divisions, it is right to ask in what sense such societies can appropriately be understood as instances of community. One answer is to stress their 'imagined' character, along the lines of Anderson:

'all communities larger than primordial villages of face-to-face contact (and perhaps even these) are imagined' (1983, 15).

Although the notion of speech *community* is used analytically within socio-linguistics it cannot escape the kinds of problems that apply to its use in other contexts. Indeed, it is difficult in practice to divorce its application from other kinds of community such as the nation. A speech community, for instance, typically requires for its operation the existence of a standard dialect or some superposed variety (such as Mandarin Chinese or classical Arabic). The very existence of such a variety then serves to encourage or promote national aspirations; or is used retrospectively to rationalize or justify them. Notions of nationhood and linguistic standards are often invoked in closely connected ways.

In the final analysis, therefore, we are forced to recognize that the speech community is as imagined a community as the nation itself. The bonds that make up each kind of community are imagined rather than actual. As Anderson remarks of the nation:

It is imagined because the members of even the smallest nation will never know most of their fellow members, meet them, or even hear of them, yet in the minds of each lives the image of their communion. (Anderson, 1983, 15)

Even in a small, clearly territorially-bounded country like Britain, for instance, any individual member of the speech community will meet in their lifetime only the smallest fraction of the community's full membership. They will have only the haziest sense of the full range of linguistic diversity around them. None the less, each individual carries with them a powerful image of linguistic communion in which – despite incidental differences – they consider themselves to be speakers of apparently the same language. Underpinning this sense of community - both national and linguistic – is deference to the standard dialect as a prestige variety – the one which is advocated for use, with only occasional competitors (e.g. Welsh), for all the major functions of the modern state, taught in schools and assumed to be the basic medium of instruction, the preferred dialect for national broadcasting, and codified in grammar books and dictionaries. The standard dialect of English as a supposedly unified and well-defined linguistic system helps to confirm the existence of the nation as the community who 'speak the language'. Paradoxically, of course, this standard is as imagined an entity as the nation itself. Prescriptive grammar books, guides to usage, dictionaries, and so on, through an elaborate process of codification, give it a far more tangible prominence than any of the other varieties with which it competes. But in the final analysis not many of us actually speak the standard, even though most of us either think that we do or believe that we should.

The authority of the standard is most precarious in times of the breaking of nations. When nations fragment, struggles ensue over what actually constitutes the standard. The resurgence of Scottish nationalism in the eighties, for instance, has led within Scotland to a renewed interest in Scots, not as a dialect of English, but as an independent linguistic formation, sharing with English a common linguistic ancestor, but with its own separate history and possible future role in an emerging Scottish state. Scots, some would claim, is a language as different from English as Bulgarian is from Russian, or Croatian is from Serbian, or Urdu is from Hindi.

Comparisons such as these help to demonstrate how closely issues of national and linguistic identity are tied together, and why questions such as 'What counts as a language?' 'How does a dialect become the standard?' are ultimately political and social as well as linguistic questions. 'A language is a dialect with an army and a navy' as someone once remarked. By the same token a question such as 'What makes a speech community?' is also a social and political question. And in the contemporary world we have to remember that a speech community is rarely, if ever, self-sufficient or self-standing. There is, in that sense, no such thing as a self-contained English speech community; there are only speech communities in overlapping and sometimes contradictory relationships.

Background sources and further reading

Bartsch, R. (1987) *Norms of Language*, London: Longman.
Coates, J. and Cameron, D. (eds) (1988) *Women in their Speech Communities*, London: Longman.

Gumperz, J. (1972) 'The speech community' in Giglioli, P.P. (ed.) *Language and Social Context,* Harmondsworth: Penguin.

Milroy, J. and Milroy, L. (1985) *Authority in Language*, London: Routledge & Kegan Paul.

Romaine, S. (ed.) (1982) *Sociolinguistic Variation in Speech Communities,* London: Edward Arnold

Saville-Troike, M. (1982) *The Ethnography of Communication: an Introduction,* Oxford: Basil Blackwell.

Trudgill, P. (ed.) (1984) *Language in the British Isles*, Cambridge: Cambridge University Press.

Warburg, J. (1968) 'Notions of correctness' supplement II in Quirk, R. *The Use of English,* London: Longman.

PART THREE
LANGUAGE AND
SOCIAL INTERACTION

Word is a two-sided act. It is determined
equally by whose word it is and for *whom*
it is meant. . . . Each and every word
expresses the 'one' in relation to the
'other'. . . . A word is a bridge thrown
between myself and
another.

(Volosinov*)

*Volosinov, V.N. (1973) *Marxism and the Philosophy of Language*, London:
Seminar Press.

10 LANGUAGE AND SOCIAL INTERACTION

Asking questions is often thought to be impertinent or intrusive . . . whatever questions I ask are bound to seem belligerent to somebody somewhere.

(Robin Day, the *Observer*, 18 November 1984)

The colonel sat down and settled back, calm and cagey suddenly, and ingratiatingly polite.

'What did you mean,' he inquired slowly, 'when you said we couldn't punish you?'

'When, sir?'

'I'm asking the questions. You're answering them.'

'Yes, sir. I—'

'Did you think we brought you here to ask questions and for me to answer them?'

'No, sir. I—'

'What did we bring you here for?'

'To answer questions.'

'You're goddam right,' roared the colonel. 'Now suppose you start answering some before I break your goddam head.'

(Joseph Heller, *Catch 22*)

Doing things with words: utterances perform actions

Every utterance adopts a stance of some kind in relation to its recipient. The most obvious kind of action performed by utterances is that of 'stating' or 'informing'. It is pre-eminently this kind of action that is performed, for example, by railway station announcements of the type, 'The train arriving on platform one is the eight twenty-five to London Paddington. A buffet car may be found in the middle of the train.' But this is clearly not the only kind of action undertaken by utterances. Take, for example, everyday random bits of verbal communication such as the following:

'Please lower your head when leaving your seat.'
'No smoking.'
'Okay.'
'Sorry.'
'Hello.'
'Excuse me.'
'Clear off.' (Or words to that effect.)

These examples variously, acknowledge, apologize, greet, command, and request a recipient to do something. None of them, strictly speaking, declares, states, or gives information. Utterances, indeed, are capable of performing a wide range of actions, of which 'informing' is but one. The range includes activities as diverse as 'warning', 'complimenting', 'inviting', 'disputing', 'commenting', 'complaining', 'exemplifying', 'challenging', as well as those mentioned above. Significantly, for many of these actions, it is difficult to envisage how else they might be performed except in words. How else, for example, can someone 'comment', 'dispute', 'compliment', or 'complain', except by means of an utterance of one form or another? Yet each of these utterance–actions represents a specific alignment or counter-alignment adopted by one speaker towards another. In this way speakers define and assume roles in an interaction and actually constitute their social relations in terms of myriad reciprocal interchanges of actions such as these.

The normal coherence of talk: the actions performed by utterances typically cohere, one with another

A central concern in the study of verbal interaction is to explain and account for how participants can recognize the action performed by another's utterance and match it with a contribution of their own in an appropriate and coherent fashion. The fact that most talk runs off as a fairly fluent joint accomplishment does not in itself make the whole process obviously self-explanatory. Indeed, the relatively rare occasions where trouble does occur can provide illuminating insights into the procedures that make possible the normal coherence of talk. The following interchange, for example, is puzzling in several respects:

EXAMPLE 10.1

TURN 1 A: What is your name?
TURN 2 B: Well, let's say you might have thought you had it from before, but you haven't got it anymore.
TURN 3 A: I'm going to call you Dean.
Source: from Laffal (1965). Cited by Labov (1970).

A major difficulty lies in the failure of Turn 2, by B, to provide a satisfactory reply to A's question ('What is your name?'). Indeed, the peculiarity of B's 'non-answer' at Turn 2 provides for the relevance of A's proposal at Turn 3 ('I'm going to call you Dean'). But this itself is slightly odd in two ways. Why does A ask B his name at Turn 1, if he is able to supply him with the name Dean in Turn 3? And why is there no explicit and overt recognition on A's part at Turn 3 of the peculiarity of B's contribution at Turn 2? (Why, for example, does A not say 'Pardon?' or 'Sorry, I don't quite follow you' or produce some other indication of difficulty?)

Some of the apparent oddities of this interchange might seem to be reduced if it is revealed that speakers A and B are doctor and psychiatric patient respectively. Interestingly enough then, the notion of psychiatric disturbance can itself be used to make sense of things that are apparently incoherent (which is presumably why the doctor is not bothered overmuch by what the patient says at Turn 2). And conversely, we take apparent conversational incoherence to be one sign of psychiatric disturbance. In the normal course of events, however, we expect turns at talk to proceed without such clear and obvious difficulties, precisely because they conform to certain types of patterned regularity which the example above fails to observe.

Formats for providing coherence: the two-part structure or 'adjacency pair'

The basic norm broken by the example is that questions expect answers – that given the production of a question by one speaker, the next speaker should provide a turn which can be heard as embodying an answer to that question. Should an answer not be provided, then its absence will be noticeable and notable. In this respect the relationship between question and answer is one in which the former strongly predicts or implicates the latter. The kind of close relationship involved is, in fact, shared by other pairs of utterance–types such as:

SUMMONS   →   ANSWER
A: 'John'   B: 'yeah'

GREETING   →   GREETING
A: 'Hi'   →   B: 'Hi'

In each of these cases the production of either a summons or a greeting, because of its status as the first part of a pair, has strong implications for the next turn in sequence: so much so that we can say that a summons by A sequentially implicates an answer from the addressee B. Should B not answer, then inferences will be made on the basis of its noticeable absence – perhaps that B is momentarily deaf, out of earshot, or offended. The importance of these pairings lies in the way they provide a kind of local, small-scale organizing device within the flow of talk – islands of predictability where conversational participants know where they stand. The peculiarity of the patient's reply in our example lies precisely in the way it subverts this predictability.

How do we recognize what an utterance is doing: in particular, what counts as a question?

These observations might seem almost self-evident, except for two basic complications. First of all, questions (or any other utterance–action, for that matter) turn out to be an extremely elusive; phenomenon to define. Secondly, even those utterances that we feel fairly confident in calling questions turn out to have a bewildering variety of additional purposes.

How do we know a question when we hear one? Partly on the basis of its formal composition: that is, either because of the particular items chosen or the way they are arranged. Thus 'John did go home early' is a statement, whereas 'Did John go home early?' is a question, and what distinguishes one from the other is the way their respective items are arranged. Similarly 'There's the typewriter' is a statement, whereas 'Where's the typewriter?' is a question by virtue of the fact that the latter contains a special question item and the former does not. And there are, of course, many other questioning words such as 'when', 'why', 'who', 'which', 'what', 'how', and tag constructions such as 'will you', 'does he', 'hasn't she', and so on, which help to mark utterances as questions. However, the criterion of formal composition is not sufficient in itself unambiguously to mark an utterance as a question, because it is quite common to find utterances which are equivalent in form performing different functions.

Compare, for example, the following two utterances:

EXAMPLE 10.2:

I went to Spain for the summer.

EXAMPLE 10.3:

You went to Spain for the summer.

The first example (10.2) is most likely to be a statement but the second, depending on situational factors, is quite likely to be a question, even though both utterances are formally very similar and no formal markers of questioning are present in either case.

Furthermore, even when formal markers of questioning are in fact present, an utterance can turn out to be performing some other function – as can be seen with the following two examples:

EXAMPLE 10.4:

Will you visit Spain again.

EXAMPLE 10.5:

Will you get a move on, Richards.

Here, example 10.4 is under most conditions likely to be a question, whereas example 10.5 is more likely to have the force of a command, especially when issued by a dominant participant to a subordinate (e.g. teacher to pupil). We can test this out to some extent by inspecting possible responses to the two utterances. Compare, for instance:

A: Will you visit Spain again.
B: I hope so.

with:

Q: Will you get a move on, Richards.
R: I hope so.

In the latter case 'I hope so' sounds distinctly odd, precisely because it treats something that is more likely to be intended as a command as if it were a question. (Conversely, 'If you say so' would be rather odd as a response to 'Will you visit Spain again', assuming the latter to be intended as a question.) Thus, we can see that formally equivalent pairs of utterances may well prove to be functionally contrastive; and turn out to be – as in the examples above – statement (10.2) and question (10.3), or question (10.4) and command (10.5) respectively.

To hear an utterance as a question, then, is as much a matter of situational factors as it is of formal properties of the utterance itself. It is not so much that the formal markers of utterance–action – of statement, question or command – are positively misleading. Rather is it the case that such features are reinterpreted according to the context of situation. Of special importance here is the distribution of knowledge within the encounter and the distribution of power.

The distribution of knowledge and questions

The distribution of knowledge, for example, can help to explain how some statement-like utterances come to sound like questions: if A addresses B with an utterance of this type, and in it B is made the grammatical subject of some event concerning which B (rather than A) has primary and first-hand knowledge, then it may be interpreted as a question – as in the following:

EXAMPLE 10.6

    A: You'll visit Spain again.
    B: I hope so.

or:

EXAMPLE 10.7

    A: Done an IBM 029 and 059 at College
    B: 029 only
    A: You haven't done the 059
    B: No, IBM 029 only
    A: Not even at College
    B: No
Source: Fowler *et al.* (1979).

In the latter example B responds to A's 'You haven't done the 059' as if it were equivalent in form to 'Haven't you done the 059?'

Thus – while the activity of 'questioning' is crucial to the conduct, organization and maintenance of verbal interaction – what counts as a question is not as easily specifiable as common sense perhaps would indicate; in fact, it is – as we've suggested above – often the outcome of a subtle interplay between the form of an utterance and the situation in which it is spoken. This introduces a high degree of flexibility into the whole interactive process: the interplay between form and situation allows an immensely wide variety of things to count as questions. In addition to this, however, there is another kind of flexibility at stake. Questions themselves are capable of performing many different types of interactive work over and beyond merely requesting a verbal response.

For, contrary to what one might expect, questions are not invariably used by one participant to seek information from another. Consider for example, the following exchanges between teacher and pupils in a primary school:

EXAMPLE 10.8

    T: What would you use for cutting wood?
    P: Saw
    T: A saw, good boy

or:

EXAMPLE 10.9

    T: What name did we give these three, Abdul?
    P: Materials
    T: Good boy, two team points, yes
Source: Sinclair and Coulthard (1975).

Here, in each case the second turn by the teacher explicitly evaluates the pupil's answer, thus implying that the teacher already had some kind of answer in mind at the moment of asking the question. The questions, therefore, are clearly not being used to seek what might be for the teacher new, previously unknown information from the other participants. They are being used to test whether the pupils know what the teacher knows already: and also to establish the positively evaluated answers as knowledge for any pupils in the class who may not have been able to answer the questions in the first place.

This use of questions may be seen as symptomatic of instructional contexts: it occurs for instance between adults and young children, as was noted in chapter 2. The following is a typical example:

EXAMPLE 10.10

    A: did you have ice cream for dinner today?
    C   yeah
    A: you didn't!
    C   yeah (.)
        ice cream (to)day

A: not today
      you had it yesterday didn't you?
(see data extract 2.9, p. 40)

The adult here is clearly not asking the question out of any real need to know, for she performs a series of overt corrections on the child's answers. The corrections on matters of fact, however, provide opportunities for oblique instruction; for example, on the difference between 'yesterday' and 'today'.

'Known-answer' questions and power relations

The asking of 'known-answer' questions, however, is symptomatic of more than merely instructional contexts. It seems generally to be associated with situations where one participant assumes power and authority over another, a relationship which will often be displayed in the follow-up turn from the questioner, where prior knowledge of the answer will be revealed. Consider, for example, the following interchange between a mother and teenage daughter:

EXAMPLE 10.11

M: what time did you get in last night?
D: oh about half eleven
M: no it wasn't I heard you coming in around twelve-thirty

Or consider the following sequence from a doctor–patient consultation: the patient is attending for an annual check-up and the doctor is reviewing his notes from the previous occasion:

EXAMPLE 10.12

D:	well carrying on then (.) no family changes	1
P:	└no	2
D:	since we last met (.) er no time off work	3
P:	er a couple of days off work I think . . .	4
D:	yes (.) you had lymphengitis	5
P:	lymphengitis?	6
D:	was that last year or the year before?	7
P:	yes	8
D:	really nothing significant this time?	9
P:	no (.) a cold I think and that was about it	10

D:	⌐and then	11
	you got backstrain	12
P:	oh yes that was right	13

On the face of it the doctor is merely bringing his records up to date or checking their accuracy, but over the course of a series of questions (frequently of the type examined in examples 10.6 and 10.7, p. 197) the doctor's record proves more detailed than the patient's memory so that the questions come more and more to sound like those of the known-answer type.

It is not so much the asking of a question when the answer is already known that is indicative of power or authority; rather is it the display of this foreknowledge in a subsequent follow-up turn, especially by evaluation or correction. But if an obvious known-answer question is used against the bias of prevailing power relations, then it typically has the effect of challenging or subverting them. It is this that helps to explain some of the peculiarities of the following sequence, which occurred between a teacher and a class during their first week in secondary school, and where in fact the usual current of known-answer questions being asked by the teacher is reversed. The teacher had just given detailed instructions concerning the completion of a written exercise, including the information that underlinings should be done in blue or black ink rather than any other colour:

EXAMPLE 10.13

P:	What colour do we use to underline, miss?	1
	((laughter from pupils))	2
T:	That is a stupid question, I've only just	3
	this minute said	4
P:	I know, miss	5
	((laughter from pupils))	6
T:	What is your name?	7
P:	Ian Smith	8
T:	Well, you're not a very polite boy, are you?	9
P:	No, miss	10
T:	In fact you seem a very rude, very stupid kind	11
	of boy	12

P:	I am, miss	13
	((laughter))	14
T:	I see	15

Source: Beynon (1985).

It is just possible, of course, that the pupil asked his initial question because he'd failed to hear the teacher's instructions. This in itself, however, would constitute grounds for admonishment, since it is a taken-for-granted feature of talk delivered generally to the class by the teacher that it is supposed to be attended to and closely monitored by all. To display ignorance of something the teacher has just said is thus to court rebuke or punishment: hence the teacher's response, 'That is a stupid question, I've only just this minute said'. The pupil's next turn, 'I know, miss', claims that the opening question *was* of the known-answer type and that in effect the pupil had no need to ask it. It is doing some other kind of work altogether than seeking information: coming from a pupil, it constitutes an incipient challenge to the prevailing power relations. The teacher undoubtedly hears it as such, hence her remarks 'you're not a very polite boy' and 'you seem a very rude, very stupid kind of boy'. And the class hears it as such, hence their laughter.

Thus, even the type of question we have called the known-answer question can have a variety of uses, though generally the one who uses the known-answer question will be the one who has power in the encounter. The pupil's use of it in the foregoing example may thus be seen as a claim against the power of the teacher.

'What is your name?'

The diversity of work performed by known-answer questions is matched, of course, by the variety of purposes performed by genuine requests for information. The teacher's 'What is your name?' in the extract above, for example, is likely to be a genuine information seeker, since it occurs on the first or second occasion that she has met the class. It is interesting, however, to speculate on why this particular information is sought at this moment in the encounter. In immediate terms, eliciting the boy's name may be seen as a preliminary to holding him identifiably accountable for his actions: the teacher, for instance, would find it useful to know the boy's name if she wished to proceed by invoking some institutional sanction against him (for example, 'Well, Ian Smith, you will report for detention after school tomorrow').

In more general terms, however, the direct and uncushioned request for an addressee's name is broadly suggestive of institutional contexts; or of contexts where the speaker is acting in an institutional capacity. On p. 111, for example, we have a policeman asking a bystander, 'What's your name, boy?' and on p. 193 we have a psychiatrist asking a patient, 'What is your name?' Indeed, precisely because the direct request for a name is suggestive of institutionalized power relations, then it will be avoided in non-status-marked settings: so much so that various mitigating procedures have evolved for eliciting an interlocutor's name in casual conversation – for example, 'My name's Smith, what's yours?' or 'Sorry, I didn't catch your name' .

Accordingly, when the teacher responds to the pupil's challenge by asking him in the full direct form 'What is your name?' she is in broad terms invoking and affirming her institutional position with respect to her interlocutor just as surely as the policeman or the psychiatrist is doing in the other examples.

Questions and 'blaming'

Thus, a variety of purposes may be fulfilled *both* by known-answer questions *and* by genuine requests for information. Indeed, in certain situations it may be routinely ambiguous as to whether or not the answer is known in advance to the questioner. Lines of questioning in court proceedings provide a case in point. Whether directed to a defendant or to a witness, they may well be heard as going further than merely 'establishing the facts of the case'. The following sequence, for example, is taken from the official transcript of the Scarman Tribunal and features a cross-examination by counsel of a police witness:

EXAMPLE 10.14

C:	You saw this newspaper shop being bombed on the	1
	front of Divis Street?	2
W:	Yes.	3
C:	How many petrol bombs were thrown into it?	4

W:	Only a couple. I felt that the window was already	5
	broken and that there was a part of it burning and	6
	this was a rekindling of the flames.	7
C:	What did you do at that point?	8
W:	I was not in a very good position to do anything.	9
	We were under gunfire at the time.	10

Source: Atkinson and Drew (1979).

On the face of it the questions posed to the witness would seem to amount to straightforward enquiries about matters of fact. The last two questions in the sequence, however, prompt replies that go beyond the minimum that would be required to answer. In reply to the question concerning how many petrol bombs were thrown, the witness could have replied, 'Two'. In reply to the question concerning what he did then, he could have said, 'Nothing'. But let us consider what the cumulative impact of such a sequence might be:

C:	You saw this newspaper shop being bombed on the	1
	front of Divis Street?	2
W:	Yes.	3
C:	How many petrol bombs were thrown into it?	4
W:	Two.	5
C:	What did you do at that point?	6
W:	Nothing.	7

Had such replies been forthcoming, it is not difficult to hypothesize that a likely next question from counsel might have been: 'You mean to tell me that you saw two petrol bombs being thrown into a shop in Divis Street and you did nothing? ' Such a question would most likely be heard as accusing the police witness of either plain incompetence or of some kind of bias in his relations with the public. The hypothetical case may, therefore, be seen as throwing into sharp relief what the *actual* replies of the witness seem designed to do. They would seem precisely to be designed to forestall this accusatory question and to avoid a projected 'blaming' by counsel. Thus, the reply to the query concerning how many bombs were thrown both minimizes the number involved ('only a couple') and the damage caused ('the window was *already* broken . . . there was a part of it burning and this was a *re*kindling of the flames'). The next question ('What did you do at that point?') implies that some relevant action both *could* and *should* have been taken by the witness, and it is these implications which the reply is explicitly designed to counter ('I was not in a very good position to do anything. We were under gunfire at the time'). It is not so much that the actual questions in themselves amount to accusations by counsel against the witness. Rather does it seem to be the case that they can be heard by participants in this situation as projecting forward in the discourse towards a possible accusation and are consequently often responded to by the witness as if they were – potentially at least – 'blame-implicative'.

Questions, therefore, vary in the functions that they perform: certainly, by no means is their only use to elicit information. The occurrence of known-answer questions, for example, serves to alert us to the many other uses of questions apart from seeking information – uses such as accusing, complaining, invoking institutional power and so on.

Questions, situation and utterance-action

Although the focus has been almost exclusively on questions, similar points could be made concerning other utterance types such as statements and commands. What counts as a statement or a command (or a complaint or a compliment, for that matter) is a product of the way features of the form of an utterance interact with aspects of its situation. Participants, accordingly, as a matter of course use their understanding of the current situation to infer what any particular utterance is doing at any one moment in an interaction.

Doing things with words and recognizing what others are doing in the same interaction is central to the production of social relations. Indeed, the relationship of one participant to another is made palpable and realized in the actions that their utterances perform. In this sense we have been examining how some of the actions performed by words are inherently interpersonal in character.

Doing things with words: managing the discourse

This insight obtains even when we consider a specialized type of utterance-function that seems restricted in its orientation merely to

204

managing the talk itself rather than the accomplishment of inter-personal purposes. This type of utterance is particularly evident in institutional settings, for example, which often have associated with them predictable stages or phases; and managing the shift from one phase to another is usually the acknowledged responsibility of one participant. In doctor–patient interviews, for example, there will be recognizably different phases of talk associated with diagnosis, with prescription, and with leave-taking; and it is the doctor who will most typically shift the encounter from one stage or phase to another. Common ways of effecting the shift from one stage to another are by use of a marker such as 'right', 'okay', 'now', 'anyway', especially when they are pronounced with full stress and followed by some reference to the nature of the forthcoming activity.

Openings

Such devices are illustrated in the following extract from a medical consultation, where a doctor shifts from opening pleasantries to the business in hand by the use of 'anyway' and loosely indicating the procedure to be followed ('going through the whole thing'):

EXAMPLE 10.15

	((Doctor leads patient into the consultation room, talking as he does so))	
D:	that's only the clutter in the (.) background	1
	(.)	2
P:	yeah	3
D:	no problem	4
	(.)	5
	so (.) take your coat off	6
P:	sure	7
	(4.0) ((Doctor helps patient to remove his	8
	coat))	9
	thanks	10
D:	don't think Philip's got any clothes pegs in	11
	here so uh (1.5) ((Doctor hangs up coat))	12
	I don't usually use thi— sit down	13
P:	fine	14
D:	I don't usually use this room its erm (.)	15

205

Philip's	16
(1.0)	17
P: yes of course	18
D: anyway (.) going through the whole thing	19
(2.0)	20
you've changed your job (.) in effect	21
(.)	22
P: well (.) an additional responsibility	23

What ensues is a stage or phase in the encounter in which the doctor checks out details of the patient's file using a series of questions such as:

'You're still chief engineer?'
'How much are you away now?'
'You're personally coping with that?'
'No family changes?'

This phase as a whole might be described as *checking the file*, and is recognizably different in character from the *opening* phase. Utterances here tend to bear a different functional load. Whereas the *opening* was distinguished by commands ('sit down') and statements ('I don't usually use this room'), *checking the file* is much more dependent on information-seeking/checking questions ('You're still chief engineer?'). None the less, whilst the two phases are clearly different in character, line 19 ('anyway (.) going through the whole thing') is crucial for signalling and effecting the transition from one to the other. In this respect its role is intrinsic to the management of the verbal component of the encounter: it plays a role intrinsic to the discourse itself.

In the extract above, the *opening* may have looked somewhat random and haphazard, partly because the doctor and patient are already in conversation as they enter the room; but *openings* to doctor–patient interviews are typically composed of elements such as greetings, identifications, invitations to sit, and a routine generalized opening query (e.g. 'How are you?'). Since the latter element is a routine politeness form in openings generally (cp. telephone conversations) and as such is not taken as a serious enquiry into health, the use of it in doctor–patient interviews can prove to be ambiguous. The patient in the following extract plays on this for humorous purposes:

EXAMPLE 10.16

D:	(morning) ((Doctor standing at his desk as patient	1
	enters room))	2
P:	(morning)	3
D:	how are you? ((Patient removes coat))	4
P:	I'm very well thank you doctor	5
	are *you* all right?	6
D:	yes ((Doctor arranging record cards on his desk)	7
P:	that's the main thing if *you're* all right	8
	(2.5) ((Joint laughter))	9

D:	now ((Doctor looks at patient)) (0.5) ((Sits down))	10
	just er check up on this (0.5)	11

	your erm (1.0) ((Patient sits down)) breathing thing	
	was (4.0)	12
	a year ago?	13
P:	was it a year?	14

The laughter (l. 9) is the outcome of some quite subtle interactive work. When the patient responds to the doctor's query (l. 4) with 'I'm very well thank you doctor' he treats it as a mere politeness formula, one not to be taken literally. (He is actually not very well at all, having a severe breathing problem.) But he treats his own query to the doctor (l. 6), and the doctor's response to it (l. 7), as if they *were* genuine, by virtue of his comment – 'that's the main thing if *you're* all right'. The doctor's way of shifting out of this phase of opening pleasantries into the consultation proper is once again by means of a marker ('now') followed by some kind of procedural signal ('just er check up on this'). It is noticeable in this case that effecting the transition from one section to the other coincides here with major shifts of posture (from standing to sitting) on the part of both doctor and patient.

Transition to the closing phase is accomplished in similar ways, though in fact there may be several unsuccessful attempts to move to closing. In the following extract the onset of closing has been delayed while the patient slowly and with some difficulty puts his coat back on, in the course of which he recapitulates the history of the condition that led to the difficulty:

EXAMPLE 10.17

	((Patient replacing coat; doctor standing at desk))	
P:	I s'pose y'ave to be grateful (.) it coulda	1
	gone worse couldn't it?	2
D:	oo aye (3.0) ((Doctor rearranging items at	3
	desk))	4
	anyway (.) there y'are (.) ((Hands patient prescription))	5
P:	thanks very much doctor (.)	6
D:	└very good	7
P:	much obliged to you ((Turns to go))	8
D:	have a nice Christmas	9
P:	yes same to you	10
D:	└and erm (.) see you make an appointment	11
	for some time (.)	12
P:	└all right	13
D:	just after Christmas	14
P:	'bout a week an' a half after Christmas	15
D:	bye ((Patient exits))	16
P:	bye	17

The doctor's 'anyway' at l. 5 and 'very good' at l. 8 are both markers shifting the encounter on towards closing. The first follows directly on a three-second silence (see l. 3) and signals that – from the doctor's viewpoint, at least – talk around the patient's difficulty with arm and hand has been exhausted. This then leads on to the handing-over of the prescription (l. 5), a feature quite typical of the later stages of a medical consultation. The marker at l. 7 ('very good') moves the encounter into its closing phase with its valediction (l. 9: 'have a nice Christmas'), its invitation to return

(l. 11: 'see you make an appointment') and its final leave-taking (ll. 16 and 17: 'bye'). It is not unusual for a closing phase, once begun, to become suspended by the revival of further topical talk. But in this instance both participants push firmly on to final closure. The patient signals his readiness to depart by postural shift at l. 8; and the doctor's subsequent turns at talk tend to overlap with those of the patient as each new but predictable element of the closing follows closely on the last. (From l. 7 onwards, where pauses occur, they tend to come within turns rather than between them.)

Social relations and the management of discourse

Thus, we can see how utterances such as:

'anyway (.) going through the whole thing' (Ex. 10.15: l. 19)
'now (0.5) just er check up on this' (Ex. 10.16: ll. 10–11)
'anyway (.) there y'are' (Ex. 10.17: l. 5)

seem specifically to be designed to move the talk on, to effect transitions between one kind of talk or activity and another. In this respect, as was noted earlier, their role is intrinsic to the talk itself and seems less interpersonal in its orientation than utterance types such as apologies or compliments. Even here, however, we have in the last analysis to recognize an interpersonal dimension. It tends, after all, only to be certain kinds of key participants in institutionalized encounters who use such devices – those with some kind of ratified responsibility for the way the talk, and the encounter generally, proceeds. In organizing the talk in these particular ways a doctor, or teacher, or committee chairperson produces social relations of a determinate type. Using an utterance such as 'anyway (.) going through the whole thing' is part of *doing* 'being a doctor' and creates for the interlocutor interactive space that is best filled by *doing* 'being a patient' .

The strength of the expectations that go with particular types of utterance in particular situations can be indicated by considering the hypothetical instance of a patient who says to a doctor in the early stages of an encounter, 'Are *you* all right?', only to be told, 'Well (.) I had this slight lesion develop on my finger and next thing I got this kind of burning sensation in my right leg.' The patient might justifiably complain that he was attending to present his own symptoms, not to hear about the doctor's. Conversely, it would be most unusual in the course of casual conversation for one participant to announce 'Well (.) that's enough about your holidays (.) let's move on to your job how's it going these days?' Anyone addressed in such a fashion by a fellow conversationalist would no doubt find it a peculiar arrogation of a role appropriate to certain institutional settings but not appropriate to everyday talk.

Social relations, language, and culture

Thus, we can see that talk is intimately implicated in the day-to-day making and taking of roles and in establishing, confirming and maintaining relations between people. This general point should not, of course, blind us to the way in which different cultures vary in the way they use language in the conduct of relationships. To put this in slightly different terms, the way in which different cultures draw upon language in the conduct of their everyday interactions does in fact make possible characteristically different modes of relationship between members of a culture.

Speech and silence

At a very basic level, for example, it has to be recognized that some cultures are simply 'more verbal' than others, in the sense that people spend more time talking in some cultures, less in others. There are quite clear differences within Europe in the degree to which silence is tolerated and valued in interactive settings. In the words of one writer: 'As one goes north in the Scandinavian peninsula, particularly in Sweden, what is called "the difficulty in expressing one's feelings" and the need for honesty and sincerity increase, whilst the amount of speech per hour decreases' (Reisman, 1974, 113).

This kind of variation is used by Reisman to explain the following incident:

> The extreme silence of my own experience was with some Lapps in Northern Sweden. . . . We spent some days in a borrowed sod house in the village of Rensjoen. . . . Our neighbours would

drop in on us every morning just to check that things were all right. We would offer coffee. After several minutes of silence the offer would be accepted. We would tentatively ask a question. More silence, then a 'yes' or a 'no'. Then a long wait. After five or ten minutes we would ask another. Same pause, same 'yes' or 'no'. Another ten minutes, etc. Each visit lasted approximately an hour – all of us sitting formally. During that time there would be six or seven exchanges. Then our guests would leave to repeat the performance the next day. (ibid., 112–13)

If one moves beyond continental Europe the range of variation increases further. The Paliyans of south India, for instance, 'communicate very little at all times and become almost silent by the age of 40. Verbal, communicative persons are regarded as abnormal and often as offensive' (Gardener, 1966, 398). And commentators of various kinds have often drawn attention to the 'reticence' of North American Indians.

Behind such broad statements, however, we often find a more complicated picture, not so much of one culture valuing speech and silence in general differently from another, but of each culture having a different sense of the contexts in which it is appropriate to use speech. An anthropologist, Keith Basso, has pointed out how the Western Apache, for example, have an extremely precise sense of when it is best 'to give up on words'. Thus they will fall silent on occasions such as 'meeting strangers', 'courting', 'children coming home', 'getting cussed out' and 'being with people who are sad'. In the case of courtship, only after several months' steady companionship will a courting couple be expected to begin lengthy conversations. Indeed, a courting couple may stand or sit, sometimes holding hands, for as long as an hour without exchanging a word. Prolonged discussion is thus avoided early in the relationship. Basso comments:

This is especially true for girls, who are informed by their mothers and older sisters that silence in courtship is a sign of modesty and that an eagerness to speak betrays previous experience with men. In extreme cases, they add, it may be interpreted as a willingness to engage in sexual relations. Said one woman, aged 32: 'This way I have talked to my daughter. "Take it easy when boys come around this camp and want you to go somewhere with them. When they talk to you, just listen at first. Maybe you won't know what to say. So don't talk about just anything. If you talk with those boys right away, then they will know you know all about them. They will think you've been with many boys before and they will start talking about that.'" (Basso, 1972, 74)

Ritual put-downs: 'sounding'

Nor is it just a question of different cultures varying in how much and when to talk. Speech itself will be used for characteristically different purposes in different cultures. There are, for instance, certain kinds of linguistic performance in Afro-American and Afro-Caribbean cultures that have no strict parallel in white middle-class culture in either Britain or the US. Black Americans have a speech event called *sounding, signifying*, or *playing the dozens* which involves a ritualized exchange of insults. The insults are highly formalized (sometimes involving rhyming couplets), extravagant, and untrue. Black teenage youths in New York draw on a wide range of formats, a range which can only be suggested by the following:

(1) *Your mother is (like)*
'Your mother look like Flipper.'
'Your mother's a rubber dick.'
(2) *Your mother got*
'Your mother got braces between her legs.'
'Your mother got three titties: chocolate milk, white milk and one half and half.'
(3) *Your mother raised you (on)*
'Your mother raised you on ugly milk.'
'Your mother raised you with big lips.'
Source: Labov (1972c, 309–19).

Many other formats exist (including absurd and bizarre ones such as 'Your mother play dice with the midnight mice'), the skill being to match or top your opponent with an appropriately selected 'sound' or insult which denigrates your opponent's origins (mother, occasionally father) or current circumstances (house, living conditions). This leads to rounds of insults between players, each successful sound being greeted with laughter or approving comment (e.g. 'Oh lord!', 'Oh shit!'), in such a way that the exchange typically produces clear winners and losers. Indeed, status within the male peer group is often linked to skill at sounding. A crucial feature of its performance, however, is that the insults are ritual and not personal – they are not to be intended or taken literally. Remarks that border on the personal are ruled out of court.

Ritual build-ups: boasting

Whereas ritual insults put down the recipient, *boasting* in the Caribbean 'builds up' the speaker. Just as in sounding, however, the practice of boasting revolves around extravagant claims, some highly formalized, with no necessary respect for the truth. They are, for instance, a typical component of self-introductions at speech competitions called singing meetings. One particular competitor would introduce himself on the way to the podium with quatrains such as:

> I am the champion of champions
> From my head to my toes
> I must remain a champion
> Wherever I goes.

They have also filtered into calypso, from which the following instance is taken:

> Is me the village ram
> I don't give a damn
> If any woman say that I
> Leave she dissatisfy
> She lie, she lie, she lie.

And they may occur in more everyday contexts, of which the following is an instance:

> mi no ke wa mi du
> kaz mi big, mi bad an mi buos
> an mi jain di polis fuos
>
> (I don't care what I do,
> because I'm big, I'm bad and I'm the boss,
> and I join the police force)

The boxer Mohammed Ali's early rhyming declamations such as:

I am the greatest!
I fly like a butterfly, sting like a bee;
and I'll knock him out in round three.

which produced such conflicting responses in his public, probably had their source in speech events such as boasting.

It is not the case, of course, that members of the white middle classes of Britain or America never boast or insult each other: quite clearly they do. And probably quite a bit of conversational work in certain circles goes into building oneself up obliquely and putting the other person down. But there are not easily identifiable verbal rituals for doing so in a way that is partly informal artistic performance and partly the displacement of interpersonal tension in an extravagant, semi-humorous and verbally dexterous fashion.

Nor equally is it the case that users of Black English only ever build themselves up or put others down in ritual fashion. The oblique and indirect boast or put-down in ordinary conversation can work for them too. But it probably is enlivened by the background presence of the ritual tradition. The following account very neatly illustrates both the boast and the put-down played out one against the other in an off-the-cuff interchange:

A man coming from the bathroom forgot to zip his pants. An unescorted party of women kept watching him and laughing among themselves. The man's friends hip [inform] him to what's [sic] going on. He approaches one woman – 'Hey, baby, did you see that big Cadillac with the full tires, ready to roll in action just for you?' She answers, 'No, mother fucker, but I saw a little gray Volkswagen with two flat tires.' (Kochman, 1969, 27)

The man's boasting question has been turned by the woman to provide the basis for a precisely matched put-down. The term signifying, which we previously mentioned as an alternative term for sounding, is also used to refer to this kind of elegant and witty, sharp and funny backchat, so that two types of talk are clearly seen to be related. It may well be that what we see in examples such as these is a greater emphasis on speech as a focus of entertainment, of aesthetic display and personal assertion among the Black subcultures of America and the Caribbean.

Conclusion

Thus we can see that talk can enter the everyday communicative economy of different cultures in subtly different ways. It can carry different kinds of communicative loads and pressures from culture to culture: and it can be used for doing different kinds of things between people in the different cultures. In this way it opens up for its users differing modes of relatedness, differing ways of connecting. In some cultures the emphasis may be more on talk as a form of artistic and personal display, but this will depend upon specialized speaking practices, the presence of which in turn will favour particular ways of relating. But each culture will mould, and be moulded by, the interactive possibilities of its favoured ways of talking. For in the last analysis, of course, relationships are made in talk, are made by doing things with words, and it is in this respect that 'word is a two-sided act . . . a bridge thrown between myself and another'.

Background sources and further reading

In preparing this chapter, I have drawn freely but selectively on three distinct (but sometimes overlapping) traditions of work: discourse analysis, conversational analysis, and the ethnography of speaking.

Discourse analysis

Although originating in linguistics, this tradition focuses not so much on what goes into making up an utterance, but rather on how utterances fit together to constitute a discourse. Discourse analysis, then, does not break an utterance (or sentence) down into smaller units but sees it as a whole entity in itself contributing to larger-scale patterns or structures of linguistic organization. 'The fundamental problem of discourse analysis', as one notable scholar in the field has put it, 'is to show how one utterance follows another in a rational, rule-governed manner – in other words how we understand coherent discourse' (Labov, 1970). The tradition is represented by work such as the following:

Labov, W. (1970) 'The study of language in its social context', *Studium Generale*, vol. 23, 66–84. Reprinted in Giglioli, P.P. (ed.) *Language and Social Context*, Harmondsworth: Penguin.

See especially the section 'Some invariant rules of discourse analysis'.

Labov, W. (1972) 'Rules for ritual insults', in Labov, W. *Language in the Inner City: Studies in the Black English Vernacular*, Philadelphia: University of Pennsylvania Press.

Labov, W. and Fanshel, D. (1977) *Therapeutic Discourse: Psychotherapy as Conversation*, London: Academic Press.

Sinclair, J. McH. and Coulthard, R.M. (1975) *Towards an Analysis of Discourse: the English Used by Teachers and Pupils*, Oxford: Oxford University Press.

For an adept summary of Sinclair and Coulthard which signposts its intellectual antecedents, see:

Burton, D. (1981) 'The sociolinguistic analysis of spoken discourse', in French, P. and MacLure, M. (eds) *Adult–Child Conversation*, London: Croom Helm.

For developments based on Sinclair and Coulthard see:

Coulthard, M. and Montgomery, M.M. (eds) (1981) *Studies in Discourse Analysis*, London: Routledge & Kegan Paul.

For an overview of different kinds of work in discourse analysis

Coulthard, M. (1977) *An Introduction to Discourse Analysis*, London: Longman.

Halliday, M.A.K. and Hasan, R. (1989) *Language, Context, and Text: Aspects of Language in a Social-Semiotic Perspective*, Oxford: Oxford University Press.

Stubbs, M. (1983) *Discourse Analysis: the Sociolinguistic Analysis of Natural Language*, Oxford: Basil Blackwell.

Conversational analysis

This tradition of work originates in sociology – in particular in ethnomethodology. Exponents of conversational analysis study conversation as a rich source of observable material on how members of society achieve orderliness in their everyday interactions with each other. They view conversations as jointly constructed, practical accomplishments, and seek to display from the close analysis of transcribed data the methods adopted by participants in achieving this orderliness – the conversational structures to which participants attend, the interpretive work which they undertake. Important papers in conversational analysis are collected in:

Atkinson, J. and Heritage, J. (eds) (1984) *Structure of Social Action: Studies in Conversation Analysis*, Cambridge: Cambridge University Press.

Psathas, G. (ed.) (1979) *Everyday Language: Studies in Ethnomethodology*, New York: Irvington.

Schenkein, J. (ed.) (1978) *Studies in the Organization of Conversational Interaction*, New York: Academic Press.

Sudnow, D. (ed.) (1972) *Studies in Social Interaction*, New York: Free Press.

See also papers by Sacks and Schegloff in:

Gumperz, J. and Hymes, D. (eds) (1972) *Directions in Sociolinguistics*, New York: Holt, Rinehart & Winston.

Turner, R. (ed.) (1974) *Ethnomethodology*, Harmondsworth: Penguin.

For a sustained application of the method to transcripts of court proceedings see:

Atkinson, J.M. and Drew, P. (1979) *Order in Court*, London: Macmillan.

Discourse and conversational analysts are interested in essentially similar phenomena, but often see their respective approaches as distinct, even incompatible. Discourse analysis is interested in verbal interaction as a manifestation of the linguistic order and is concerned to describe and explain it in terms of comprehensive models of utterance-exchange. It has tended to concentrate mostly on institutional settings. Conversational analysis is more concerned with verbal interaction as instances of the situated social order. It eschews the practice of setting up general models of analysis and undertakes instead to characterize small-scale local features of conversational organization, e.g. preferred responses to compliments. For collections that include papers from both camps (and elsewhere) see:

French, P. and MacLure, M. (eds) (1981) *Adult–Child Conversation*, London: Croom Helm.
Werth, P. (ed.) (1981) *Conversation and Discourse*, London: Croom Helm.

An extremely well-informed and thoughtful account of both approaches – critical of discourse analysis – may be found in:

Levinson, S. (1983) *Pragmatics*, Cambridge: Cambridge University Press.
Schiffrin, D. (1994) *Approaches to Discourse*, Oxford: Blackwell.

The ethnography of speaking

This tradition of work probably owes most to anthropology, in as much as it is particularly occupied with questions of cross-cultural differences in speaking practices and the degree to which language enters differently into the life of different societies to sustain and reproduce them. Important papers in this tradition may be found in:

Bauman, R. and Sherzer, J. (eds) (1974) *Explorations in the Ethnography of Speaking*, Cambridge: Cambridge University Press.
Gumperz, J. (ed.) (1985) *Discourse Processes*, Vols 1 & 2, Cambridge: Cambridge University Press.
Gumperz, J. and Hymes, D. (eds) (1972) *Directions in Sociolinguistics*, New York: Holt, Rinehart & Winston.
Hymes, D. (ed.) (1964) *Language in Culture and Society*, New York: Harper & Row.

For overviews of this work see:

Hymes, D. (1974) *Foundations in Sociolinguistics: an Ethnographic Approach*, Philadelphia: University of Pennsylvania Press.

Saville-Troike, M. (1982) *The Ethnography of Communication: an Introduction*, Oxford: Basil Blackwell.

Fieldwork projects

(1) The following text (a transcribed request by phone for an appointment to see the doctor) is drawn from a discussion of discourse structure in Halliday and Hasan (1989). See if you can specify which of the numbered elements are optional within the total discourse, which elements are obligatory? Consider also if any of the elements can be reordered. By this means see if you can specify what role the elements are playing within the overall discourse.

RECEPTIONIST: good morning	1
Dr Scott's clinic	2
may I help you	3
CALLER: oh hello	4
good morning	5
this is Mrs Lee speaking	6
I wonder if I can see Dr Scott today	7
RECEPTIONIST: um well	8
let me see	9
I'm afraid Mrs Lee I don't have much choice of time today	10
would 6.15 this evening suit you	11
CALLER: yes yes	12
that'll be fine	13
RECEPTIONIST: may I have your address and phone number please	14
	15
CALLER: 24 May Avenue, North Clyde and the number is 527.2755	16
RECEPTIONIST: thank you	17
so that's Mrs Lee for Dr Scott at 6.15 this evening	18
CALLER: mm	19
yes thanks	20
RECEPTIONIST: thank you ma'am	21

(2) Identify a type of encounter (e.g. some kind of service encounter) that recurs fairly frequently and is usually of restricted duration. Record and transcribe a set of them – say five or six – and see if you can delineate its basic structure. What seem to be the minimal recurring elements for accomplishing this type of encounter?

PART FOUR
LANGUAGE AND REPRESENTATION

Consciousness takes shape and being in the
material of signs created by an organized
group in the process of its social intercourse.
The individual consciousness is nurtured on
signs; it derives its growth from them; it
reflects their logic and laws.

(Volosinov*)

*Volosinov, V.N. (1973) *Marxism and the Philosophy of Language*, London:
Seminar Press.

11 LANGUAGE AND REPRESENTATION

We see and hear and otherwise experience very largely as we do because the language habits of our community predispose certain choices of interpretation.

(Edward Sapir*)

We dissect nature along lines laid down by our native languages. . . .We cut nature up, organize it into concepts, and ascribe significances as we do, largely because we are parties to an agreement to organize it in this way – an agreement that holds throughout our speech community and is codified in the patterns of our language.

(Benjamin Lee Whorf*)

Language and representation

Language enables us to talk *with* each other. At the same time it enables us to talk *about something*. It provides us with not just a mode of interaction, but also with a capacity for representation.

*Sapir, E. (1949) *Selected Writings of Edward Sapir in Language, Culture and Personality*, edited by Mandelbaum, D.G., Berkeley: University of California Press.
*Whorf, B.L. (1956) *Language, Thought and Reality: Selected Writings*, edited by Carroll, J.B., California: MIT Press.

In the foregoing chapter we considered some of the interpersonal possibilities of language. Here we turn (in the terms of chapter 2) to the *ideational* possibilities of language. It is these which provide us with the means for apprehending and comprehending, to ourselves and with others, the world in which we live.

We are immediately faced, however, with a fundamental question: do all human languages represent the world in the same way; or do different languages (by virtue of their different vocabularies and structures) provide different ways of experiencing and understanding the world, rather as different kinds of speaking practice make possible different modes of interpersonal relationship?

Two conflicting positions: the 'universalist' versus the 'relativist'

Fundamentally, we can understand the way in which language represents the world to us, in terms of two opposing positions. According to one view, human beings generally (whatever their culture or language) are endowed with a common stock of basic concepts – 'conceptual primes' as they are sometimes known – out of which more elaborate conceptual systems and patterns of thought can be constructed. Language, according to this view, is merely a vehicle for expressing the conceptual system which exists independently of it. And, because all conceptual systems share a common basis, all languages turn out to be fundamentally similar. They will all, for instance, find some way of expressing such conceptual primes as relative height (e.g. 'up', 'down'), relative distance (e.g. 'near', 'far'), relative time (e.g. 'now', 'then'). According to this position, thought determines language; and consequently separate languages represent the world in closely equivalent ways. We might characterize this view as the 'universalist' position.

The alternative position maintains that thought is difficult to separate from language; each is woven inextricably into the other. Concepts can only take shape if and when we have the words and structures in which to express them. Thinking depends crucially upon language. Because the vocabularies and structures of separate languages can vary so widely, it makes no sense to posit conceptual primes of a universal nature. Indeed, it is not at all likely that different languages represent the world in equivalent ways. On the contrary, habitual users of one language will experience and understand the world in ways peculiar to that language and different from those of habitual users of another language. The latter viewpoint might be termed the 'relativist' position.

Vocabulary differences between languages

In support of the relativist position it is clear that the continuum of experience is differently dissected by the vocabularies of different languages. The Hopi Indians of North America have one word '*masalytaka*' to designate all flying objects (apart from birds). Thus, they actually call an insect, an aeroplane, and an aviator by the same word, where English provides quite separate lexical items. And on the other hand, where we have at most three lexical items to distinguish types of snow ('snow', 'slush', 'blizzard'), Eskimos have at least five, in order to distinguish between 'falling snow', 'wind-driven flying snow', 'snow on the ground', 'snow packed hard like ice', and 'melting snow'.

Even quite closely related languages make distinctions in experience in different ways. French, for example, makes a distinction between a river which flows into a river ('*rivière*') and one which flows into the sea ('*fleuve*'), a distinction which has no lexical counterpart in English where the same word 'river' is used in both cases. On the other hand in French the word '*mouton*' is used to designate both 'sheep' and 'sheep's meat prepared for the table'.

Some of the most striking differences between the vocabulary of separate languages are displayed in their use of colour terms. Whereas English operates with eleven basic colour terms ('black', 'white', 'red', 'green', 'yellow', 'blue', 'brown', 'purple', 'pink', 'orange' and 'grey'), some languages operate with more, some with fewer. Russian and Hungarian, for example, deploy twelve, the former making a distinction between two types of blue, the latter between two types of red. The Philippine language of Hanunoo, however, makes do with four basic colour terms:

(*ma*)*biru*	=	black, dark tints of other colours
(*ma*)*lagti*?	=	white, light tints of other colours
(*ma*)*rara*	=	maroon, red, orange
(*ma*)*latuy*	=	light green, yellow, and light brown

And Jale, a language of the New Guinea highlands, basically makes do with one term for white, one for black. The way in which the colour spectrum is segmented can thus vary quite dramatically from language to language.

Grammatical differences between languages

However, the really fundamental differences between languages operate at a further level than that of vocabulary: they operate within the grammar of the language itself. Thus, differences between languages may be found in the way they are structurally patterned to handle such basic notions as time, cause and effect, agency, spatial relations, and so on. The linguist with whom the relativist claim is most associated – Benjamin Lee Whorf – argued, for example, that time is handled very differently in English than in Hopi. Whereas English grammar provides for at least two tenses, Hopi seems to have none. Instead, its verb forms distinguish between what is subjective and what is objective, the subjective form including both the future and everything that is 'mental'. Nor does Hopi seem to distinguish between distance in time and distance in space.

This does not make English a better language than Hopi, since Hopi makes other distinctions that are lacking in English. (Indeed, Whorf said English compared to Hopi was 'like a bludgeon compared to a rapier'.) But it did lead Whorf to propose:

> a new principle of relativity, which holds that all observers are not led by the same physical evidence to the same picture of the universe, unless their linguistic backgrounds are similar, or can in some way be calibrated. . . . Users of markedly different grammars are pointed by their grammars toward different types of observations and different evaluations of externally similar acts of observation, and hence are not equivalent as observers but must arrive at somewhat different views of the world. (Whorf, 1956, 214, 221)

Difficulties in the relativist position

Over forty years have elapsed since Whorf originally wrote these words. Yet, with occasional shifts in the terms of debate, controversy around these issues has remained strong ever since. Evaluating the respective merits of the relativist and universalist positions would really require a book in its own right. There are, it must be admitted, certain basic difficulties in the relativist position. In its extreme form it assumes distinctions in experience and understanding on the basis of linguistic distinctions. So it assumes, for example, that Russians experience the colour spectrum, particularly in the domain of 'blueness', rather differently than English speakers do, because the linguistic terms are different. It assumes, for example, that because the Hopi linguistic system of tense differs from our own, therefore they must have a different understanding of time. But evidence to establish incontrovertibly these supposed differences in experience and understanding has been notoriously difficult to come by. And if one reconsiders the Eskimo example, it is not difficult to see why. There may only be in English three individual lexical items that relate in particular to 'snowness'; but it does not necessarily follow that these three items thereby exhaust our capacity to distinguish a range of different types of 'snowness'. An English speaker may well be sensitive in experience to differences in 'snowness' ranging through, for example, fine powdery snow, hard-packed snow, deep-lying snow, and so on, even when the language lacks a single separate word for each kind of separate 'snowness' condition.

Any claim, therefore, that we can experience *only* that for which our native language provides explicit categories and distinctions proves difficult to sustain. In certain circumstances we can always think our way around the edges of the categories supplied by our own language, and in this respect language is not an absolute strait-jacket – it does not totally constrain our ways of seeing and experiencing. For these and other reasons I would wish to avoid espousing a simple and total linguistic determinism. I would still want to claim, however, that language plays an active and crucial – if qualified – role in shaping (though not completely determining) the processes of representation, by 'pointing us toward different types of observation' and 'predisposing certain choices of interpretation'.

It should be noted, of course, that it is easiest to describe the outlines of the relativist position by comparing one discrete and usually remote language with another. In practice, languages rarely, if ever, turn out to be uniform entities – as we saw in part two. They are subject to quite wide ranges of internal variation – by social class, by age, by area, and so on. They are also subject to situational specialization – advertising, legal, medical language, and so on. Relativism can be seen otherwise than purely in terms of the shift from language to language (the precise boundaries of which are difficult to define anyway); it can also be seen as implicated in the shift from variety to variety. The way one variety, such as a social dialect, or indeed an anti-language, depicts the world will often involve subtle differences in mode of representation. So much so that, concerning evaluative reactions to accents, it has been commented that people are not so much reacting to the sound in itself, but rather to the sound as socially symbolic of a different way of looking at the world. 'I don't like his accent' amounts to a deeper sense of mistrust of the preferred modes of representation that habitually go with that pattern of pronunciation.

The 'interested' character of linguistic representation

What the relativist position emphasizes, then, despite certain difficulties associated with it, is that the world is not given to us directly and straightforwardly in experience. In apprehending, comprehending and representing the world we inevitably draw upon linguistic formulations. One might say that because of this we always see it slightly askew. But it is not so much a question of bias that is at stake here. What it amounts to in fact is that there is no absolutely neutral and disinterested way of apprehending and representing the world. Language always helps to select, arrange, organize, and evaluate experience, even when we are least conscious of it doing so. In this sense representation is always interested: the words chosen are selected from a determinate set for the situation at hand and have been previously shaped by the community, or by those parts of it, to which the speaker belongs.

Vocabulary and the depiction of gender

We can see something of the interested nature of representation by looking at the distribution of English vocabulary items around the notions of 'woman' and 'man', 'female' and 'male'. In a study (Stanley, 1977), based primarily on American English, it was found, for example, that there were more words for men than there were for women. Despite this kind of imbalance, however, there were many more words for a woman in her sexual aspect than there were for a sexually active man. Thus, for women there are in excess of 200 expressions such as 'bint', 'judy', 'tart', 'skirt', 'piece', 'bitch', 'tight-bitch', 'slag', 'scrubber', 'piece-of-ass', 'cunt', 'bird', 'broad', 'lay', 'pick-up', 'prick-teaser', and so on. Many of the terms sound pejorative. An equivalent list for men is much more difficult to compile, but would include less than fifty items such as 'stud', 'dirty old man', 'randy old goat', 'philanderer', 'Casanova', 'trick', 'lecher', and so on. Not only are there fewer of them in total but proportionally less of them are explicitly pejorative. Some, indeed, have positive overtones.

Why should 'woman-as-sexual-being' require such a proliferation of lexical items? Such terms can hardly be said to be representing reality in disinterested ways. Indeed, it would clearly be wrong to suppose that there is anything in the sexual nature of women themselves that warrants such an accumulation of codings. The items themselves, of course, give some kind of clue to their origins. They mostly have resonances of certain all-male subcultures: the adolescent male peer group, the locker-room and the building-site subculture. As such they are more likely to be used by men of women than by women of women. Also, there is an overriding tendency in items of this type towards metonymic representation, where a part is made to stand for the whole: it can be an anatomic element ('ass', 'cunt'); or an element of dress ('skirt'); it can be an element of the act itself ('lay', 'screw'); or a preliminary to it ('pick-up'). The cumulative effect of these metonyms is to objectify and depersonalize in a reductive fashion.

Obviously, not all men necessarily use such items. And those that do so will probably use them only in certain restricted contexts. And even then, the items will not always and inevitably be used in a reductive and objectifying fashion. But the presence in the language of such a skewed distribution of lexical items generates and confirms a pressure in favour of modes of representation that ultimately help to portray women as a commodity for consumption (e.g. 'tart').

A similar pattern of representation seems to be in play around paired items in the language, where by derivation the pairs were once roughly equivalent in meaning except for a difference in gender. Such pairs include the following:

bachelor	spinster
courtier	courtesan
king	queen
lord	lady
master	mistress
sir	madam

Thus, one meaning for 'king' and 'queen' is monarch or sovereign, male and female respectively. But, whereas the former has retained exclusively its honorific orientation towards pre-eminent', the latter item is now available for use in designating 'a male homosexual who dresses and acts effeminately', in which sense it is quite likely to be used derogatorily. Similarly, 'master' and 'mistress' could once be used equivalently to refer to the male and female heads of a household. More recently, however, mistress came to be used almost exclusively to designate 'kept woman' or 'illicit lover'. In like manner 'courtesan' now refers exclusively to 'high class prostitute'; and 'madam' is just as likely to refer to 'woman brothel keeper', unless it is being used of a child ('she's a right little madam') in which case it carries derogatory overtones of pertness and conceit. All these items once helped to map an area of meaning to do with social rank and position. They still do, despite social shifts away from courtly hierarchies. As boundaries become blurred, however, what we find typically is the male term retaining some, at least, of its status characteristics, but the female term in a pair becoming increasingly open to pejorative usage or usage for non-status-marked positions.

It is quite normal, of course, for words to change their meaning. Nor is it at all unusual for some words in some situations to be

used for pejorative purposes. It is striking, however, that words associated with women should be consistently downgraded in this way.
Such a tendency lends support to the claim that English, at least,
is systematically skewed to represent women as the 'second sex'.

Vocabulary and the depiction of nuclear 'weaponry'

Another way in which we can see the interested nature of representation is by examining the vocabulary that emerges in the area
of modern warfare and nuclear weaponry in particular. Inspecting
the range of expressions reveals certain kinds of regularity in their
formation. First of all there is a set of pseudo-technical expressions
such as 'delivery system', 'circular error probable', 'collateral damage', 'flexible response', 'dual-key system', and so on. At first sight
they seem to have the status of specialized terms developed to serve
rational analysis, calculation, and debate. On closer inspection they
prove instead to be obscurantist and euphemistic, creating an
illusory sense of precision. Thus:

To mount a strike – to attack (and, if nuclear weapons are used,
    presumably to destroy)
A surgical strike – destroying an individual target
A pre-emptive strike – destroying the enemy first to prevent their
    destroying you (otherwise known as 'getting your retaliation in
    first')
Flexible response – the capacity to deliver all types of strike; ration-
    alization for more, and more varied, nuclear weaponry
Strategic nuclear weapon – 'large' nuclear bomb of immense
    destructive power
Tactical nuclear weapon – 'small' nuclear bomb of immense destruc-
    tive power
Enhanced radiation weapon – neutron bomb (destroys people, not
    property)
Demographic targeting – killing the civilian population
Collateral damage – killing the civilian population
Throw-weight – destructive power
Circular error probable – likely proportion of missiles to land within
    a designated zone

Generally such expressions have the effect of anaesthetizing one to the full reality being referred to. Many such expressions, of course, are susceptible to lettered abbreviation such as the following:

ICBM	Inter-Continental Ballistic Missile
SLBM	Submarine-Launched Ballistic Missile
ABM	Anti-Ballistic Missile
ERW	Enhanced Radiation Weapon
TNW	Theatre Nuclear Weapon

Sometimes the lettered abbreviations can be pronounced as a single syllable to give acronyms such as:

MIRV	Multiple Independently-targeted Re-entry Vehicle
SALT	Strategic Arms Limitation Talks
PAL	Permissive Active Link
START	Strategic Arms Reduction Talks
MAD	Mutually Assured Destruction

While the use of abbreviations and acronyms is a fairly generalized process in the language, in this case it serves to insulate yet further the expression from the reality it designates.

One term conspicuously absent from recent official discourse about nuclear weaponry is the term 'bomb'. There are many ways of referring to the devices which engender such explosions. They may be referred to as the nuclear arsenal; or as nuclear devices, warheads, missiles, weapons, weaponry or armaments; but they are rarely, if ever, referred to as 'bombs'. To do so would now sound rather archaic or even melodramatic. Yet it is curious that this should be the case. It might be argued that 'bombs' by definition need to be dropped from aircraft, and since so little modern nuclear weaponry is designed to be delivered in this way the term has consequently become obsolete. But 'bomb' has never been thus restricted in its usage. It is still used currently in media accounts to refer to objects and events such as 'the embassy bombing', 'car bombs', 'bomb factory', 'sectarian bombings', 'bomb disposal experts', 'petrol bomb', none of which need necessarily imply aircraft. According to the dictionary, 'bombs' may even be delivered by artillery fire, as in 'bombshell'. Furthermore, in 1944 when London was hit by several rocket propelled projectiles – the V1 and the V2 – they were known then as 'flying bombs'. Indeed, the V1, because of its characteristic sound, was known by the general public as the 'buzz bomb'. These weapons were direct forerunners of current missile systems. Indeed, the V1 flying bomb might well be seen as a prototype for today's cruise missile. But, whereas the earlier weapon could be described as a 'bomb', the preferred term now is clearly 'missile'.

Various factors might underlie the abandonment of the term 'bomb' from official discourses on nuclear weapons. For one thing, the word 'bomb' tends to stress explosive and destructive properties. It can also be used for both the action and the entity, as both verb and noun, as in 'we bombed Hiroshima', and in 'the Hiroshima bomb'. Indeed it provides the stem for various cognate forms such as 'bombers' and 'bombing'. In this respect the name for the entity implies also both the action and someone to perform it. By contrast, the items that are selected turn out to be either non-specific, general terms such as 'weaponry', 'armaments', 'arsenal', or terms that emphasize technological sophistication ('device') or method of delivery ('missile', 'vehicle'), rather than destructive power. In none of these instances is there any suggestion either of action or of someone to perform it.

Indeed, in recent times, if ever the term 'bomb' has been used in a nuclear context by members of the defence establishments on either side of the Atlantic, they have probably come to regret having done so on public relations grounds. On two occasions in particular its use has provoked sharp reactions. The first occasion involved attempts to win acceptance for basing a new 'battlefield nuclear weapon' in Europe. It was a weapon that, by its high level of radiation, was designed to destroy people, not property; and it was called – unusually – 'the neutron *bomb*'. The idea of the weapon was found offensive by even moderate opinion in Europe ('the ultimate capitalist weapon' as one commentator, somewhat sardonically, referred to it). Such adverse reactions prompted a high-ranking British officer on a late-night current affairs programme to lament the public relations ineptitude of calling it a 'bomb' at all. He argued that there would have been much less opposition to it if it had been presented from the outset as an 'Enhanced Radiation Weapon', or ERW for short. And in official circles, at least, that – not surprisingly – is how it came to be known.

Another case involved President Ronald Reagan making impromptu jokes in front of the microphone, while warming up for his weekly radio broadcast. He announced that he had signed legislation that would outlaw Russia for ever: 'We begin bombing in five minutes.' The joke appalled many, the reference to 'bombing' only serving to increase its offensiveness.

Otherwise, of course, we find distinctions being made within the abstract generality of nuclear weaponry by the use of various code names and nicknames. These in themselves can prove noteworthy, as may be seen from the following examples:

FAT MAN – uranium bomb detonated over Hiroshima
LITTLE BOY – plutonium bomb detonated over Nagasaki
HONEST JOHN – short-range missile from the 1950s
MINUTEMAN – long-range missile
TOMAHAWK – cruise missile
PERSHING – medium-range missile
TRIDENT – submarine-launched missile
POSEIDON – largest American submarine-launched missile
POLARIS – submarine-launched missile
TITAN – largest American missile of the 1950s
THOR – medium-range American missile of the 1950s and 1960s
SKYBOLT – missile project cancelled in the 1960s
VULCAN – British long-range nuclear bomber

Some terms draw on national folklore. Thus, the name *Minuteman* (an American long-range missile) originally referred to members of the heroic militia of the American War of Independence who earned their title by virtue of their ability to turn out at a minute's notice. *Tomahawk* (the cruise missile) has resonances of the frontier days of American history. *Fat Man* and *Little Boy* sound curiously and inappropriately like Laurel and Hardy.

Other terms tend to be drawn from classical mythology, particularly from those myths in which figures with divine or supernatural powers are depicted. Thus, *Poseidon* (the submarine-launched missile) is named after the Greek god of the sea, who (as an encyclopedia of mythology puts it):

was master not only of the sea but of the lakes and rivers. In a sense even the earth belonged to him, since it was sustained by his waters and he could shake it at will. Indeed, during the war with the Giants he split mountains with his *trident* [another submarine launched missile] and rolled them into the sea to make the first islands. . . . Often . . . the appearance of *Poseidon* was accompanied by wild tempests, a manifestation of the god's furious rage. (*New Larousse Encyclopedia of Mythology*, 1968, 133; emphases added)

The *Titan* (largest American missile of the 1950s) derives its name from the early race of gods who waged war on Zeus after he had supplanted them. In the struggle between Zeus and the Titans:

The fertile earth shuddered and burned; vast forests flamed and all things melted and boiled . . . sky and earth were confounded, the earth shaken on its very foundations, the sky crashing down from its heights. Such was the mighty uproar of this battle among the gods!

Finally defeated by Zeus, they were 'cast into the abysmal depths of the earth' (ibid., 92).

Vulcan (British nuclear bomber) was one of the oldest of the Latin gods. In his earliest forms he 'possessed warlike functions and may have preceded Mars as god of battles. . . . [He] was god of the thunderbolt and of the sun, then the god of fires.' His son, finding doubts being cast on his paternity at a public games held in his honour, invoked his father 'and the crowd was immediately surrounded by flames' (ibid., 205).

Thus, it may be clearly seen that the mythical figures who have been drawn upon are distinguished by their awesome destructive power. To some extent then, the re-introduction of their names into the sphere of nuclear weaponry seems to have been done with a certain grotesque appropriateness. At the same time, however, the names are quite mystificatory, since they consistently tend to 'super-naturalize' the weapons, depicting them in ways which help to remove them conceptually from processes which involve human agency and technical inventiveness. These same weapons, however, are designed, developed and produced for profit by large armaments industries. There is, presumably, a human finger on the button.

One cannot help but sense, therefore, some crucial abdication of human responsibility and control in this naming process, which reinterprets modern nuclear weapons in terms of heroic supernatural struggles as played out by the gods of the myths of antiquity.

These two areas, then, help us to see something of the interested character of representation. The selection of items, the emergence of a specialized vocabulary, its establishment as the currency of discussion and debate, none of these processes can be understood as neutral and disinterested. Indeed, more important than the individual lexical items is the way in which they build into complex but, as we have seen, systematically patterned vocabularies. This process does not have to be a matter of conscious contrivance for it to have important consequences for thought, understanding and action.

Sentences and representation

It is not just lexical items, however, that have fundamental consequences for the mode of representation. Also crucial is the structured arrangement of such items into utterances, in part at least because we are even less conscious about choice of structure than we generally are about choice of words. Linguistic structure is built up out of the basic patterns that utterances must conform to if they are to be meaningful. Some of these patternings have to do with representing time, some with reporting speech, and so on. One particularly crucial set of patterns (as we saw in chapter 1) is concerned with representing actions and their concomitant persons and circumstances. The domain of linguistic structure constituted by these patterns is known primarily as *transitivity* – basically, for any one clause, 'who (or what) does what to whom (or what)'.

Transitivity

Exploring an example may help to illustrate the notion of *transitivity*. Imagine a situation involving two entities (in this case, persons), one of them a policeman, the other a miner. Let us further suppose that in this hypothetical situation one entity (person) has placed the other under legal restraint one day prior in time to the moment of utterance. What we have so far specified about the situation thus includes two *entities* ('miner', 'policeman'), an *action* or *process* ('arrest') and information concerning the *circumstances* of the action. If these elements are brought together into an utterance, the most likely form it would take would be:

(1) The policeman arrested the miner yesterday.

This, of course, is not the only possible arrangement the items can take. Other possible arrangements are:

(2) Yesterday the policeman arrested the miner.
(3) The policeman yesterday arrested the miner.

Apart from some slight shifts in emphasis, no one of these forms differs significantly from the others in meaning. They all crucially convey the proposition that 'the policeman' is an *agent* with respect to a *process*, 'arrest'; and the 'miner' is the *affected* entity with respect to that same *process*. Further alteration of the order in which the items are arranged is likely either to produce nonsense such as:

(4) The yesterday policeman miner the arrested.

Or, it is likely to result in some quite fundamental change in meaning that would really imply a totally different situation, as in:

(5) The miner arrested the policeman yesterday.

In this last example the roles of *agent* and *affected* have been reversed, so that 'the miner' becomes the *agent* of the *action* and 'the policeman' the *affected* entity. But, of course, we are now in a very different, somewhat anomalous, but just conceivable situation of a miner performing a citizen's arrest on an errant policeman.

These examples, with the exception of (4), display a common relationship in English of one entity (the *agent*) acting upon another (the *affected*), in which the respective roles are signalled partly by word order. It is perhaps the most fundamental type of transitivity relation, though by no means the only one. (In chapter 1 we saw some of the other possibilities as they were being developed by the child.)

The passive

In fact, the particular kind of relationship which we have been considering can be represented in English by an alternative ordering of items in which the *agent* no longer comes before the *process*, as long as other elements are added in the course of the rearrangement. Thus:

(1) | The policeman | arrested | the miner | yesterday. |
    | *agent* | *process* | *affected* | *circumstance* |

can become:

(6) | The miner | was arrested | by the policeman | yesterday. |
    | *affected* | *process* | *agent* | *circumstance* |

with little change in meaning, although the two constructions are clearly very different. The first (1) is the *active* form, and the second (6) is the *passive*. The *passive* construction has in effect, by expanding the *process* to include 'was' and by introducing 'by' alongside the *agent*, reversed the order of *agent* and *affected* and allowed the *affected* to come first. Not only may the *affected* come before the *process* in *passive* constructions; the *agent* may remain unspecified, as in:

(7) | The miner | was arrested | yesterday. |
    | *affected* | *process* | *circumstance* |

This allows for subtle differences in focus and emphasis. For instance, (7) might be produced in a context where it was so obvious who had arrested the miner that there was no need to specify it further. Alternatively – to take a slightly different example – a construction such as:

(8) | Three miners | were injured | yesterday. |
    | *affected* | *process* | *circumstance* |

may be used in order to leave the question of *agency* completely unspecified.

Transitivity and the depiction of civil disorder

The *active* and *passive* constructions provide, therefore, alternative patterns for expressing the same basic transitivity relationship. With this in mind we can see how quite crucial shifts of emphasis can emerge in newspaper reports from one paper to another and from

238

day to day. Here are the opening lines of two reports from similar British newspapers of 2 June 1975, both describing the same event:

The Times

> RIOTING BLACKS SHOT DEAD BY POLICE AS ANC LEADERS MEET
> Eleven Africans were shot dead and 15 wounded when Rhodesian police opened fire on a rioting crowd of about 2,000 in the African Highfield township of Salisbury this afternoon.
>
> The shooting was the climax of a day of some violence.

The *Guardian*

> POLICE SHOOT 11 DEAD IN SALISBURY RIOT
> Riot police shot and killed 11 African demonstrators and wounded 15 others here today in the Highfield African township on the outskirts of Salisbury. The number of casualties was confirmed by the police.
>
> Disturbances had broken out. . . .
> *Source*: Trew (1978) 39.

There are some important differences in the selection of lexical items *The Times*, for instance, has 'RIOTING BLACKS' where the *Guardian* refers to 'African demonstrators'. *The Times* refers to 'violence' whereas the *Guardian* refers to 'disturbances'. But probably the most significant differences emerge in the contrasting structures of the headline and opening line from each paper. *The Times* uses the *passive*:

RIOTING BLACKS	SHOT DEAD	BY POLICE
affected	*process*	*agent*

This places in the foreground not so much those who perform the action as those who are on the receiving end of it (described, incidentally, as 'rioting'). The *Guardian*, on the other hand, uses the active construction:

This clearly emphasizes the agency behind the action. Indeed, the *Guardian* report generally makes no attempt to displace responsi-

239

bility away from the police. By contrast, the first line of the *Times* report is not only in the *passive*:

Eleven Africans	were shot dead and	15	wounded
affected	*process* &	*aff*	*process*

the *agent* of the *process* is left unspecified in this clause, to be identified by implication in the next,

when	police	opened fire on	a rioting crowd
	agent	*process*	*affected*

But here, although the police are clearly the agent in an active construction, it is one in which they 'open fire on', a process which is significantly more neutral as to its consequences than 'shooting dead'.

The next day the *Times* printed a report which began as follows:

SPLIT THREATENS ANC AFTER SALISBURY'S RIOTS
After Sunday's riots in which 13 Africans were killed and 28 injured, a serious rift in the ranks of the African National Council became apparent today.

The events of two days before become simply 'riots', in which

13 Africans	were killed	and	28	injured
affected	*process*	&	*aff.*	*process*

The *agent* now remains completely unspecified. This vagueness is reinforced if anything by the selection of 'were killed' rather than 'were shot' which would at least have implied someone to do the shooting. Indeed, in the absence of any specified agent the cause of the deaths could almost be the riots themselves, rather than armed policemen. This kind of shift is in fact not uncommon in media representation of civil disorder. It is a crucial one. In this case it effectively insulates the account from the conditions that produce the rioting. The possibility that they were the outcome of a distorted and frustrating social and political process is consequently closed off from discussion.

Industrial disputes and civil disorder: the miners' strike (1984–5)

The coverage of industrial disputes in the media tends to focus predominantly on the disruptive consequences of strike action, rather than upon the conditions that generate the dispute (see Glasgow University Media Group, 1976, 1980, 1982; and Hartley, 1982). The miners' strike of 1984–5 was no exception in this respect. A significant proportion of the coverage was devoted to reporting the conduct of picketing – mostly at mines, but also at coal depots and docks. The most newsworthy dimension to picketing was, not surprisingly, the degree of violence associated with it, so that papers even quite remote from each other in political sympathy would commonly headline stories as follows:

WORST DAY OF VIOLENCE (*Daily Telegraph*: 19 June 1985)
SCARGILL INJURED IN WORST CLASHES YET (*Morning Star*: 19 June 1985)

However, underlying this common concern with the degree of violence are some quite significant differences. In part, these differences operate in the sphere of vocabulary. The *Daily Mail*, for instance, somewhat distinctively drew on a vocabulary more typically associated with military campaigning – a vocabulary in which pickets 'stage an ambush', demolish a wall for 'ammunition', and 'bombard the police'. The latter undergo a 'barrage', but send in 'the mounted brigade on two flanks' who 'charge dramatically', narrowly missing a 'tank trap', and so on . However, it is not just in the sphere of vocabulary that distinctive traits emerge. There are subtle but significant differences in the way that the respective roles of participants were actually constructed in the syntax of different newspaper accounts, especially – say – when the *Morning Star* on the one hand is compared with the *Daily Mail* and *Telegraph* on the other.

The syntax of 'picketing' and 'policing' in the Daily Mail *and the* Daily Telegraph

The *Daily Telegraph* tended to depict the respective roles of police and pickets in the following way. Where 'police' are focused on as the subject of a clause, it is often in the passive, their role within the clause being that of affected. Thus:

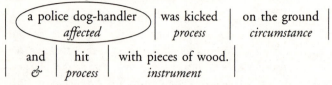

| a police dog-handler
 affected | was kicked
 process | on the ground
 circumstance |

| and
 & | hit
 process | with pieces of wood.
 instrument |

This tendency includes not only police personnel but also their vehicles. Thus:

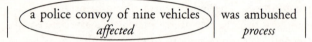

| a police convoy of nine vehicles
 affected | was ambushed
 process |

The tendency is even more marked in the *Daily Mail* where it is extended to include the animals (dogs and horses) used by the police, as can be seen in the following examples:

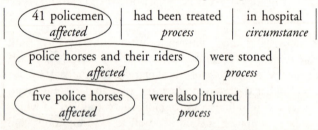

| 41 policemen
 affected | had been treated
 process | in hospital
 circumstance |

| police horses and their riders
 affected | were stoned
 process |

| five police horses
 affected | were |also| injured
 process |

Hence, it was not unusual for a story of 'picket-line violence' in the *Daily Mail* to open as follows (under the headline THE THIN BLUE LINE HOLDS FIRM): 'They were bombarded with stones and bricks, ball bearings and nails, and even fencing staves.' The emphasis, as distributed by the syntax, falls clearly upon the police ('they') as recipients (*affected*) of *action processes* involving a variety of material objects. Interestingly enough, here, as happens quite frequently in those passive clauses which figure the police as *affected*, the *agents* of the action remain unspecified. In context the most obvious inference open to readers would involve attributing *agency* to 'the pickets'.

'Pickets', of course, do figure as overtly specified *agents* in some clauses, these clauses usually being *active* with 'pickets' as subject. Thus:

| (pickets *agent*) | demolished *process* | a wall *affected* |

Or:

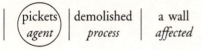

| (pickets *agent*) | bombarded *process* | the police *affected* | with bricks, stones, sticks *instrument* |

The main exception to this tendency may be found in clauses where the process is one of 'arrest', as can be seen in the following examples. Here in both cases 'pickets' occur as *affected* in *passive* constructions where no *agent* is specified.

'About a hundred pickets were arrested.'

'More than 100 miners' pickets were arrested.'

Otherwise we find a basic syntactic patterning whereby 'pickets' on the one hand are inscribed within *action processes* as *agent* often in the *active* voice, thus:

'The pickets started throwing missiles.'

'Police', on the other hand, are often inscribed within *action processes* as *affected*, usually in the *passive* voice, thus:

'One of them [police] was struck by a stone.'

And when the police *do* initiate action it is usually with some reluctance:

'Senior officers, their patience exhausted and fearing for the safety of their men, sent in the mounted brigade on two flanks.'

These are broad tendencies, therefore, in the coverage of picketing in both the *Daily Mail* and the *Daily Telegraph*. But this patterning of linguistic choice is not inevitable or incontestable, as we can see if we consider the habitual patterns of syntactic selection adopted in a paper written from a different perspective.

The syntax of 'picketing' and 'policing' in the Morning Star

In the *Morning Star* we find that the police typically appear as *agents* of *active* clauses, in which case they occupy the position of subject, thus:

| police *agent* | attacked *process* | isolated groups of miners *affected* |

Or:

| fifteen police *agent* | dragged *process* | him *affected* | to a waiting police van *location* |

'Pickets', however, (now more typically referred to as 'miners'), appear not only as *affected* in *active* constructions (as illustrated above), but also quite commonly as *affected* in *passive* constructions, thus:

| several miners *affected* | were hit *process* | with truncheons *instrument* |

Or:

| one miner *affected* | was pounced on *process* | by other policemen *agent* |

If miners/pickets do appear as *agents*, it is frequently in clauses involving some kind of movement or change of location, such as:

| the majority of the pickets *agent* | withdrew *process* | in orderly fashion *circumstance* |

Or:

| the miners *agent* | massed *process* | round the entrance *location* |

Or:

| 3,000 pickets *agent* | yesterday *circumstance* | gathered *process* | outside Cortonwood Colliery *location* |

Overall, then, in the *Morning Star* the emphasis is on the police as agents by the use of clauses where, typically, their actions have clear consequences. The miners, on the other hand, either exercise a limited *agency* in respect of processes involving movement, or appear as *affected* with respect to the actions of the police. All this we find in contrast to the *Daily Mail* and the *Daily Telegraph*, where 'police' tend to figure as *affected* alongside the unrestrained *agency* of

244

'miners'. Thus, the actions of police and pickets are represented in quite contrary ways, involving contrasting patterns of linguistic choice.

One possible reaction to these divergent patterns of linguistic choice is to try and establish which pattern or set of patterns most accurately reflects 'what really happened'. After all, it is clearly possible for accounts actively to distort, misreport and mislead. But my point here is more fundamental than matters of factual accuracy – or even of loaded vocabulary. It is rather that particular linguistic choices (in this case those of *transitivity* and *voice*) make sense of, and give significance to, the phenomenon of picketing in strikingly different ways. Now it might be said that such choices merely reflect contrasting ideological positions with their attendant framework of beliefs and expectations. But I think it is also true that in an important sense such patterns of choice *are* the ideologies and the belief systems. In effect, certain dominant styles of linguistic construction prefer certain ways of seeing and thinking about an event. And the more widely and pervasively a structure circulates, especially in privileged communicative contexts such as mass circulation daily newspapers, the more difficult it becomes to select differently – and hence to see and think differently about the depicted events.

Language in the news: violent men and crimes against women

Take, for instance, accounts in tabloid newspapers of crimes of violence by men against women. A study by Kate Clark (see Toolan (ed.), 1991, pp. 154–78) of reports carried by the *Sun* newspaper in the late 1980s highlights particular kinds of linguistic patterning that tend to shift the blame from the perpetrator to his victim. These patterns operate at the level of both syntax and vocabulary.

Vocabulary for the victim ranges from items that depict the victim in familial (and hence respectable) terms, such as 'bride', 'wife', 'mum', 'housewife', 'daughter', 'mother of two', to items that depict the victim in extra-familial terms, such as 'call-girl', 'Lolita', 'prostitute', 'blonde divorcee', with a range of more neutral (but age-related) terms in between such as 'schoolgirl', 'girl', 'young woman'. The opposite ends of this range of items amount to a contrast between depicting women as either in relationships which are socially approved (mother) or not (Lolita). The perpetrators, on the other hand, are described in terms ranging from the socially neutral (name, occupation) to the extra-human: 'monster', 'fiend', 'beast', 'maniac'.

Two types of contrasting account seem to grow out of the contrast in vocabulary: where the victims are coded neutrally, or as 'respectable', the perpetrator becomes 'extra-human', hence:

DOUBLE MURDER MANIAC PROWLS CITY OF TERROR

or

FIEND STRANGLES ONLY CHILD, 7

Conversely, however, where the victim is coded as disreputable then the 'extra-human' vocabulary is less evident. Compare, for example,

FIEND STRANGLES ONLY CHILD, 7

with

SEX-STARVED SQUADDIE STRANGLED BLONDE, 16
Love ban by teenage wife

The patterning of vocabulary, therefore, tends to exonerate the male perpetrators.

The syntax also contributes to this general tendency in ways similar to those discussed above in the reports of police shootings in southern Africa. It is not unusual for these accounts of male violence to draw upon the *passive voice* with its attendant possibilities for deleting the male *agent* of the action, as in the following headline and lead sentence:

GIRL 7 MURDERED WHILE MUM DRANK AT PUB
Little Nicola Spencer was strangled in her bedsit home – while her Mum was out drinking and playing pool in local pubs.

The headline and the report begins with the *affected*, the girl, and the only *agent* encoded in these two sentences is not the criminal but 'mum', *agent* of a process, 'drank' in the headline – a process further elaborated in the subsequent sentence.

246

This kind of patterning can be seen more clearly over a longer passage such as the following, taken from the *Sun's* account of the actions of a particularly brutal rapist and murderer.

Two of Steed's rape victims – aged 20 and 19 – had a screwdriver held at their throats as they were forced to submit. His third victim a 39 year old mother of three was attacked at gunpoint after Steed forced her car off the M4. Two days later, he gunned down call-girl Jacqueline Murray, 23, after picking her up in London's Park Lane.

We can list the basic clauses of this account as follows:

two victims	had a screwdriver held at their throats
affected	
they	were forced to submit
affected	
a third victim	was attacked at gunpoint
affected	
Steed	forced her car off the M4
agent	
he	gunned down call girl ... after picking her up in Park
agent	Lane

The first three of these clauses are passive constructions which focus on the victims without explicitly encoding the *agent* at all. When Steed does become encoded as the *agent* in the last two clauses it is in relation to forcing a car off the road and then gunning down a call-girl. *Agency*, therefore, is most clearly ascribed to Steed either in relation to an inanimate object (forcing a car) or where the victim is coded as not socially respectable (a call-girl).

These patterns of vocabulary and syntax are part of particular ways of making sense of dreadful events and as such they raise very important questions. Are there, for instance, more appropriate patterns for making sense of these events? If so, why have these patterns prevailed? Whose interests do they serve? Are the same patterns current today?

It is not possible to address all these questions in detail here: the issues they raise are extremely complex. It is hard, however, not to conclude that the overall tendency of these patterns is to make the victim and the crime salient rather than the perpetrator. In cases where the perpetrator *is* made salient it is usually within a super-naturally evil or sub-humanly bestial paradigm – one which has wider currency in popular culture (the film *Silence of the Lambs* would be a case in point) and which treats such violence as by definition exceptional and extraordinary. All the evidence, however, indicates that it is much more common than the beast/fiend paradigm would suggest. Either way, the result is to deflect attention away from men who are violent and from what might be the causes of this violence.

Conclusions

One common kind of reaction to analyses such as those presented above is to raise in various ways issues of intentionality: are those who compose these texts aware of what they are doing? are the patterns planned and deliberate? First of all, it is important to recognize that deliberation and awareness amount to two separate issues. You can be aware of a feature of your linguistic behaviour without deliberately planning it. Take, for instance, a speech impediment such as stammering. Speakers can be painfully aware of it, even to the extend of knowing in advance when it is likely to occur, without deliberately planning it.

However, in the case of the kinds of patterns discussed above questions of deliberation or awareness in their production seem simply to miss the point. For one thing these texts are commonly produced by more than one author. Sub-editors, for instance, routinely re-write copy provided by journalists or press agencies. For another thing, even if it could be decided which writer's intentions were paramount, it is not easy to see how they can be identified reliably: after all, the way in which social actors report their actions and intentions need not always be consistent with their actual actions and intentions. It is not the intention behind these linguistic patterns that counts; it is their intrinsic significance, how they are interpreted, and their effect on patterns of thought and behaviour that matters. Indeed, they may be all the more effective for being unconsciously produced and reproduced. Questions of intention, deliberation and awareness, therefore, are irrelevant.

Another common kind of reaction is to raise questions about the conditions under which the texts were produced by referring to aspects of the routine practice of journalism as a craft or a profession and the way in which these impose constraints upon the writer. Thus, there may exist a range of pressures on tabloid journalists, including rules governing the reporting of criminal cases, and requirements to be both entertaining and economical. Admittedly, some quite specific features of the above texts can be explained in this way. For instance, why has the fourth victim been named in the following account but not the other three.

> Two of Steed's rape victims – aged 20 and 19 – had a screwdriver held at their throats as they were forced to submit. His third victim a 39 year old mother of three was attacked at gunpoint after Steed forced her car off the M4. Two days later, he gunned down call-girl Jacqueline Murray, 23, after picking her up in London's Park Lane.

On the face of it, it looks as if the naming of the fourth victim is part of the overall asymmetrical presentation of respectable versus non-respectable victims. Against this, it could be argued – invoking craft or professional pressures – that the difference in naming is due to the conventions governing the reporting of rape' cases where victims who testify in court are supposed to have their anonymity guaranteed. This rule does not apply to the fourth victim, because she was murdered; and it is for this reason that she gets named. Arguments such as this are invoked to undermine notions of ideological motivation. Put simply they rest on claims such as: (1) if an alternative motivation for a feature can be found, then it ceases to be ideological; and (2) texts are only ideological if they are ideologically motivated.

Such claims are spurious. It is quite possible to offer more than one explanation for the occurrence of a feature or pattern without these explanations necessarily becoming self-cancelling. It is quite possible, for instance, for aspects of the journalist's craft to affect the composition of the text in ideological ways. Moreover, claiming that features of the verbal design of text are not ideological on the grounds that some other motive can be attributed to them merely rehearses the intentional fallacy, exposed above, which mistakenly attempts to insist that a text can only mean what its author(s) intended it to mean, neither more nor less.

A much more fundamental difficulty relates to how we interpret these patterns and more broadly to the effects of certain kinds of recurrent interpretation. Put simply, do readers of the *Sun*, for instance, as a result of reading its rape reports, come to think of rape victims as implicated in their own ordeal, as somehow to blame for what happens to them? This kind of question about effects is notoriously difficult to answer, as can be seen from the many conflicting reports about the effects of pornography or violence on television. We do know enough, at least, from these studies to reject any simplistic correlation of cause and effect. And, if we do not have clear answers to the question of the effectivity of modes of representation, we do know enough to begin to think of ways in which it can be fruitfully studied.

In the meantime, however, this chapter has aimed to give some substance to claims about how choices of vocabulary and sentence structure give particular shape to experience, affecting how reality is depicted in deep and significant ways. Basically, reality is not 'out there', easily available to be grasped in any straightforward and simple way; it is socially constructed, with language playing a centrally important role, so that the patterning of vocabulary and sentence structure shows us reality in a particular light and guides our apprehension of it. This is how linguistic relativity operates: 'the language habits of a community predispose certain choices of interpretation' (Sapir). Language habits, such as those from the *Sun* discussed above, may in part underlie the disturbing fact that in prosecutions for rape 'it remains the case that in order to be sure of obtaining a conviction, the victim should be a respectable married woman and the assailant unknown to her' (Grant, 1994). Certainly, the attribution of blame, as seen in the outcome of court cases, seems to march in step with a recurrent kind of linguistic patterning.

Whorf (1956) claimed that 'we ascribe significances as we do, largely because we are parties to an agreement [that] ... is codified in the patterns of our language.' Some accounts of Whorf derive from his work a kind of linguistic determinism in which the patterns of the language become a prison house enabling us to see

250

reality in one way only. However, when it is claimed that 'the language habits of a community predispose certain choices of interpretation' we need to be clear about which community we are referring to. As we saw above in the discussion of the speech community (pp. 175–86) it is increasingly difficult in the modern world to conceptualize the notion of community as self-contained and self-standing. In the case of English we are faced with various speech communities in overlapping and contradictory relationships. Neither languages nor speech communities are stable uniform entities. Thus, the patterns which we have discussed above do not obtain everywhere that English is spoken or written: patterns that prevail in one part of the speech community can be contradicted by those prevailing in another. In drawing attention to these patterns, however, we have raised the possibility that they can be changed or at least challenged and brought into question.

Everything in this book may be seen in this light. Language informs the way we think, the way we experience, and the way we interact with each other. Language provides the basis of community, but also the grounds for division. Systematic knowledge about language and practical awareness of how it works is fundamental to the process of building mature communities.

Background sources and further reading

Linguistic relativity

Whorf, B.L. (1956) *Language, Thought and Reality* (ed. by John B. Carroll), Massachusetts: MIT Press.

This contains the major statement of the relativist position and explores it in detailed comparisons between North American Indian languages (particularly Hopi) and European languages.

Leech, G.N. (1974) *Semantics*, Harmondsworth: Penguin.

Includes a neat review of the arguments concerning relativism and universalism (31–4; and chapter 11).

Palmer, F. (1976) *Semantics*, Cambridge: Cambridge University Press.

Succinctly states the case against linguistic relativity (55–8).

Pinxten, R. (ed.) (1976) *Universalism and Relativism in Language and Thought*, The Hague: Mouton.

Orwell, G. (1946) 'Politics and the English Language', in Orwell, S. and Angus, I. (eds) (1970) *The Collected Essays, Journalism and Letters of George Orwell*, Harmondsworth: Penguin, vol. 4, (156–70).

Orwell's concern with language and thought found subsequent expression in his novel *1984*, in which an official language called 'Newspeak' is developed 'not only to provide a medium of expression for the world view and mental habits proper [for members of society] but to make all other modes of thought impossible'.

Words and women

Stanley, J.P. (1977) 'Paradigmatic woman: the prostitute' in Shores, D.L. and Hines, C.P. (eds) (1977) *Papers in Language Variation*, Alabama: University of Alabama Press.

This is the seminal paper on words with connotations of sexuality for men and women. It is reported in:

Spender, D. (1980) *Man Made Language*, London: Routledge & Kegan Paul.

This book ranges broadly over issues relating to the position of women in language. It is a committed and comprehensive treatment, thoughtfully reviewed by:

Black, M. and Coward, R. (1981) 'Linguistic, social and sexual relations: a review of Dale Spender's *Man Made Language*' in *Screen Education*, 39, Summer.

Key, M.R. (1975) *Male/Female Language*, New York: Scarecrow Press.

Contains good summaries of literature and a very full bibliography.

Lees, S. (1983) 'How boys slag off girls', *New Society*, 13 October 1983, 51–3.

The vocabulary of nuclear weapons

Chilton, P. (1982) 'Nukespeak: nuclear language, culture and propaganda' in Aubrey, C. (ed.) *Nukespeak, the Media and the Bomb*, London: Comedia.

Paul Chilton has written several important papers on how nuclear weapons are depicted in language. The above is one of the more generally accessible. The collection in which it appears contains other material of interest, including a glossary of terms, drawn upon on pp. 231–6 above.

Beedham, C. (1983) 'Language indoctrination and nuclear arms' *UEA Papers in Linguistics*, 19, 15–31.

A further useful paper on the vocabulary of nuclear weapons. It has some perceptive points to make about the use of 'bomb', noting, for example, that fears of an Islamic 'nuclear capability' would typically be couched in terms of an 'Islamic bomb'.

Nash, H.T. (1980) 'The bureaucratization of homicide' in Thompson, E.P. and Smith, D. (eds) *Protest and Survive*, Harmondsworth: Penguin.

This gives an insider's view on how the language adopted by defence establishments actually obscures what is going on, as much for those inside those establishments as for the general public.

Sentences and representation

Fowler, R., Hodge, R., Kress, G. and Trew, T. (1979) *Language and Control*, London: Routledge & Kegan Paul.

Kress, G. and Hodge, R. (1979) *Language as Ideology*, London: Routledge & Kegan Paul.

These companion volumes include important discussions of ways in which world views and ideologies are implicated in our choice of sentence structure. The examples from *The Times* and the *Guardian* discussed above on pp. 239–40 are drawn from:

Trew, T. (1978) 'Theory at work', *UEA Papers in Linguistics*, 6, 39–60.

This contains fuller discussion of transitivity in the examples and also raises general issues of ideology, theory and language.

Burton, D. (1982) 'Through glass darkly: through dark glasses', in Carter, R. (ed.) *Language and Literature: an Introductory Reader in Stylistics*, London: George Allen & Unwin.

Related issues are worked through from a feminist perspective by analysis of the transitivity patterns in a prose text by Sylvia Plath.

Critical linguistics

Other books that use linguistics as a tool of critical analysis in addition to Kress and Hodge (1979) and Fowler *et al.* (1979) listed above are:

Fowler, R. (1991) *Language in the News*, London: Routledge.
Fairclough, N. (1989) *Language and Power*, London: Longman.
Fairclough, N. (1992) *Discourse and Social Change*, Oxford: Basil Blackwell.

Fieldwork projects

(1) What degrees of overlap and difference might exist between groups of speakers of different ages and gender in the words with sexual connotations for men and women that they (a) know, and (b) use? In what circumstances and for what purposes would the vocabulary be used? Can you develop a questionnaire that would elicit this information? What difficulties would you anticipate in administering the questionnaire? How would you explain any differences that might emerge?

(2) Jot down as many medical terms as you can think of for physical illness (e.g. 'tonsillitis', 'appendicitis', 'pneumonia' . . .). Now jot down as many medical terms for mental illness as you can (e.g. 'schizophrenia', 'paranoia' . . .). Which list is longer? Do you think that for most people the list for physical illness is likely to be longer than that for mental illness? Why?

(3) (a) The following examples are from the British press coverage of the miners' strike (September 1984):

The *Guardian*
> 'Pickets, policemen, the Labour MP Mr Kevin Baron and an ITN journalist were injured in further clashes between the police and miners at Maltby colliery near Rotherham yesterday.'

The *Morning Star*
> 'Police in riot gear smashed into a picket line at Maltby colliery in South Yorkshire yesterday, injuring a number of miners and an MP who needed hospital treatment.'

Who are the *agents* and *affected* in each account. What has happened to the *agent* in the *Guardian* account?

(b) What is the effect of the following kind of formulation selected from a range of British newspapers during the miners' strike:

> 'Picket – police *battle*   *flares*   in Kent . . .'.
> '   *Conflict was building up* yesterday . . .'.
> '   More *violence broke out*   on miners' picket
>   lines today . . .'.
> '*Clashes* between police and pickets *led to* eighteen
>   arrests . . .'.

(c) Collect together a range of accounts from different newspapers of an event involving civil disorder either at home or abroad. How do these accounts represent the roles of the various participants? Who does what to whom and how? Do different newspapers favour different modes of representation? In what way? Why?

REFERENCES

Adlam, D. and Salfield, A. (1980) 'Sociolinguistics and "linguistic diver-
· sity"', *Screen Education*, 34, Spring, 71–87.

Alleyne, M.C. (1971) 'Acculturation and the cultural matrix of creolization', in Hymes, D. (ed.) (1971).

Aitchison, J. (1987) *Linguistics*, Teach Yourself Books, Sevenoaks: Hodder
& Stoughton.

Anderson, B. (1983) *Imagined Communities: Reflections in the Origins and
Spread of Nationalism*, London: Verso.

Atkinson, J.M. and Drew, P. (1979) *Order in Court*, London: Macmillan.

—— and Heritage, J. (eds) *Structures of Social Action: Studies in Conversation
Analysis*, Cambridge: Cambridge University Press.

Aubrey, C. (ed.) (1982) *Nukespeak: the Media and the Bomb*, London:
Comedia.

Bartsch, R. (1987) *Norms of Language*, London: Longman.

Basso, K. (1972) '"To give up on words": silence in Western Apache
culture', in Giglioli, P.P. (ed.) (1972).

Bauman, R. and Sherzer, J. (eds) (1974) *Explorations in the Ethnography of
Speaking*, Cambridge: Cambridge University Press.

Beedham, C. (1983) 'Language, indoctrination and nuclear arms', *UEA
Papers in Linguistics*, 19, 15–31.

Bernstein, B. (1971) *Class, Codes and Control: vol. 1, Theoretical Studies
Towards a Sociology of Language*, London: Routledge & Kegan Paul.

—— (ed.) (1973) *Class, Codes and Control: vol. 2, Applied Studies Towards
a Sociology of Language*, London: Routledge & Kegan Paul.

Beynon, J. (1985) *Initial Encounters in a Comprehensive School: Sussing,*

Typing and Copying, Barcombe, near Lewes: The Falmer Press.

Black, M. and Coward, R. (1981) 'Linguistic, social and sexual relations: a review of Dale Spender's *Man Made Language*', *Screen Education*, 39, Summer.

Bloom, L. (1970) *Language Development: Form and Function in Emerging Grammars*, Massachusetts: MIT Press.

—— (1973) *One Word at a Time*, The Hague: Mouton.

Bolinger, D. (1980) *Language the Loaded Weapon*, London: Longman.

Bolinger, D. and Sears, D.A. (1981) *Aspects of Language*, New York: Harcourt Brace Jovanovich.

Brouwer, D., Gerritsen, M. and Dettaan, D. (1979) 'Speech differences between women and men: on the wrong track?', *Language in Society*, 8, 33–50.

Brown, G. and Yule, G. (1983) *Discourse Analysis*, Cambridge: Cambridge University Press.

Brown, P. and Levinson, S. (1978) 'Universals in language usage: politeness phenomena', in Goody, E. (ed.) (1978).

—— and —— (1979) 'Social structure, groups and interaction', in Giles, H. and Scherer, K.R. (eds) (1979).

Brown, R. (1976) *A First Language: the Early Stages*, Harmondsworth: Penguin.

Bullowa, M. (ed.) (1979) *Before Speech*, Cambridge: Cambridge University Press.

Burton, D. (1981) 'The sociolinguistic analysis of spoken discourse', in French, P. and MacLure, M. (eds) (1981).

—— (1982) 'Through glass darkly: through dark glasses', in Carter, R. (ed.) (1982).

Cameron, D. (ed.) (1990) *The Feminist Critique of Language: A Reader*, London: Routledge.

—— (1992, 2nd edn) *Feminism and Linguistic Theory*, London: Macmillan.

—— , McAlinden, F. and O'Leary, K. (1988) 'Lakoff in context: the social and linguistic functions of tag questions', in Coates, J. and Cameron, D. (eds) (1988).

Carter, R. (ed.) (1982) *Language and Literature: an Introductory Reader in Stylistics*, London: George Allen & Unwin.

Cecco, J.P. de (ed.) (1961) *The Psychology of Language, Thought and Instruction*, New York: Holt, Rinehart & Winston.

Cheshire, J. (1982) *Variation in English Dialect*, Cambridge: Cambridge University Press.

Chilton, P. (1982) 'Nukespeak: nuclear language, culture and propaganda', in Aubrey, C. (ed.) (1982).

—— (ed.) (1985) *Language and the Nuclear Arms Debate*, London: Frances Pinter.

Chomsky, N. (1959) 'Review of Skinner's *Verbal Behaviour*', *Language*, 35, 26–58. Reprinted in de Cecco, J.P. (ed.) (1961).

Clark, E.V. (1973) 'What's in a word? On the child's acquisition of semantics in his first language', in Moore, T.E. (ed.) (1973).

Clark, K. (1992) 'The linguistics of blame', in Toolan, M. (1992).

Coates, J. (1986) *Women, Men and Language*, London: Longman.

—— and Cameron, D. (eds) (1988) *Women in their Speech Communities*, London: Longman.

Coulthard, M. (1977) *An Introduction to Discourse Analysis*, London: Longman.

—— and Montgomery, M.M. (eds) (1981) *Studies in Discourse Analysis*, London: Routledge & Kegan Paul.

Cruttenden, A. (1979) *Language in Infancy and Childhood*, Manchester: Manchester University Press.

Crystal, D. (1976) *Child Language, Learning and Linguistics*, London: Edward Arnold.

—— and Davy, D. (1969) *Investigating English Style*, London: Longman.

Culler, J. (1976) *Saussure*, London: Fontana.

Dale, P.S. (1976) *Language Development: Structure and Function*, New York: Holt, Rinehart & Winston.

Demisse, T. and Bender, M.L. (1983) 'An argot of Addis Ababa unattached girls', *Language and Society*, 12, 339–47.

Deutsch, W. (ed.) (1981) *The Child's Construction of Language*, New York: Academic Press.

Dittmar, N. (1976) *Sociolinguistics*, London: Edward Arnold.

Dubois, B.L. and Crouch, I.C. (1975) 'The question of tag questions in women's speech: they don't really use more of them do they?', *Language and Society*, 4, 289–94.

Dyer, G. (1982) *Advertising as Communication*, London: Methuen.

Edwards, A.D. (1976) *Language in Culture and Class*, London: Heinemann.

Edwards, V.K. (1979) *The West Indian Language Issue in British Schools*, London: Routledge & Kegan Paul.

—— (1983) *Language in the Multicultural Classroom*, London: Batsford.

Ervin-Tripp, S. (1972) 'Sociolinguistic rules of address', in Pride, J.B. and Holmes, J. (eds) (1972).

—— and Mitchell-Kernan, C. (eds) (1977) *Child Discourse*, New York: Academic Press.

Fairclough, N. (1988) 'Register, power and socio-semantic change', in Birch, D. and O'Toole, M. (eds) (1988) *Functions of Style*, London: Pinter Publishers.

—— (1989) *Language and Power*, London: Longman.

—— (1992) *Discourse and Social Change*, Oxford: Basil Blackwell.

Ferguson, C.A. and Slobin, D.I. (eds) (1973) *Studies in Child Language Development*, New York: Holt, Rinehart & Winston.

Fishman, P.M. (1983) 'Interaction: the work women do', in Thorne, B., Kramarae, C. and Henley, N. (eds) (1983).

Fiske, J. (1982) *An Introduction to Communication Studies*, London: Methuen.

Fletcher, P. and Garman, M. (eds) (1979) *Language Acquisition*, Cambridge: Cambridge University Press.

Flexner, S.B. (1976) *I Hear America Talking*, New York: Touchstone.

Foss, B.M. (ed.) (1969) *Determinants of Infant Behaviour IV*, London: Methuen.

Foster, S. (1990) *The Communicative Competence of Young Children*, London: Longman.

Fowler, R. (1991) *Language in the News*, London: Routledge.

—— , Hodge, R., Kress, G. and Trew, T. (1979) *Language and Control*, London: Routledge & Kegan Paul.

French, P. and MacLure, M. (eds) (1981) *Adult–Child Conversation*, London: Croom Helm.

Friedrich, P. (1972) 'Social context and semantic feature: the Russian pronominal usage', in Gumperz, J. and Hymes, D. (eds) (1972).

Gardener, P.M. (1966) 'Symmetric respect and memorate knowledge: the structure and ecology of individualistic culture', *South Western Journal of Anthropology*, 22, 389–415, cited in Hymes, D. (1972).

Garvey, C. (1984) *Children's Talk*, London: Fontana.

Giglioli, P.P. (ed.) (1972) *Language and Social Context*, Harmondsworth: Penguin.

Giles, H. (1979) 'Ethnicity markers in speech', in Giles, H. and Scherer, K.R. (eds) (1979).

—— and Powesland, P.F. (1975) *Speech Style and Social Evaluation*, London: Academic Press.

—— and Saint-Jacques, B. (eds) (1979) *Language and Ethnic Relations*, Oxford: Pergamon Press.

Glasgow University Media Group (1976) *Bad News*, London: Routledge & Kegan Paul.

—— (1980) *More Bad News*, London: Routledge & Kegan Paul.

—— (1982) *Really Bad News*, London: Writers' and Readers' Co-operative.

Goodwin, M.H. (1980) 'Directive-response speech sequences in girls' and boys' task activities', in McConnell-Ginet, S., R. Borker and N. Furman (eds) (1980) *Women and Language in Literature and Society*, New York: Praeger.

Goody, E.N. (ed.) (1978) *Questions and Politeness: Strategies in Social Interaction*, Cambridge Papers in Social Anthropology, 8, Cambridge: Cambridge University Press.

Goody, J. and Watt, I. (1972) 'The consequences of literacy', in Giglioli, P.P. (ed.) (1972)

Graddol, D. and Swann, J. (1983) *Gender Voices*, Oxford: Basil Blackwell.

Grant, L. (1994) 'Sex and the single student', in Dunant, Sarah (ed.) *The War of the Words: the Political Correctness Debate*, London: Virago.

Gregory, M. and Carroll, S. (1978) *Language and Situation*, London: Routledge & Kegan Paul.

Gumperz, J. (1972) 'The speech community', in Giglioli, P.P. (ed.) (1972).

—— (ed.) (1985) *Discourse Processes, Vols 1 & 2*, Cambridge: Cambridge University Press.

—— and Hymes, D. (eds) (1972) *Directions in Sociolinguistics*, New York: Holt, Rinehart & Winston.

Hall, R.A. Jr (1966) *Pidgin and Creole Languages*, Ithaca and London: Cornell University Press.

Halliday, M.A.K. (1975) *Learning How to Mean*, London: Edward Arnold.

—— (1976) 'Antilanguages', *American Anthropologist*, 78 (3).

—— (1978) *Language as Social Semiotic: the Social Interpretation of Language and Meaning*, London: Edward Arnold.

—— and Hasan, R. (1989) *Language, Context, and Text: Aspects of Language in a Social-semiotic Perspective*, Oxford: Oxford University Press

Harris, J. (1990) *Early Language Development*, London: Routledge.

Harris, S. and Morgan, K. (1979) *Language Projects: an Introduction to the Study of Language*, London: Edward Arnold.

Hartley, J. (1982) *Understanding News*, London: Methuen.

Hasan, R. (1973) 'Code, register and social dialect', in Bernstein, B. (ed.) (1973).

Hewitt, R. (1986) *White Talk Black Talk: Inter-Racial Friendship and Communication amongst Adolescents*, Cambridge: Cambridge University Press.

Hockett, C.F. (1958) *A Course in Modern Linguistics*, New York: Macmillan.

Holmes, J. (1984) 'Hedging your bets and sitting on the fence: some evidence for hedges as support structures', *Te Reo*, 27, 47–62.

Hudson, R.A. (1980) *Sociolinguistics*, Cambridge: Cambridge University Press.

—— (1984) *Invitation to Linguistics*, Oxford: Basil Blackwell.

Hughes, A. and Trudgill, P. (1979) *English Accents and Dialects*, London: Edward Arnold.

Hymes, D. (ed.) (1964) *Language in Culture and Society*, New York: Harper & Row.

—— (ed.) (1971) *Pidginization and Creolization of Languages*, Cambridge: Cambridge University Press.

—— (1972) 'Models of the interaction of language and social life', in Gumperz, J. and Hymes, D. (eds) (1972).

—— (1974) *Foundations in Sociolinguistics: an Ethnographic Approach*, Philadelphia: University of Pennsylvania Press.

Key, M.R. (1975) *Male/Female Language*, New York: Scarecrow Press.

Kochman, T. (1969) '"Rapping" in the black ghetto', *Trans-Action*, February, 26–34, cited in Mitchell-Kernan, C. (1972).

Kress, G. and Hodge, R. (1979) *Language as Ideology*, London: Routledge & Kegan Paul.

Labov, W. (1966) *The Social Stratification of English in New York City*, Washington D.C.: Centre for Applied Linguistics.

—— (1970) 'The study of language in its social context', *Studium Generale*, 23, 66–84. Reprinted in Giglioli, P.P. (ed.) (1972).

—— (1972a) 'Rules for ritual insults', in Labov, W. (1972c).

—— (1972b) 'The logic of nonstandard English', in Labov, W. (1972c).

—— (1972c) *Language in the Inner City: Studies in the Black English Vernacular*, Philadelphia: University of Pennsylvania Press.

—— (1972d) *Sociolinguistic Patterns*, Philadelphia: University of Pennsylvania Press.

—— and Fanshel, D. (1977) *Therapeutic Discourse: Psychotherapy as Conversation*, London: Academic Press.

Laffal, J. (1965) *Pathological and Normal Language*, New York: Atherton Press.

Lakoff, R. (1975) *Language and Woman's Place*, New York: Harper & Row.

Leech, G.N. (1966) *English in Advertising: a Linguistic Study of Advertising in Great Britain*, London: Longman.

—— (1974) *Semantics*, Harmondsworth: Penguin.

Lees, S. (1983) 'How boys slag off girls', *New Society*, 13 October 1983, 51–3.

Leith, D. (1983) *A Social History of English*, London: Routledge & Kegan Paul.

Le Page, R.B. (1981) *Caribbean Connections in the Classroom*, York: Mary Glasgow Language Trust.

Levinson, S. (1983) *Pragmatics*, Cambridge: Cambridge University Press.

Lock, A. (ed.) (1978) *Action, Gesture and Symbol: the Emergence of Language*, London: Academic Press.

Macaulay, R.K.S. (1977) *Language, Social Class and Education: a Glasgow Study*, Edinburgh: Edinburgh University Press.

—— (1981) *Generally Speaking: How Children Learn Language*, Rowley: Newbury House.

Menyuk, P. (1971) *The Acquisition and Development of Language*, New Jersey: Prentice Hall.

Milroy, J. and Milroy, L. (1985 [1991]) *Authority in Language: Investigating Language Prescription and Standardisation*, London: Routledge.

Milroy, L. (1980) *Language and Social Networks*, Oxford: Basil Blackwell.

Mitchell-Kernan, C. (1972) 'Signifying and marking: two Afro-American speech acts', in Gumperz, J. and Hymes, D. (eds.) (1972).

Moore, T.E. (ed.) (1973) *Cognitive Development and the Acquisition of Language*, London: Academic Press.

Nash, H.T. (1980) 'The bureaucratization of homicide', in Thompson, E.P. and Smith, D. (eds) (1980).

Nichols, P. (1983) 'Linguistic options and choices for Black women in the rural South', in Thorne, B., Kramarae, C. and Henley, N. (eds) (1983).

Ong, W.J. (1982) *Orality and Literacy: the Technologizing of the Word*, London: Methuen.

Orwell, G. (1954) *1984*, Harmondsworth: Penguin.

Orwell, S. and Angus, I. (eds) (1970) *The Collected Essays, Journalism and Letters of George Orwell*, vol. 4, Harmondsworth: Penguin.

Painter, C. (1984) *Into the Mother Tongue: a Case Study in Early Language Development*, London: Frances Pinter.

—— (1985) *Learning the Mother Tongue*, Victoria: Deakin University Press.

Palmer, F.R. (1976) *Semantics*, Cambridge: Cambridge University Press.

Pinxten, R. (ed.) (1976) *Universalism and Relativism in Language and Thought*, The Hague: Mouton.

Pride, J.B. and Holmes, J. (eds) (1972) *Sociolinguistics*, Harmondsworth: Penguin.

Psathas, G. (ed.) (1979) *Everyday Language: Studies in Ethnomethodology*, New York: Irvington.

Quirk, R. (1968) *The Use of English*, London: Longman.

Reisman, K. (1974) 'Contrapuntal conversations in an Antiguan village', in Bauman, R. and Sherzer, J. (eds) (1974).

Romaine, S. (ed.) (1982) *Sociolinguistic Variation in Speech Communities*, London: Edward Arnold.

Rosen, H. (1972) *Language and Class: a Critical Look at the Theories of*

Basil Bernstein, Bristol: Falling Wall Press.

Ryan E. and Giles, H. (eds) (1982) *Attitudes towards Language Variation*, London: Edward Arnold.

Sacks, H., Schegloff, E. and Jefferson, G. (1974) 'A simplest systematics for the organisation of turn-taking in conversation', *Language*, 50, 696–735.

Safder, A. and Edwards, V. (eds) (1991) *Multilingualism in the British Isles Vols 1 & 2*, London: Longman.

Saporta, S. (ed.) (1961) *Psycholinguistics: a Book of Readings*, New York: Holt, Rinehart & Winston.

Saussure, F. de (1974) *Course in General Linguistics*, London: Fontana.

Saville-Troike, M. (1982) *The Ethnography of Communication: an Introduction*, Oxford: Basil Blackwell.

Scannell, P. and Cardiff, D. (1977) *The Social Foundations of British Broadcasting*, Open University Course: *Mass Communication and Society*, 1–6.

Schenkein, J. (ed.) (1978) *Studies in the Organization of Conversational Interaction*, New York: Academic Press.

Scherer, K.R. and Giles, H. (eds) (1979) *Social Markers in Speech*, Cambridge: Cambridge University Press.

Schiffrin, D. (1994) *Approaches to Discourse*, Oxford: Blackwell.

Shores, D.L. and Hines, C.P. (eds) (1977) *Papers in Language Variation*, Alabama: University of Alabama Press.

Sinclair, J. McH. and Coulthard, R.M. (1975) *Towards an Analysis of Discourse: the English Used by Teachers and Pupils*, Oxford: Oxford University Press.

Skinner, B.F. (1957) *Verbal Behaviour*, New York: Appleton Century Crofts, 1–12 reprinted in de Cecco, J.P. (ed.) (1961) as 'A functional analysis of verbal behaviour'.

Snow, C. and Ferguson, C.A. (eds) (1977) *Talking to Children*, Cambridge: Cambridge University Press.

Spender, D. (1980) *Man Made Language*, London: Routledge & Kegan Paul.

Stanley, J.P. (1977) 'Paradigmatic woman: the prostitute', in Shores, D.L. and Hines, C.P. (eds) (1977).

Stubbs, M. (1976) *Language, Schools and Classrooms*, London: Methuen.

—— (1980) *Language and Literacy: the Sociolinguistics of Reading and Writing*, London: Routledge & Kegan Paul.

—— (1983) *Discourse Analysis: the Sociolinguistic Analysis of Natural Language*, Oxford: Basil Blackwell.

Sudnow, D. (ed.) (1972) *Studies in Social Interaction*, New York: Free Press.

Sutcliffe, D. (1982) *British Black English*, Oxford: Basil Blackwell.

Tannen, D. (1991) *You Just Don't Understand*, London: Virago.

Thompson, E.P. and Smith, D. (eds) (1980) *Protest and Survive*, Harmondsworth: Penguin.

Thorne, B. and Henley, N. (eds) (1975) *Language and Sex: Difference and Dominance*, Rowley, Mass.: Newbury House.

——, Kramarae, C. and Henley, N. (eds) (1983) *Language, Gender and Society*, Rowley, Mass.: Newbury House.

Todd, L. (1974) *Pidgins and Creoles*, London: Routledge & Kegan Paul.

Tolson, A. (1976) 'The semiotics of working class speech', in *Working Papers in Cultural Studies*, 9, University of Birmingham: Centre for Contemporary Cultural Studies.

Toolan, M. (ed.) (1992) *Language, Text and Context: Essays in Stylistics*, London: Routledge.

Trew, T. (1978) 'Theory at work', *UEA Papers in Linguistics*, 6, 39–60.

Trudgill, P. (1974) *The Social Differentiation of English in Norwich*, Cambridge: Cambridge University Press.

—— (ed.) (1978) *Sociolinguistic Patterns in British English*, London: Edward Arnold.

—— (ed) (1984) *Language in the British Isles*, Cambridge: Cambridge University Press.

Turner, R. (ed.) (1974) *Ethnomethodology*, Harmondsworth: Penguin.

de Villiers, P.A. and de Villiers, J.G. (1979) *Early Language*, London: Fontana .

Wanner, E. and Gleitman, L.R. (eds) (1982) *Language Acquisition: the State of the Art*, Cambridge: Cambridge University Press.

Warburg, J. (1968) 'Notions of correctness', supplement II in Quirk, R. (1968).

Wells, G.C. *et al.* (1981) *Learning Through Interaction: the Study of Language Development*, Cambridge: Cambridge University Press.

Wells, J.C. (1982) *Accents of English*, vols 1–3, Cambridge: Cambridge University Press.

Werth, P. (ed.) (1981) *Conversation and Discourse*, London: Croom Helm.

West, C. and Zimmerman, D. (1983) 'Small insults: a study of interruptions in cross-sex conversations between unaquainted persons', in Thorne, B. Kramarae, C. and Henley, N. (eds) (1983).

Whorf, B.L. (1956) *Language, Thought and Reality* (ed. by John B. Carroll), Cambridge, Mass.: MIT Press.

Williams, R. (1974) *Television: Technology and Cultural Form*, London: Fontana.

Wolff, P.H. (1969) 'The natural history of crying and other vocalizations in early infancy', in Foss, B.M. (ed.) (1969).

Wooton, A. (1975) *Dilemmas of Discourse*, London: George Allen & Unwin.

Zimmerman, D. and West, C. (1975) 'Sex roles, interruptions and silences in conversation', in Thorne, B. and Henley, N. (eds) (1975).

INDEX